Foundations
of
Northeast Archaeology

This is a volume in

Studies in Archaeology

A complete list of titles in this series appears at the end of this volume.

Foundations
of
Northeast Archaeology

edited by

Dean R. Snow
Department of Anthropology
State University of New York
Albany, New York

 ACADEMIC PRESS 1981
A Subsidiary of Harcourt Brace Jovanovich, Publishers

New York   London
Paris   San Diego   San Francisco   São Paulo
Sydney   Tokyo   Toronto

ACADEMIC PRESS, INC.
111 Fifth Avenue, New York, New York 10003

United Kingdom Edition published by
ACADEMIC PRESS, INC. (LONDON) LTD.
24/28 Oval Road, London NW1 7DX

Library of Congress Cataloging in Publication Data
Main entry under title:

Foundations of northeast archaeology.

(Studies in anthropology)
Based on papers delivered at a conference held Feb.
29-Mar. 1, 1980, at the State University of New York
at Albany.
Includes bibliographical references and index.
Contents: Prehistoric social and political organiza-
tion, an Iroquoian case study / Bruce G. Trigger --
Paleoenvironmental reconstruction in the Northeast, the
art of multidisciplinary science / Dena F. Dincauze --
Approaches to cultural adaptation in the Northeast /
Dean R. Snow -- [etc.]
1. Indians of North America--Northeastern States--
Antiquities--Congresses. 2. Indians of North America--
Canada--Antiquities--Congresses. 3. Northeastern
States--Antiquities--Congresses. 4. Canada--Antiquities
--Congresses. I. Snow, Dean R. II. Series.
E78.E2F68   947'.01   81-17666
ISBN 0-12-653960-X   AACR2

PRINTED IN THE UNITED STATES OF AMERICA

81 82 83 84   9 8 7 6 5 4 3 2 1

CONTENTS

CONTRIBUTORS

Numbers in parentheses indicate the pages on which the authors' contribution begin.

GEORGE J. ARMELAGOS (229), *Department of Anthropology, University of Massachusetts, Amherst, Massachusetts 01003*

M. PAMELA BUMSTED (229), *Department of Anthropology, University of Massachusetts, Amherst, Massachusetts 01003*

DENA F. DINCAUZE (51), *Department of Anthropology, University of Massachusetts, Amherst, Massachusetts 01003*

FRANCIS P. McMANAMON (195), *Division of Cultural Resources, National Park Service, North Atlantic Region, 15 State Street, Boston, Massachusetts 02109*

DEBRA L. SCHINDLER (229), *Department of Anthropology, University of Massachusetts, Amherst, Massachusetts 01003*

DEAN R. SNOW (97), *Department of Anthropology, State University of New York at Albany, Albany, New York 12222*

WILLIAM A. STARNA (139), *Department of Anthropology, State University of New York at Oneonta, Oneonta, New York 13820*

BRUCE G. TRIGGER (1), *Department of Anthropology, McGill University, 855 Sherbrooke West, Montreal, Quebec H3A 2T7, Canada*

DOUGLAS H. UBELAKER (175), *Department of Anthropology, National Museum of Natural History, Smithsonian Institution, Washington, D.C. 20560*

PREFACE

Archaeology in its infancy was little more than a treasure hunt. In its protracted adolescence it has been sometimes the means by which culture history might be discovered, sometimes merely the illustrator of culture history already known. The relatively recent emergence of processual issues in archaeology has at once emphasized its development as a discipline and reaffirmed its dependence upon the larger parent discipline of anthropology. As the papers in this volume illustrate, the emergence of processual archaeology has also reaffirmed and refined the relationships between archaeology and a variety of nonanthropological sister disciplines. What emerges is a new vision of archaeology in which the problems are basically anthropological ones, and archaeology is one necessary (sometimes the only possible) means for their solution.

The purpose of this collection of papers is to discuss the emergent new paradigm in terms of unique problems that attend its application in the Northeast. The core of the region is comprised of New England, New York, and the adjacent portions of Ontario, Quebec, and the Maritime Provinces. For decades archaeologists have been defining themselves according to the regions of the world in which they have chosen to work. The emergence of archaeology as a discipline has allowed us to break free from these territorial constraints. Consequently, this volume defines the foundations of archaeology in the Northeast not so much in terms of the known and presumed content of Northeast prehistory, but in terms of the special problems and potentials that attend the application of archaeology in this region. We hope that by discussing both the unique features of Northeast archaeology and archaeological principles having universal application, we have produced a volume that will be of value both within and outside the region.

A volume that discusses the fundamentals of Northeast archaeology is necessary, not because we still cling to an empirical, regionally content-oriented notion of archaeological specialization, but because the nature of prehistory, preservation, and current data acquisition are regionally unique in ways that constrain the kinds of problems we can undertake to solve. We need a regional epistemology, as does every other archaeological region, one that recognizes the unique opportunities and limitations of archaeology in the Northeast.

The collection of seven papers is the outgrowth of a conference held on February 29 and March 1, 1980 on the campus of the State University of New York at Albany. The conference was funded through the Conversations in the Disciplines program, and we thank the State University of New York for that essential support. All but one of the authors, Francis McManamon, were conference participants, albeit the delivery of Bruce Trigger's paper was postponed some weeks due to illness. Two of the conference participants, Bert Salwen and Robert Schuyler, were unable to provide written versions of their presentations, and the chapter by Francis McManamon was solicited to fill the gap left by their withdrawal. Unfortunately, the change also removed the integrative connections between the papers published here and a very informative presentation by James Adovasio. Consequently, the present volume is more theoretical and methodological, less tactical and technical in tone, than the 1980 conference from which it derives.

Trigger is no stranger to theoretical debate, but for Chapter 1 he has chosen to take a largely empirical approach to the potentials and limits of prehistoric anthropology in the Northeast. He evaluates propositions in terms of what we know and can potentially know in the way of relevant evidence. He finds most to be as yet inadequately tested, some probably untestable. But he also finds many to be testable archaeologically, handing the discipline a set of what are at once intriguing possibilities and formidable challenges. Few of the lines of research he proposes will yield results either quickly or cheaply, and less expensive approaches cannot be made sufficient to resolve the outstanding issues. His discussion applies directly to Iroquoians, but can be extended to other Northeast cultures as well. At the same time, it shows that if it is to yield valid and interesting results, archaeology in the Northeast cannot proceed without detailed reference to ethnology and ethnohistory. If this makes archaeology less a discipline in its own right and more a set of special anthropological techniques, so be it.

Dincauze's use of the word "art" is deliberate and appropriate. It implies that in archaeology, as in any science, there is room for reasonable disagreement and variation in what we might call scholarly style. What she does in Chapter 2 is limit a range of possible problems, possible research strategies, and possible solutions in Northeast archaeology more precisely and clearly than has been the case in the past. That is the larger purpose of the book. Within the limits she sets, however, there is still room for disagreement. Confronted with the same data base, two archaeologists might come to different conclusions if one has only a slightly more determinist view of the environment than the other. The selection of fundamental principles is an art indeed, and variation at this basic level will supply us with controversy even in the unlikely event that we come to a unanimous agreement on less fundamental epistemological and procedural issues. All of the papers in this volume contribute to the clarification and circumscription of the epistemological foundations of Northeast archaeology. It is the collective hope of the authors that our contributions will not eliminate controversy, but will serve to limit it and even organize it within productive areas of research. Like Trigger, Dincauze shows us that we understand much less about an area of archaeological interest than we have thought we do, and that to understand it as well as we would like will be both difficult and expensive.

My own Chapter 3 attempts to show how we might better come to grips with issues of adaptation by carefully choosing the correct scale of investigation. Attention to proper scale is not unique to this chapter; indeed, it may be the strongest common thread running through all seven of them. Like the other authors, I see a need to scale down theoretical constructs and scale up the data base in order to close the gap between theory and empirical archaeology. Most attempts to discuss cultural adaptation to well-defined environments have been framed in terms of simple ethnographic analogy, very often intuitively rather than explicitly. We have all done it, and we should probably continue to do it at lower levels of analysis. An obsession with explicit objectivity can lead to endless arguments over trivial issues. However, at higher levels of analysis and explanation we can do much better than we have done. Arguments based upon undefined private understandings of the ethnographic literature do little to advance our understanding of adaptation.

Starna explores the epistemology of the same issues in Chapter 4. While clarifying the logical structure of contemporary archaeology, he exposes its conceits as well. He shows how an obsession with simplification or rigor can be as debilitating as an avoidance of them. It is frighteningly easy to imagine a muscle-bound archaeology of the future, its strict scientific canons perpetually unsatisfied by its meager data base. Fortunately, he also shows us how we can use the data we have without abandoning scientific principles. While his is essentially a theoretical approach, the congruence between this chapter and the more empirical and methodological chapters by Trigger and Dincauze is heartening.

Ubelaker summarizes the problems and potentials of demographic archaeology in the Northeast in Chapter 5. The chapter introduces the reader to emerging literature on this subject, and links it to issues of adaptation, ecology, and cultural processes raised in other chapters. It is likely that demographic issues will be a permanent part of archaeology in the Northeast in coming decades, such that no approach to anthropological archaeology will be possible without their consideration.

McManamon's Chapter 6 is an excellent example of the current state of cultural resource management and the kinds of archaeological information it is producing. The issues are largely empirical ones, with attention centered

upon problems of sampling and the subsequent validity of statistical operations. Sampling and statistics serve to clarify, define, and verify observations.
Consequently, McManamon's purpose is to define the epistemological limits
of empirical field archaeology. His conclusions parallel those of Chapters 1
and 2, where the limits of other empirical approaches are defined. They also
indicate that problems at the large scale discussed in Chapter 3 are indeed empirically testable, and that the gaps discussed in Chapter 4 can in fact be
bridged. Discovery and excavation, once the only objective of Northeast archaeology, has clearly advanced to a new level of sophistication, and is an
essential part of contemporary processual archaeology. Far from being a
nonacademic departure from legitimate archaeology, cultural resource
management is likely to produce the data base anthropological archaeology
will need to realize its aims over the coming decades.

The chapter by Schindler, Armelagos, and Bumsted revives osteology as a
legitimate and potentially informative subdiscipline of anthropology in the
Northeast. Few academic enterprises have been as victimized by a history of
fundamentally flawed lines of research. Chapter 7 is a refreshing reappraisal
of the epistemological limits of their subdiscipline of anthropology, and an
assessment of its data base in the Northeast. It combines with Chapter 5 to
show us the potential insights offered by the analysis of human skeletal remains, a class of remains too often misused or even deliberately avoided by
archaeologists. Chapters 5 and 7 both draw upon examples far removed from
even the most liberal definition of the Northeast in order to illustrate the
kinds of problems we could undertake to solve, but have only begun to approach here.

As always, reasonable people will differ, yet there is remarkable congruence of thought among the following chapters. This is clear evidence that
the new archaeological paradigm is widely shared, for there was little communication between authors while the chapters were being written. The agreement seen here therefore results from neither prior arrangement nor subsequent editorial standardization. What disagreement remains is often both
subtle and fundamental. For example, the special significance of environmental reconstruction to Dincauze is revealed in her discussion of culturally ex-
plainable residuals, which she assumes to be minimal and of last resort. Starna, citing Gunn, expresses another point of view, in which environmental and
cultural factors cannot be ranked or prioritized. Only further work will
clarify and resolve such differences. In the meantime they give life to archaeology, a range of valid options rather than the small choice of rotten
apples.

Dean R. Snow

1

PREHISTORIC SOCIAL AND POLITICAL ORGANIZATION: AN IROQUOIAN CASE STUDY

BRUCE G. TRIGGER
McGill University

Social organization is no less primordial a part of our human heritage than are subsistence activities. The earliest manifestations of both antedate the development of culture and even the appearance of a distinct hominid line. Although some anthropologists have maintained that social organization is a dependent variable determined entirely by environmental factors, technology, subsistence activities, or the economy, such propositions appear doubtful. Changes in subsistence economies have always occurred in preexisting social contexts and seem to have been shaped by these contexts as much as they have transformed them. Synchronically this implies that, while social and economic variables are functionally interdependent, aspects of social organization play roles that are no less determining than economic ones (Earle 1978). This has been explicitly recognized by traditional Marxist theory, which defines the deterministic "infrastructure" or "base" as embracing the relations as well as the means of production (Marx 1964). It is also implied by most ecological approaches, which stress that human beings do not relate to their environment as individuals but only as members of social groups. This suggests a lesson that archaeologists have been reluctant to acknowledge; namely, that, even in situations where, as a result of historical continuity, detailed ethnographic analogies seem to apply, prehistoric social organization cannot be reconstructed or explained creatively as an epiphenomenon or by-product of subsistence activities. Instead, it must be studied on its own merits as an aspect of broader sociocultural systems.

OBJECTIVES OF A SOCIOPOLITICAL APPROACH

Unlike social anthropologists, archaeologists are unable to observe directly either social behavior or the beliefs and values associated with it. Both must be inferred from their material products and correlates, insofar as these have been preserved in the archaeological record. In general, it is easier to infer actual patterns of behavior from such data than it is the ideal constructs that are assumed to govern them. These limitations seem overwhelming to social anthropologists, who frequently have assumed that archaeological data are too limited and ambiguous to contribute significantly to a better understanding of human behavior. Yet the very abundance of data available to social anthropologists and the relative ease with which they are collected may encourage interpretations that are theoretically less rigorous than those now being attempted by archaeologists. Perhaps the greatest danger confronting archaeologists and leading to misunderstanding of their work is the temptation to confuse the analytical categories that are appropriate to their data with those conventionally used by social anthropologists. As David Aberle (1968:358) has reminded us, archaeological data may yield much solid information about prehistoric residence patterns but it is a mistake to believe that they will equally inform us about "fancier" ethnological concepts, such as descent systems.

Despite their limitations, archaeological data have the potential of providing enough information about significant dimensions of human behavior to make the analysis of prehistoric social and political systems worthwhile. Much can be learned from human skeletal remains about the age and sex composition of populations, as well as about conditions of health and causes of mortality (see Chapter 7). The analysis of settlement data will produce additional demographic information concerning household size and composition, community size, and the distribution of population across the landscape. From the study of tool kits, manufacturing techniques, and the distribution of activity debris, it is possible to identify some of the tasks that were performed, as well as where and by whom. In this fashion, much may be learned about the division of labor: what tasks were performed by either sex and the degree of economic specialization and interdependence within and between households, communities, and regions. Factors considered to be of importance for understanding relatively simple social organization are the relative economic importance of tasks performed by either sex and the degree to which husbands and wives worked alongside each other or separately as members of sexually-defined work teams (Fitting and Cleland 1969).

Studies of artifacts, especially their stylistic elements, may permit residence patterns to be inferred. It may also be determined in what manner extended-family groupings did or did not engage in collective economic or ritual activities. It has been frequently suggested that patterns of community or group exogamy ought to be reflected in the stylistic homogeneity of artifacts associated with one sex and the heterogeneity of those associated with the other (Wright 1965). Exogamous marriage patterns may also be discerned in physical anthropological studies, which show members of one sex in a community to be more closely related physically than are members of the other (Ossenberg 1976; Land and Sublett 1972). Artifact distributions also provide information about ranking, hierarchical organization, and differential access to goods and services that cut across descent groups. Houses may differ in size and quality of construction and prestige artifacts (often made of materials of exotic origin) may be associated with specific houses or living areas within houses (Tyyska 1968). .

Much attention also has been paid in recent years to the analysis of burial customs from this point of view. The association of unusually elaborate burials or large amounts of grave goods with young adults has been construed as evidence of a society in which achieved status was of major importance; whereas societies in which unusually elaborate mortuary treatment was associated with a minority of burials and some children were buried with large amounts of goods have been interpreted as ones in which hereditary status was of greater importance (Brown 1971; Tuck 1976; Trubowitz 1977). Skeletal studies have produced evidence of physical differences reflecting varying marriage or nutritional patterns that had a class basis (Haviland 1967).

Most archaeological studies of political organization are concerned with chiefdoms or even more complex societies (Trigger and Longworth 1974). The study of prehistoric political organization at the tribal level is less advanced and in many respects inherently far more difficult, since political relationships are not clearly differentiated institutionally from the basic network of kinship relations. Patterns of warfare may be reflected fairly directly in some cases, in village defenses and the positioning of communities in relationship to one another. Increasing population densities, even in small-scale societies, appear to require more formal regulatory mechanisms and hence a more formal political organization (Trigger 1976b), although an understanding of this problem has not yet reached the point where demographic data can serve as more than a very general predictor of political systems.

GENERAL STATE OF NORTHEASTERN ARCHAEOLOGY

The archaeology of the Northeast has not been characterized by any spectacular breakthroughs in the study of prehistoric social or political organization. Since the 1950s, however, sustained, if slow, progress has been made with these topics, both in the formulation of new problems and in the actual practice of field archaeology. This paper evaluates these developments, particularly as they refer to the evolution of Iroquoian cultures in the vicinity of the lower Great Lakes. In view of the unusually long period during which Iroquoian archaeology has been studied systematically and the important role played by Iroquoian ethnology in the development of North American anthropology, it seems appropriate to focus on these cultures. My own knowledge of recent developments is more complete for southern Ontario and Quebec than for other areas. This, however, has been the most active center of innovative Iroquoian research in recent years.

Iroquoian archaeology, like other regional manifestations of the discipline, is hampered as well as assisted by the data and local interpretations of data that are a heritage of its own past. Specific interpretations of many aspects of Iroquoian prehistory, including ones that long ago should have been seen to be of doubtful validity, have survived unchallenged, even after the paradigms or general interpretative frameworks in which they evolved have been repudiated and forgotten (Trigger 1970). Because of this, the swifter progress made by archaeology on a continental or international level has to be assimilated and understood afresh in each region.

Iroquoian archaeology developed in the nineteenth century utilizing a series of assumptions that were common to North American archaeology. On the basis of what White Americans judged to be their unsatisfactory reaction to White domination, the native peoples of America were believed to be either biologically incapable of cultural development or for some reason incorrigibly predisposed against it. It appeared to follow from this that native cultures had been equally uncreative and static in prehistoric times. Where temporal variations were evident in the archaeological record, it was assumed that these were the result, not of cultural change and development, but of the replacement, as a result of migration, of one people and their unchanging culture by another (Trigger 1980). Thus what we would now call the Middle Woodland (300 B.C.-A.D. 600) cultures of the lower Great Lakes region were believed to have been produced by Algonquian-speaking peoples who had later been expelled by Iroquoian horticulturalists, who had invaded the area from the southwest. Hence these earlier cultures were interpreted as being historically related to those of the Algonquian peoples who inhabited New England, central Ontario, and Michigan in the early historic period. It was also speculated that the still-earlier Archaic cultures might be attributed to an Eskimo-like people (Parker 1922). Because of this, it was generally assumed that the traditional cultures being described or reconstructed by ethnographers represented the full range of native cultures present in North America at all but the earliest period of native settlement. Intellectually, this view implied total stagnation for archaeology, since it left no special subject matter for it to explain and no role but to illustrate the material content of cultural patterns that were thought to be well-known.

The growing attention that was paid to establishing cultural chronologies throughout North America after 1914 revealed the unsuspected complexity of prehistoric cultural sequences in most areas. This was accomplished in the Iroquoian area by William Ritchie's (1944) research on the so-called pre-Iroquoian cultures of New York State. At first, culture change continued to be explained in terms of migration, but gradually diffusion came to be relied on to account for much that was observed in the archaeological record. Yet, in spite of this, earlier concepts of ethnicity persisted without alteration. For example, the Owasco culture, although horticultural and today interpreted as early Iroquois, continued to be viewed as ethnically Algonquian, although it was argued that it had been influenced by contact with invading Iroquoians. Gradually, however, archaeologists became aware of marked continuities in local sequences of development. In the Iroquoian area, this culminated in Richard MacNeish's (1952) *in situ* theory, which postulated that the historic Iroquoian cultures of the region had developed from local so-called Algonquian ones. Yet, while "pre-Iroquoian" cultures were recognized as being ethnically Iroquoian, archaeologists continued to interpret late horticultural manifestations in this sequence in terms of what was known about historic Iroquoian ones, and preagricultural ones, regardless of their presumed ethnicity, in terms of what was known about the historic Algonquian cultures of central Ontario, especially that of the Ojibwa. Even though these prehistoric cultures are no longer viewed as ethnically Algonquian, they are still widely regarded as being like Algonquian ones in terms of their economy and social structure.

This line of thinking was reinforced at a crucial point in the development of Iroquoian archaeology by the unilinear scheme of "Primary Types of Community Patterning" devised by the Seminar on the Functional and Evolutionary Implications of Community Patterning held under the chairmanship of Richard Beardsley (1956) in 1955. Four of the seven developmental stages outlined by that seminar were widely accepted as representing significant phases in the prehistoric development of the Northeast. The Free Wandering period appeared to summarize the essential features of the economy and social organization of the Paleo-Indian period, the Restricted Wandering and Central-Based Wandering ones various Archaic through Middle Woodland cultures, and the Semi-Permanent Sedentary the slash-and-burn horticultural villages of the Iroquoians. Through the work of Ritchie (1956) and Ritchie and Funk (1973) these terms became part of the intellectual currency of Northeastern archaeology. The use of analogy in the absence of historical continuity to interpret archaeological data was also sanctioned by Fred Eggan's (1966:78-111) employment of data concerning historical Algonquian cultures to reconstruct aspects of prehistoric Iroquoian social organization. This approach maintained the old concept of limited cultural variation and the idea that the total diversity of cultures in prehistoric times did not exceed their diversity in the early historic period. It also drew parallels of doubtful validity between societies existing in very different environments. It seems highly unlikely, for example, that prehistoric hunter-gatherers living in the rich Carolinian biotic province of extreme southwestern Ontario would have had a seasonal round or social organization precisely similar to that recorded in historic times for the Ojibwa of central and northern Ontario. As David Clarke (1979:61) has reminded us, archaeology would be a feeble science indeed, if it subscribed to a uniformitarianism that assumed that the variation in prehistoric societies was no greater than that attested in present day ones. In his far-fetched example, this would forever preclude the chance of discovering that in Neanderthal society women had done "the hunting, clustered in bands of up to 300, each served by only a handful of males."

There is also a growing realization among archaeologists and ethnologists that ethnographic data concerning traditional cultures in the Northeast are neither as complete nor as reliable as they once were assumed to be. Iroquoian ethnographies are based on historical documents of varying completeness and reliability and on recollections and survivals of what were assumed to be traditional cultures that were recorded by several generations of ethnographers. Eyewitness accounts of the Iroquois cultures of New York State prior to 1650 are very limited. In the past ethnologists generally assumed that at this period these cultures must have been very similar to that of the neighboring Huron people, which is well-documented. Recently, however, archaeological and ethnohistorical studies have shown that the Huron and Iroquois differed culturally in many specific ways in the early seventeenth century. These differences extended to their subsistence patterns, technology, settlement patterns, house types, religion, and burial rituals (Trigger 1963). Other northern Iroquoian groups about whom even less was recorded seem to differ no less in the archaeological record. To ignore these differences and accept a composite picture of any one Iroquoian society as a valid description of all of them is a procedure that is as misleading as it is unproductive of deeper insights into the similarities and differences in northern Iroquoian cultural patterns.

There is also increasing awareness of the limitations of existing ethnographic and ethnohistorical information concerning relatively well-reported groups, such as the Huron between 1615 and 1650. Even data about matters that required no special linguistic skills are often meager and imprecise. For example, we are told almost nothing about the technical details of Huron house construction, although various French writers had the Huron build houses for them. Similarly, we are told that Huron women planted, tended, and harvested the crops but not whether each woman did this on her own or the female members of households or larger kinship groupings worked together. Nor is it stated whether the women of a longhouse pooled their corn harvest or each woman stored and used hers separately. While we are informed that women made pottery and in general terms what techniques they employed, it was never specified whether or not all women engaged in this craft, how many pots each of them made, and how these pots were distributed to the women who eventually used them. Archaeological studies of interments within Ontario Iroquoian villages have amplified and amended to a considerable degree the limited ethnohistorical data relating to this practice (Kapches 1976; Fitzgerald 1979).

Most ethnohistorical information takes the form of broad generalizations, with little in the way of supporting case studies, such as might be found in a report on modern ethnographic research. We are told, for example, that a Huron longhouse normally had 4-5 fires, usually 2-3 paces apart, with a family living on either side of each hearth (JR 15:153; 16:243; 17:177). We are also informed that after marriage Huron men usually lived with their wives' families (Boucher 1664:103). Yet there is no information whether or not there were special arrangements that permitted chiefs, who inherited their office matrilineally, to live in a longhouse belonging to their own clans, despite rules requiring clan exogamy.

Even when the early historical accounts are sufficiently detailed to allow case studies to be assembled, the data are mostly too vague and ambiguous, or their context too uncertain, for conclusive results to be obtained. For example, Cara Richards (1967) was able to assemble descriptions of twenty-four Huron and Iroquois families from the first half of the seventeenth century. She concluded that the majority of these families were based on virilocal rather than matrilocal residence patterns and that, if matrilocal residence ever occurred with any regularity, it was after 1650 and as a direct consequence of the situation resulting from European contact. In fact, however, because of various ambiguities, including uncertainty whether kinship relations are being reported in each instance in a framework of European or Iroquoian nomenclature, there are only eight solid cases of nonmatrilineal residence in Richard's study (Trigger 1978:56). Several of these refer to chiefly families, where an exceptional form of avunculocal residence might have been practiced to permit young men to live with uncles whose offices they were eligible to inherit.

Significant efforts are being made to overcome the limitations of ethnohistorical data. Archaeologists are attempting to learn more about how Iroquoian houses might have been constructed by building and trying to maintain full-scale models of what they believe they might have been like (Wright 1974:293-302; Pearce 1979). While still inconclusive, this work has increased an awareness of the structural problems that are involved in building longhouses and of the significance of many hitherto ignored architectural details that can be observed in the archaeological record. These experiments also indicate the snow loads and wind pressure that different types of structures can withstand and the durability of the various materials that were used (R. Williamson, personal communication). Archaeological evidence of repair, when recognized, can provide valuable clues as to how long a time a structure might have been used.

Archaeologists are also constructing sophisticated simulation models, in which archaeological and ethnohistorical information concerning historic Iroquoian groups is supplemented by carefully quantified data derived from modern studies concerning crop yields, soil fertility, and the availability of game and firewood, and by estimates of the time or energy required to perform specific tasks. The geographer Conrad Heidenreich (1971) has been particularly successful in building an elaborate model that quantifies the labor that would have gone into the clearing of land, the relocating of villages, and the changing annual crop yields of Huron field systems. His research provides valuable information concerning the factors involved in timing the relocation of Iroquoian villages. Even for this purpose, however, Heidenreich's model is not complete. More experimental work is needed to determine how much wood an Iroquoian village would have required for heating and cooking, and how much effort would have had to be expended to provide it. Research is currently under way on this problem (Smith et al. 1979). Yet, whatever specific criticisms may be made of it, Heidenreich's model provides the basis for discussing Iroquoian subsistence patterns in a far more precise manner than was possible previously. Unfortunately, the high standards set by this research have not been maintained in some recent investigations of this type. For example, Webster's (1979) study of the energy inputs involved in Huron deer hunting is vitiated by gross errors in understanding the ethnohistoric documents and their descriptions of hunting parties (Trigger 1981). The approach also seems to offer more rigorous insights only into those areas where greater quantitative rigor can be derived from the biological and physical sciences or by estimating human energy expenditures; hence its main potential contribution is likely to be to the study of Iroquoian ecology. It does not seem clear how, given the nature of the ethnohistorical record, this approach can be used in such a way as to make significant direct contributions to the study of Iroquoian social or political organization.

There has also been growing awareness in recent years that the earliest ethnohistorical data do not describe Iroquoian cultures prior to when they began to be modified by European influences. Instead they describe societies involved in a process of change resulting from direct or indirect European contact. Although the first description of Huron life is based on eye-witness observations made as early as 1615, archaeological data suggest that European goods may have begun to reach southern Ontario almost a century earlier (Trigger 1979). Archaeological data document major changes in Huron culture during the sixteenth century, many of which seem to be related to the gradual development of the fur trade at this time. These include the resettlement around the beginning of the seventeenth century in a small area at the southeastern corner of Georgian Bay of proto-Huron peoples who formerly had been dispersed to the south and east; an event historically associated with the expansion of the Huron confederacy to embrace its full membership.

Awareness of changes of this sort has encouraged a great deal of speculative revisionism by Iroquoian ethnologists. We have already noted that Cara Richards proposed that matrilocal residence developed among the Iroquoians as a response to the fur trade. Using the same data, Wallis Smith (1970) has speculated that the fur trade had led to a breakdown in traditional matrilocal-matrilineal institutions by the first half of the seventeenth century; while Brian Hayden (1976) has suggested that Iroquoian extended families may never have been strictly lineage-based. Yet, disturbing as these claims are, we do not have and are unlikely to discover, sufficient ethnohistorical data to resolve ambiguities of this sort or to provide a picture of what any native societies in the Northeast (or possibly anywhere in North America) were like prior to significant changes being brought about as a response to the presence of Europeans. The answers to these controversies, if they are to be found at all, must be provided by archaeology. Ethnologists and ethnohistorians will have to depend on archaeology for an improved understanding of what native cultures were like prior to the impact of European presence in North America as well as for better knowledge of the diversity and nature of native cultures in the early historic period. Archaeology thus has had thrust upon it a wholly new and more important role in studying the native peoples of the Northeast. This, in turn, confronts archaeologists with new challenges and responsibilities.

NEW APPROACHES

In the past, archaeologists working in the Northeast have tended to generalize about social organization too quickly and on the basis of inadequate and poorly-defined samples of data. The latter were mostly the small collections of artifacts from sites that originally had been used to construct cultural chronologies. Recent analyses by Sanders, Parsons, and Santley (1979:491-532) of their extensive data on prehistoric settlement patterns in the Valley of Mexico indicate that no one sampling technique could adequately have represented all of the significant local variation in settlement patterns in that region. Nor could it have provided data that were appropriate to answer the many questions that they asked. A similar analysis of data from Draper, a large and almost completely excavated sixteenth century Iroquoian site near Toronto, indicates that arbitrary sampling techniques could not have produced samples that were truly representative of the variation within that site. Bellhouse and Finlayson (1979) suggest that no less than 40-45% of even large middens would have had to be excavated to achieve a maximum standard error of 1.5% or less. Even larger fractions of smaller middens would have been required to achieve a similar result with them. The once common assumption that a small part of a site can be assumed to be representative of the whole, or a single site of an entire class of sites, is yet another manifestation of the normative approach to the study of cultures that rightly has been condemned by the New Archaeology. It was an approach that was, and still is, encouraged by the difficulties involved in processing archaeological data. Yet, by masking important variations in the archaeological record, it greatly retards our understanding of prehistoric cultures.

The temporal counterpart of this spatial or geographical normativism is the assumption that all cultural change occurs as gradual evolutionary processes. This uniformitarian view sees abrupt changes as resulting only from migration or the conquest of one group by another. Yet the introduction of some highly-significant innovation, such as corn agriculture or the bow and arrow, might, in a short time, radically transform the economic and social patterns of a region and give the impression of a major discontinuity in the archaeological record. It is also being realized that abrupt and dramatic changes do not occur simply as a result of fortuitous external causes. They can come about as a result of specific combinations of variables fluctuating in a normal fashion. René Thom's (1975) so-called "catastrophe theory" attempts to provide a rigorous description of the manner in which such transformations occur (Renfrew and Cooke 1979). It is therefore unsound to assume that major and abrupt changes in the archaeological record necessarily imply ethnic changes, any more than it is safe to assume that continuities in patterns of ecological adjustments necessarily indicate ethnic continuity(see Chapter 3). The archaeological record must be studied in detail and with a special emphasis on social and political issues before alterations in population can be assumed or ruled out. Even when dealing with entities as seemingly alike as the northern Iroquoian cultures, it is an abuse of uniformitarian principles to assume that what applies at one site or at one period of time necessarily holds at another.

Archaeological data collected at an earlier period tend to be of limited usefulness for the sociopolitical interpretations that currently are being attempted (see Chapter 4). Most excavations of habitation sites concentrated on small areas of middens that it was believed would yield a sample that could be treated as representative of the whole site for working out a cultural chronology. Although efforts have been made to base social and political interpretations on such data (Whallon 1968), their limited range and the fact that most of the material comes from contexts of disposal rather than use severely limits their utility. William Ritchie (1956) recognized that this was so when he began his study of Iroquois settlement patterns in the 1950s. Yet the work done by Ritchie and his associates remains transitional in many respects between the older culture-chronological archaeology and more recent work on Iroquoian settlement patterns. In part because of financial constraints, only small portions of sites were excavated. While a few longhouses were completely excavated, many more were only partially uncovered while their remaining outlines were traced by slit trenches. Slit trenches were also used to follow the lines of village fortifications and establish village size. Many of the interpretations of Iroquoian house outlines offered in Ritchie and Funk's *Aboriginal Settlement Patterns in the Northeast* were made tentatively, either because of the multiplicity of overlapping post molds in many Owasco sites or because of the small areas that were opened. It is unfortunate that many of these interpretations are now being accepted without a review of the evidence on which they were based. An examination of Ritchie's published material clearly reveals, for example, that the patterns of hearths, pits, and post molds recorded at the Owasco Sackett site can be interpreted more satisfactorily as partially uncovered longhouses rather than as a number of small round houses (Ritchie and Funk 1973:215-216; see also Snow 1980:313).

Recent studies of Iroquoian settlement patterns have involved innovations at all three levels of analysis: (1) individual structure, (2) settlement layout, and (3) regional distribution of sites (Trigger 1968; Clarke 1977). Recent work, in particular at the Draper site, first by Hayden (1979) and more recently by Finlayson (1977), has involved as never before the detailed excavation and analysis of individual houses in an effort to define activity areas and residence groups within each structure. This work has demonstrated the value of excavating houses in areas that have not been plowed, since the latter activity generally obliterates the locational associations of artifacts that were not deposited in pits. Experimental studies have since been conducted in order to quantify the degree to which modern cultivation disturbs the location of artifacts (Latta 1979). In longhouse 2 at the Draper site, efforts were made to record in detail the location of every artifact and, by digging the floor in 3 cm levels, to detect alterations in artifact types and the use of different parts of the house during its occupation. The published study of the partial excavation of this longhouse suggests that it was inhabited by what appear to be at least two matrilineal extended families that had member families extending over three generations. It also suggests that different tasks, such as bone working, adze manufacture, and hide-working, were performed either by different nuclear families or at least in different parts of the longhouse (Hayden 1979). While the subsequent finding that one end of this longhouse was built over the remains of a palisade and midden dating from an earlier phase in the occupation of the site casts doubt on some of these conclusions, work done more recently on other houses at the Draper site promises further interesting conclusions along these lines.

After World War II, a number of Iroquoian sites were excavated quite extensively. Between 1948 and 1950, Father Thomas Grassmann (1969) excavated the historic Mohawk site of

Caughnawaga, first occupied in 1667. Wilfrid Jury produced ground plans of the Huron mission villages of St. Ignace II and St. Louis, as well as of the prehistoric Forget site. Unfortunately, no detailed final reports are available concerning any of this work. In 1959, Walter Kenyon (1968) excavated most of the groundplan of the Miller site, which belongs to the Pickering culture and was radiocarbon dated to the early twelfth century, although some archaeologists would now date it still earlier. His report did not, however, describe in detail the internal arrangements of the six houses belonging to this village.

In 1971, J.V. Wright took a major step forward with his total excavation of Nodwell, an Iroquoian site of the fourteenth century near the shores of Lake Huron that was being threatened by development. In his final report, Wright (1974) provided a vast amount of distributional data concerning the relationship of artifacts to individual houses that had well-defined internal features. One structure, later demolished and built over, was interpreted as having been occupied briefly in the spring and summer by the work party that had established the village. While Wright was unable to correlate specific clusters of attributes with particular houses in the village, he did manage, using stylistic criteria, to divide the houses into three spatially noncontiguous groupings that he labelled "conservative," "intermediate," and "progressive." The first and last of these groups have been confirmed by chemical differences in pottery fabric revealed by x-ray fluorescence analysis (Trigger et al. 1980).

The most ambitious "total" excavation carried out to date is that of Draper, a large sixteenth century Iroquoian site that experienced a series of clearly demarcated expansions during the course of its occupation (Finlayson 1979). These appear to have come about as a result of additional groups joining the community. The examination of artifact distributions within this site thus promises to reveal important aspects of patterning not only with respect to different parts of the village (including growth patterns) but also within individual houses. Although there has been considerable controversy concerning the cost of excavating the Draper site and the methods employed, the work done there has led to a growing conviction that the total excavation of an increasing number of Iroquoian sites is a necessary precondition for an improved understanding of Iroquoian social organization.

The first important regional study to be published in detail was James Tuck's (1971) examination of the Onondaga sequence in central New York State. Tuck attempted to delineate sequences of sites that had been successively occupied by the same communities and to show how, in the course of the fifteenth century, these sites came together to form the two communities that were associated with the historic Onondaga tribe. Similar studies among other Iroquois groups in New York State have been facilitated by the tendency of these groups to remain within distinctive territories over long periods. Archaeologists are now trying to work out similar sequences in Ontario, but there the situation is complicated by a tendency for some groups to move considerable distances in the course of their village relocations. The tribes of the historic Neutral and Huron confederacies both were clustered in small areas of the regions over which proto-Neutral and proto-Huron villages had been dispersed in earlier times. There is also evidence that the groups making up large Ontario Iroquoian villages may have split apart no less frequently than small villages joined together to form larger ones (Heidenreich 1971:129-132). While this may represent behavior distinctive of Iroquoian groups who were not surrounded on all sides by hostile neighbors who were also sedentary horticulturalists, it greatly complicates the interpretation of developmental sequences. Where kin groups switched frequently from one community to another the archaeologist requires a detailed knowledge of stylistic variation within sites even to work out a satisfactory culture chronology. Investigations of major importance along these lines are William Noble's (1978) still largely unpublished studies of protohistoric and historic Neutral sites in the Hamilton area and Peter Ramsden's (1977) attempt to identify prehistoric clusters of Huron settlement in the Trent Valley and north of Lake Ontario, from which the development of the historic Huron tribes may eventually be traced forward in time.

Archaeologists have long known that, in addition to their main villages, Iroquoians utilized various seasonally-occupied sites for fishing, hunting, and cultivating their fields. While such sites occasionally have been identified as such by archaeologists, until recently they have been treated very casually in the archaeological literature. There is now, however, a growing conviction that these sites must be carefully identified and studied if Iroquoian exploitation patterns are to be defined and regional populations estimated more accurately. There is also increasing awareness that patterns of subsistence and settlement may have been quite different in the early stages of the development of a horticultural economy from what they were like in the historic period. Archaeologists are now prepared to take up Marian White's (1963) challenge to determine empirically whether or not early agricultural villages were actually inhabited throughout the year. Growing attention is paid to determining during what seasons sites were inhabited and what activities went on in them. The former requires the analysis of floral and faunal remains, with the flotation of pit and midden contents facilitating the recovery of the former. There is also need of more progress in identifying specific Iroquoian tool kits and their functions, an activity largely ignored since the pioneering work of W. M. Beauchamp and W. J. Wintemberg.

The investigation of special purpose sites is now receiving considerable attention from Canadian archaeologists. Robert Pearce (1978) has studied a group of seasonal collecting sites that appear to be associated with major year-around Pickering stage villages near Peterborough, Ontario. A number of St. Lawrence Iroquoian fishing stations have also been examined. Several of these seem to have been used repeatedly over longer periods than any one agricultural village would have been occupied (Pendergast 1975; Girouard 1975; Marois 1978). One of these, the Steward site, has produced the first stratigraphic evidence covering several centuries of cultural development among the St. Lawrence Iroquoians (P. J. Wright and J. B. Jamieson, personal communication). Ronald Williamson (1979) has identified the Robin Hood site, located near Draper, as a small summer cabin site that probably was used mainly by women cultivating the adjacent fields (see Chapter 3). In addition to floral and faunal evidence indicating only warm weather occupation, the houses appeared to be open-ended, and more activity to have gone on outside than inside them. Although there were three houses at this site, they were flimsily constructed and Williamson believes that each may have been used by a single household for a few years in succession. The Robin Hood site appears more likely to be a cabin site than does the nearby White site, which previously was thought to be a possible example of this type. One of the problems encountered at the Robin Hood site was that so little ceramic material was recovered that very precise dating which might have connected it with one of the several large sites nearby was impossible.

The identification of special activity sites becomes meaningful only as part of a larger project that aims to define regional systems of settlement. This requires the systematic locating and mapping of all Iroquoian sites in a particular region, an activity that has largely been in abeyance since the work of A. F. Hunter and a few other archaeologists at the end of the nineteenth century. Despite the general failure of Iroquoian archaeologists to deal effectively with local or community differences as these are reflected in ceramic assemblages, the work of Tuck (1971), Ramsden (1977), and others demonstrates that it is possible not only to seriate main sites but to differentiate sequences of such sites that ran parallel to each other in the same area.

It is more difficult to determine how long any particular site was inhabited, a problem that cannot be dealt with effectively by assuming that each site was inhabited for some arbitrary fixed length of time. It appears likely that as communities grew larger, they exhausted their hinterland more quickly and hence were compelled to relocate more frequently. This implies that, on average, early Iroquoian communities may have had to relocate less frequently than they did in historic times. Where sufficient data have been collected, it should eventually be possible, by comparing the number of households estimated for a community with the amount of midden debris and also by taking account of post mold evidence relating to the rebuilding of houses, to estimate the approximate lengths of time that such sites were inhabited. Where artifact samples are small, it may always be difficult to correlate special activity sites with specific main villages. Nevertheless, identifying such sites permits estimates of population to be made that are not inflated by counting such sites in the main sequences.

We are unlikely to be able to recover total settlement patterns over large areas. Many sites have been destroyed by urban growth or intensive cultivation. Others, for various reasons, elude detection. Because of a lack of money and manpower, even many known sites have not been examined closely enough to be properly dated or assigned to a functional type. Yet, especially in areas such as southern Ontario, where Iroquoian populations appear to have shifted from one region to another over time, extensive and rather detailed mapping will be required before satisfactory population estimates can be made for different periods. It has been suggested, for example, that Princess Point summer camps were located along lakes and major rivers, whereas in the following Glen Meyer phase major villages were located in areas of light, fertile soil farther inland (Stothers 1977:113). This indicates that extensive site surveys are necessary before generalizations can be made about the ecological and political factors that affected prehistoric distributions of population. Exhaustive local or regional studies, of the sort Tuck pioneered in the Onondaga region, may be the best way to work toward this goal. Areas of Ontario that were intensively occupied for only a brief period are of particular value for understanding local systems of resource exploitation.

ETHNICITY

It is indicative of the failure of the old culture-chronological approach to realize even its own limited objectives that archaeologists still cannot agree concerning the ethnic origins of the Iroquoian-speaking peoples in the Northeast. Since 1952, it has generally been assumed that continuity in pottery types and other cultural traits indicates an ethnic continuity in the Iroquoian occupation of the lower Great Lakes area stretching back into Middle Woodland times. No one seems to doubt that the Princess Point people in Ontario or their Owasco counterparts in New York State were Iroquoian-speaking. James Tuck (1977), although admitting gaps in current archaeological evidence, would trace an Iroquoian presence back through the Point Peninsula culture to the Laurentian Archaic. Wright (1972, n.d.) agrees but extends the developmental sequence geographically to include the Middle Woodland Saugeen and Inverhuron Archaic cultures in southwestern Ontario. Douglas Byers (1961) suggested that the arrival of the Iroquoians in the Northeast may have corresponded with the earliest manifestations of the Lamoka culture in New York State during the Archaic period. Dean Snow (1977) has linked this event with the Frost Island culture, which he sees as ancestral to Meadowood and Point Peninsula.

David Stothers (1977), on the other hand, rejects the hypothesis of continuity between Middle and Late Woodland cultures in the lower Great Lakes region. He derives the Iroquoian-speaking peoples from Havana Hopewell groups that originally lived in Michigan, Illinois, and Wisconsin. He equates their arrival in Ontario with the early Princess Point or a still earlier Weaver culture and in New York State with the Clemson's Island culture. Yet, while Stothers sees these groups bringing corn agriculture into the Northeast, his hypothesis does not represent a complete return to the southern migrationary theories that H. M. Lloyd and A. C. Parker expounded early in the twentieth century. They saw the invading Iroquoians as possessing an horticultural way of life that was entirely different from the culture of the Algonquian-speaking hunting peoples they replaced. Stothers sees the newcomers as possessing only a rudimentary form of agriculture and a way of life that was little different from that of the Middle Woodland peoples they supposedly superseded.

The Princess Point culture (ca. A.D. 600-1000) has only recently been identified as a stage in the development of Iroquoian culture in southwestern Ontario. It precedes the Glen Meyer culture (ca. A.D. 1000-1300), which itself is not particularly well-known. Still less is known about the still earlier late Middle Woodland cultures in this region. Because of this, it is impossible to be certain whether or not there is continuity in the cultural development of this region between Middle and Late Woodland times. There is more evidence of such continuity in New York State, although more attention should be paid to the Kipp Island and Hunter's Home phases of development. Archaeological proof of ethnic continuity requires evidence of persistence, not merely in broad cultural units but generation by generation in carefully-defined social groups. This in turn requires that more attention be paid to interpreting the social significance of the distribution of various types of artifacts in the archaeological record than the culture-historical approach hitherto thought necessary or worthwhile.

Explicit attention must be paid to distinguishing archaeological similarities that are indices of ethnicity and group membership from those that indicate only a widely shared system of adaptation to a particular environment. The techniques that Ian Hodder (1978) has developed for determining the functional significance of individual artifact types by analyzing their spatial distributions, if applied to Iroquoian data, might help to define various types of social groupings. Tuck's (1978) interpretation of Maritime Archaic burial mounds as possible territorial markers erected in times of increasing stress is a move in this direction, paralleling Bradley and Hodder's (1979) analysis of the role of burial mounds in neolithic Britain. Fresh archaeological approaches of this sort can be complemented by small-scale physical anthropological studies which may differentiate neighboring populations that have tended to remain relatively isolated reproductively from each other over time.

LATE MIDDLE WOODLAND CULTURES

The rest of this paper addresses problems that currently are being encountered in studying social and political aspects of the evolution of prehistoric Iroquoian cultures. In such discussions, the ethnic origins of the Iroquoians are a matter of more than historical curiosity. It makes a great deal of difference if early Iroquoian cultures in the Northeast developed from one or more local Middle Woodland antecedents or if they developed from a Hopewellian culture that perhaps had evolved quite different social and political institutions. J. Friedman and R. J. Rowlands (1978) have pointed out that it is impossible to analyze and explain the development of societies from one period to another unless we can specify empirically their cultural contents at each stage of their development. This implies that the functional integration of cultures is not so tight or immune from external influences that social scientists can predict in detail their development over long periods. Any discussion of how or why horticultural economies developed among the Iroquoians must consider what Iroquoian cultures were like prior to that happening. The following sections will respect the majority opinion that the roots of northern Iroquoian culture are found in the late Middle Woodland cultures of Ontario and New York State. This discussion may also reveal why the problem of continuity and discontinuity remains so hard to resolve.

Despite traditional nomenclature, I am assigning the Princess Point culture, because of its well-defined horticultural economy, to the Late Woodland rather than to the Middle Woodland period. The earlier Middle Woodland cultures of southern Ontario and New York State generally have been interpreted in accordance with Julian Steward's (1955) and E. R. Service's (1962) generalizations about the structure of hunting bands, and more specifically in accordance with analogies to Algonquian-speaking peoples, such as the Ojibwa, who in historic times lived on the southern margin of the Precambrian Shield, directly north of the Iroquoians. Groups numbering 200-300 men, women, and children are believed to have gathered during the summer at major fishing locations around the lower Great Lakes and along their major tributaries, and to have dispersed to hunt game in the adjacent forests during the winter. It has also been suggested that these bands were patrilineal and probably exogamous (Hickerson 1967). Recently, however, as a result of criticism of the concept of the patrilineal hunting band by Lee and DeVore (1968) and Guemple (1972), some archaeologists have suggested that the residence patterns of Archaic and Woodland hunting bands may have been more variable and flexible. Drawing analogies with the Indians of the Northwest coast, it has also been proposed informally that some of the late Middle Woodland groups around the lower Great Lakes that depended heavily on fishing might already have been matrilineal. The testing of these theories, using archaeological evidence, has so far remained perfunctory. However, greater morphological similarities among male than among female skeletons found in studies of cemetery populations of the Middle Woodland period in the Rice Lake area of southern Ontario have been interpreted as supporting a virilocal or avunculocal residence pattern for these groups (Spence et al. 1979).

The most comprehensive study of a Middle Woodland people in the lower Great Lakes area is William Finlayson's (1977) report on the Saugeen culture that flourished along the southeastern shores of Lake Huron between 400 B.C. and A.D. 600. Wright interprets these people as ancestral to the Ontario Iroquoians, while Finlayson alternatively suggests that they might have been the ancestors of the Algonquian-speaking Ottawas. Preliminary osteological studies suggest a close similarity between the Saugeen and Princess Point peoples. Although the relevant cemeteries are not located in the same part of southwestern Ontario, this has been interpreted as evidence against the hypothesis that the Princess Point people were intrusive into southern Ontario. On the other hand, Saugeen skeletons can be distinguished from those associated with the contemporary Point Peninsula culture in southeastern Ontario, who were probably the ancestors of the historic Huron (Molto 1979:49-50). This indicates a significant degree of genetic heterogeneity among the inhabitants of southern Ontario in Middle Woodland times.

Large Saugeen groups seem to have gathered to fish near rapids along rivers flowing into Lake Huron during the spring and early summer. It has also been suggested, on the basis of small pit and fissure caries in the teeth of late Saugeen skeletons, that some horticulture might already have been practiced at that time (Molto 1979:40-41). During the autumn, the population dispersed in smaller groups to collect nuts. It is assumed that they dispersed in still smaller groups to hunt in the interior over the winter, although sites associated with that season have not yet been identified. Major fishing sites were used repeatedly over long periods, but the archae- ological record was deposited in such a manner as to make it impos- sible to distinguish the loci that were occupied in any one year. The cemeteries that have been studied at the Donaldson site (a large summer camp) appear to date from different periods. While each has a distinctive pattern of grave offerings, neither is suggestive of other than a simple egalitarian society.

Finlayson speculates that each river drainage in southwestern Ontario was occupied by one or more Saugeen bands. However, no work has been done to define such groups and identify their cultural similarities and differences. In particular, very little has been pub- lished about late Middle Woodland sites in the southern part of southwestern Ontario, where the Princess Point culture has been identified. Yet work is in progress in the latter area and results may be expected soon.

There is evidence that for at least a few centuries, a strikingly different economic and social pattern was associated with the Ontario Point Peninsula culture found in eastern Ontario, especially the Rice Lake area, during the Middle Woodland period. It is sug- gested that bands of 100-200 people lived by the lake shores during the summer, collecting fish, birds, shellfish, and plant food and, in the autumn, wild rice and nuts that would nourish them into the winter. After these supplies were exhausted, the bands dispersed in multi-family groups into the forest to hunt until spring. Each of the clusters of mounds found at intervals around Rice Lake and adjacent bodies of water has been interpreted as associated with a band and its territory. It is suggested that the death of a band leader was the signal for the construction of such a mound (Spence et al. 1979; Spence 1980). The lavish grave goods found with the principal interments are associated primarily with adult males and children. This is seen as additional evidence for the patrilineal bias of these groups. It has been suggested that the Levesconte Mound belonged to the group that played the leading role in the trading network that supplied the Rice Lake area with exotic goods. It perhaps also played the key role in the interband political organization of this region. Economic, marital, and ritual activities may have linked these bands together to form a regional band or tribe.

Although the cultural sequence linking Middle and Late Woodland times is better known for northern New York State than for Ontario, archaeologists have not studied in detail the accompanying changes in band organization. It has been suggested that the Kipp Island site in western New York might have been inhabited year-around in late Middle Woodland times, with its inhabitants also making use of summer fishing stations nearby (Ritchie and Funk 1973:353). It has also been suggested that the later White and Turnbull sites, associated with the Hunter's Home culture, were occupied throughout the year and that corn might have been grown there. Ritchie and Funk (1973:355) treat these sites as examples of Beardsley's Semi-Permanent Sedentary pattern. It is possible that the warmer and richer biotic zone of northern New York State and extreme southwestern Ontario permitted intensive collecting economies to support more permanent settlements than are exemplified by the ethnographic parallels provided by societies that in historic times lived considerably farther north. Yet it is important that before they are accepted, patterns that are not ethnographically attested should be established on a firmer basis of archaeological evidence than Ritchie and Funk have done. It is also important that band territories should be delineated in detail for some areas in northern New York State in late Middle Woodland times as a basis for understanding how these groups were altered in the early Owasco period. A model for work of this sort in New York State is provided by Joseph Granger's (1978) study of the Archaic Meadowood culture.

It has often been assumed that Middle Woodland huntergatherer groups lived in nuclear family dwellings and that extended families developed in Late Woodland times. Because of what appears to be prolonged, probably seasonal, reuse, it is often difficult to distinguish house patterns in the confusion of post molds at many of the larger Middle Woodland sites (Finlayson 1977:257). Yet many of the house plans that have been inferred are small and probably would have been occupied by nuclear families. At the Donaldson site, Wright identified two rectangular structures measuring 7.0 x 4.3 m and 5.2 x 3.4 m respectively (Wright and Anderson 1963). The larger structure had a hearth near the center and is believed to have had a gable roof and been open at the south end. A round structure 5.5-6.1 m in diameter and a rectangular one with rounded corners have been tentatively identified at the Kipp Island site in New York State (Ritchie and Funk 1973:160).

Yet ethnohistorical and ethnographic data indicate that in historic times the hunter-gatherer peoples of central Ontario and southern Quebec did not normally live in single-family dwellings. The Montagnais winter hunting parties that Paul LeJeune lived with in the 1630s had two or more brothers and their families living together in a large conical tent (JR 7:107). Champlain's description of a fortified Montagnais encampment at Tadoussac in 1603 indicates that during the summer they were living in longhouses (Biggar 1922-36, 1:98-99). The normal house type among the Algonquians who lived around Georgian Bay in the early seventeenth century appears to have been an elliptical structure equipped with two fireplaces and sheltering several families (Wrong 1939:185). E. S. Rogers (1967) has documented houses each containing several nuclear families still in use in recent times among the Mistassini Cree.

At the Summer Island site in Lake Michigan, David Brose (1970) excavated four cabins that had been inhabited seasonally in the second or third centuries A.D. One of them was an elliptical structure measuring 8.8 x 3.7 m that had two hearths along its main axis. The distribution of artifacts inside indicated that it had been lived in by two nuclear families. The other cabins at the site were round but large and at least one seems to have been occupied by an extended family. Post molds at the Kipp Island No. 4 site have been interpreted as representing a structure over 12 m long. It has been claimed as a prototype of later Iroquoian longhouses but its delineation is far from certain. Another example is a rectangular house 10.7 m long and 6.1 m wide noted at the White site (Ritchie and Funk 1973:119). A house 24.4 m long at the Juntunen site, in the Straits of Mackinac, has been interpreted as evidence of Iroquoian influence there around A.D. 1300 (McPherron 1967:103). Alternatively, it may provide a link between the incipient longhouse at the Summer Island site and the longhouses reported among the historic Nipissing, Ojibwa, and other Algonquian-speaking groups.

This suggests that small extended families may have been a widespread household type in the Northeast already in Middle Woodland times. Some may have lived in incipient longhouses; others in round or rectangular houses that, especially in winter, may have been crowded beyond the space norms suggested by Raoul Naroll (1962) and others (Cook and Heizer 1968; LeBlanc 1971; Casselberry 1974).

To determine the nature of Middle Woodland residence patterns it will be necessary to examine the use of space inside habitation structures by means of artifact distributions. This will be very difficult to do at sites where reuse makes it impossible to attribute hearths and storage pits to specific dwellings with certainty.

It is possible that in Middle Woodland times Iroquoian speakers were already living in small multi-family residences. There is also limited evidence that the band structure of at least some of these groups was patrilineal rather than matrilineal and that they tended to be exogamous. If these observations are correct, the main problem concerning the development of Iroquoian social structure in later times is not how extended families came into being, but how and under what circumstances institutions based primarily on patrilineal descent were restructured to become matrilineal.

If women moved from one band to another at marriage in late Middle Woodland times, this would have facilitated the rapid diffusion of new ceramic styles and of the elements of horticulture. Brose (1970:67-68) has suggested that because of such a marriage pattern new pottery styles had diffused so rapidly at the beginning of the Middle Woodland period that it gives the false impression of a sweeping occupation of the Great Lakes region by a new population. A similar alternative may apply to neomigrationary explanations of northern Iroquoian origins. The study of late Middle Woodland social organization is a matter of considerable urgency, both for establishing a base line for tracing the social changes that accompanied increasing reliance on horticulture and for resolving the nature of the cultural transition from the Middle to the Late Woodland pattern.

EARLY IROQUOIAN DEVELOPMENT

It remains uncertain whether agriculture was practiced to any significant degree in the lower Great Lakes region prior to the beginnings of the Princess Point culture in Ontario and the Owasco culture in New York State. The developmental sequence that we are considering in this section embraces the Princess Point, Glen Meyer, and Pickering cultures in Ontario and the entire Owasco sequence in New York State.

Three explanations have been offered why horticulture became the dominant mode of subsistence at this time. Stothers (1977) suggests that it began in the Northeast because a new people entered the region who happened to practice it. Ritchie and Funk's (1973) general interpretation of New York State prehistory could be construed as suggesting that horticulture was a response to population increases that had outstripped the carrying capacity of an intensive collecting economy. This motivated groups to adopt crops of Mesoamerican origin that were already being grown in the Ohio and Mississippi valleys. Demographic data remain extremely rudimentary and even Mark Cohen's (1977:71-84) secondary indices of population pressure have not been tested systematically against evidence for the late Middle Woodland period. Nevertheless, this interpretation is attractive to those anthropologists who see demographic pressure as the principal driving force behind cultural change (Smith 1972:418).

I have argued that the principal factor leading to the adoption of horticulture, at least in Ontario, was a desire to minimize or eliminate the period during the winter when hunter-gatherers were compelled to disperse in search of game. This was the time of year of greatest hardship and probably also of highest mortality (see Chapter 3). Nuts and wild rice were storable commodities that could help to reduce this period of dispersal. Yet these resources were concentrated in limited areas and, because of unfavorable natural conditions, wild rice harvests tended to fail about one year in three. Hence no group could depend on such resources to survive every winter. Corn had the advantage that it could be grown far more widely and in proximity to a wider range of environments that were desirable for hunting and fishing. Even in early times, the chances of losing a crop probably were less than those of a wild rice failure. Hence, even if the first varieties of corn that became available were only marginally adapted for as short a growing season as prevailed in the lower Great Lakes region, they would nevertheless have been adopted as a substitute for wild rice. No one need have expected that eventually crops would eliminate completely the period of late winter dispersal. As corn became better adapted to a shorter growing season, horticulture gradually laid the basis for a sedentary way of life (Trigger 1976a:131-134). This argument would not apply to areas that had already achieved year-around settlement utilizing local natural resources. Yet even these economies, if such existed, would have been enriched and further stabilized by the introduction of horticulture.

If this hypothesis is correct, the earliest horticultural communities probably were continuations of the hunting bands of earlier times. It may not be a coincidence that both Middle Woodland summer fishing camps and the earliest horticultural villages are estimated to have had populations of 100-300 people. The small size of early Iroquoian settlements suggests that, in general, separate bands had not yet begun to join together to form larger communities. Anthony Forge (1972) has suggested that in communities of this size, decision making can remain informal, with everyone interacting on the basis of personal knowledge of each other. Nothing more was required than a chief to coordinate decision making within the community and act as a spokesman for it when dealing with other groups. Among the northern Algonquians in historic times such offices tended to be hereditary in a particular lineage of a band. Yet, the two cemeteries at the Sackett site may indicate that a couple of matrilineal bands or clan groups lived in that village, in which case some kind of village council might have been needed to coordinate village life.

While archaeological data remain inadequate, there is presently no evidence that more early Iroquoian villages were being inhabited at any one time than there had been late Middle Woodland bands. Hence there may have been less of an increase in population at this time than often has been assumed. Careful regional surveys would be required to resolve this question definitively.

Stothers (1977:123-123) argues that during early and middle Princess Point times the annual cycle remained much as it had been in the late Middle Woodland period. The earliest horticultural villages were inhabited only during the summer and autumn, while their populations dispersed into the interior of southwestern Ontario to hunt sometime during the winter. According to Stothers, most of these sites are located in exposed positions near lakes and large rivers that would have been very uncomfortable in winter, and are often found on mud flats that would have been flooded during the spring. The middens at these sites are small and diffuse. It is significant that Roundtop, which is one of the earliest Owasco sites in New York State, was similarly located in a flood zone, while a plethora of post molds indicates that there was much rebuilding of houses at the site, perhaps reflecting repeated seasonal occupations. These observations call seriously into question Ritchie and Funk's (1973:166) stereotype of year-around horticultural villages as characterizing the entire Owasco sequence. Indeed, the confusing patterns of post molds at the Roundtop, Maxon-Derby, Kelso, Nahrwold, and other Owasco sites resemble more closely what is found on Middle Woodland sites in New York State than they do the well-defined house patterns associated with later Iroquoian villages. This rebuilding suggests either seasonal abandonment of sites or that they were occupied for much longer periods than were common in later prehistoric or historic times. Either of these might have occurred because these communities were not as dependent on horticulture and hence were not depleting their local environment as quickly as villages did later. Ritchie and Funk (1973:279) estimate that the Nahrwold site was occupied, probably sporadically, for 150 years.

According to Stothers, by late Princess Point times villages such as Porteous were being occupied year-around. These villages were located above the flood plains of adjacent streams, had deep middens, and have yielded bird and animal bones indicating procurement throughout the year. The Porteous site contained small longhouses, including one over 11 m long that had two hearths aligned down the center. Yet, unlike many later longhouses, these were built with single lines of posts and new houses frequently overlapped the locations of old ones (Noble and Kenyon 1972). Hence the similarity between subsistence patterns at this time and in the historic period should not be taken for granted. The Kelly site, a Glen Meyer one near London, Ontario, contains one longhouse, has a palisade, and appears to have been inhabited in the autumn, primarily for the purpose of collecting and processing acorns (Williamson 1980). Confusing patterns of post molds have also been noted at Glen Meyer sites, such as Reid (M. Wright 1978), and Pickering ones, such as Miller and, to a lesser degree, Bennett (Wright and Anderson 1969).

Both incipient longhouses and circular houses have been delineated on Owasco sites, although in many cases the patterns are far from clear because of overlapping post molds. We have already suggested that the small excavations at the Sackett site can be more convincingly interpreted as segments of longhouses. There is clearly much to be learned about the evolution of sedentary villages and the development of Iroquois longhouses both at this time and later.

There is no evidence that deceased Iroquoian chiefs were venerated, a practice frequently associated with the emergence of an elite stratum and political integration in less egalitarian tribal societies elsewhere in the world (Friedman and Rowlands 1978:210). Indeed, the inheritance of chiefs' names from generation to generation of office holders indicates a very different, essentially atemporal view of the political order. Moreover, all but the simplest grave goods are generally absent in prehistoric interments. Yet burial customs served to reinforce social solidarity in rather different ways among various Iroquoian groups. Among the Iroquois, from Owasco times onward, the majority of burials were made in individual graves shortly after death, but apparently frequently in cemeteries or parts of cemeteries that corresponded to clan or moiety divisions. In the Pickering culture, bodies that often had decayed over the winter, or over several years, were buried in small groups inside villages or in sites unattached to any permanent habitation. Richard Johnston (1979), who accepts Stothers' explanation of Iroquoian origins, suggests that this practice was brought into Ontario from the southwest. This does not explain, however, why the customs of the Iroquoians in New York State were different. It seems possible that

Pickering burial patterns were a continuation of little-known late Middle Woodland ones in that part of Ontario. The ritual importance attached to the Serpent Mounds site as a place of burial may be a specific reflection of such continuity. In later times, the Huron practiced scaffold burial, but reburied the bones of their dead at intervals in rituals that expressed the unity of communities, of tribes, and ultimately of an extensive intertribal trading network (Trigger 1976a:426-429). Neutral burial customs were in many respects intermediate between Huron and Iroquois ones. While they interred bodies in groups at intervals, they do not appear to have used these groupings to express solidarity at the village level (Kenyon 1979).

Robert Whallon (1968) has sought to infer aspects of prehistoric Iroquoian social organization by examining associations among stylistic attributes on pottery from sites in New York State. Following James Deetz's study of stylistic behavior in Arikara ceramics, he hypothesized that if all pottery were made locally by Iroquoian women, mutual associations of attributes would be especially strong on pots produced in communities that had a high rate of matrilocal residence. In these communities, patterns would tend to be transmitted within specific matrilocal family groups. Whallon also sought to measure the flow of women from one community to another as a result of marriage. He postulated that a strong emphasis on matrilocal residence would have correlated with a low rate of such movement and hence with greater stylistic homogeneity within each village. Whallon's findings suggest that there was considerable development of matrilocality already by early Owasco times, with this trend increasing into the late prehistoric period. He suggests that Owasco groups were simple matrilocal families, not yet organized into matrilineages embracing several extended families, such as are reported existing in historic times.

In a similar, but less elaborate study of pottery from Princess Point sites, Scott Horvath (1977) observed that a considerable degree of attribute clustering on pottery from early Princess Point sites was followed by greater randomness and then, in the late Princess Point period, by renewed clustering. He interpreted this as marking a transition from patrilocal bands in the early period to matrilocal ones by the end of this phase, with an intervening transitional period. He seems to have assumed, however, that these patrilineal bands would have been endogamous, which seems unlikely given their small size. Yet, if wives were recruited from neighboring bands, attribute clustering would have been of low frequency. Given Horvath's small samples, it is difficult to be certain whether his aggregate findings can be reinterpreted as suggesting conclusions similar to Whallon's for the Owasco.

Whallon's conclusions pose certain developmental problems. He assumed, as Ritchie did, that matrilocality in the Owasco period reflected the important role now being played by women and by female work teams in food production. While allowing for a slight increase in emphasis on horticulture in the early Owasco period, he proposed that "the organization of economic activities characteristic of the historic Iroquois was present in all essential details in the early Owasco period [Whallon 1968:241]." We now see, however, that the traditional hunter-gatherer lifestyle may not have been altered as radically during this period as was previously believed. An alternative explanation of Iroquoian matrilocality suggests that women, rather than men, began to constitute the ongoing core of extended families when, as a result of economic change, women and their children began to live in or near their villages year-around, while men spent considerable amounts of time away from them during the warmer months, hunting, fishing, and performing other tasks. Under these conditions, it made more sense for female relatives to live together than for male ones. Melvin Ember (1973) has argued that, in general, sisters find it easier to live together than do unrelated women. This suggests under what circumstances extended families may have grown larger after virilocal residence had given way to matrilocal. Yet, neither of these theories accounts for why, from Whallon's evidence, matrilocality appears to have been so strongly established by the early Owasco period.

All studies that try to elicit information about Iroquoian social organization from studies of ceramics face a common problem. It is generally assumed in these studies that each Iroquoian woman made the pots that she herself needed and that each woman was trained by her mother or by other women of her household; hence techniques and designs tended to be inherited matrilineally. Yet detailed studies of Iroquoian villages, such as Wright's (1974:308) report on the Nodwell site, have so far not demonstrated close correlations between particular pottery types or attributes and specific houses or house clusters within the community. The lack of obvious correlations of this sort has been interpreted as casting doubt on traditional views of Iroquoian residence patterns. Nevertheless, from ethnohistorical accounts, we learn little except that pots were made by women. We are told nothing about how many women made pots, whether the same women made and used them or, if not, how they were transferred from maker to user, how much they were used, how long they lasted, or how many pots the average woman possessed (see Chapter 4). Although Iroquoian pots are generally well made, the total amount of pottery found in thoroughly excavated sites does not suggest that each family was breaking and replacing a large number of pots each year. The fact that the Iroquoians manufactured only one functional type of vessel, although in different sizes, indicates that pottery played a restricted number of roles in their cultures, probably for cooking and storage. The small number of sherds from Robin Hood, a small proto-Huron agricultural camp, also suggests that relatively little use may have been made of pottery vessels during the summer, perhaps because little corn soup was being prepared in that season. If each Iroquoian woman required only a couple of new pots each year, these may have been made by a relatively small number of skilled women rather than by each woman for her own use. Perhaps only in this way could women acquire and maintain the skills that are evident in Iroquoian pottery. Whether it was manufactured by one or two women for each household or for a larger clientele remains to be determined. Wright (1974) noted refuse resulting from ceramic manufacture in all but three of the twelve houses at the Nodwell site, yet the amount of refuse was highly variable in relation to the number of broken vessels found in each house. It is clear that any interpretation of Iroquoian social organization based on pottery design elements must be preceded by studies that seek to determine who made this pottery and what was the relationship between makers and users. Problems of this sort are amenable to archaeological investigation, especially now that some Iroquoian sites have been excavated in their entirety. This proposal accords with Ruth Tringham's (1978) and Robert Dunnell's (1978) arguments that rigorous archaeological studies of the function of artifacts and how they were produced must precede higher level speculations about their social and political significance.

The same observations apply to pipes. In 1968, William Noble suggested a possible correlation between pipe types and matrilineal descent groups and that "it is possible to trace lineage totems on pipes back to ca. A.D. 1400 [Noble 1968:297]." Yet obvious correlations between pipe types and residence patterns have not been forthcoming and, in a more recent study, Noble (1979) rejected his earlier interpretation as simplistic. He lists many different factors that may have influenced individual preferences for pipe types. Woolfrey et al. (1976), employing a statistical measurement of the correlation of decorative motifs on pipes and clay vessels from sites of the Middleport period, have concluded that these artifact classes reflect two or more traditions at any one site. They suggest that these are best explained by assuming that women made the pottery vessels while men made the pipes. Very limited ethnohistorical evidence indicates that men did make pipes, although it is unclear whether the reference was meant to apply to all pipes or only to stone ones (Boucher 1664:101). On the other hand, if pottery vessels and pipes were each made by semispecialists, the interpretation that traditions of manufacture correlate with sex differences need not hold.

It is often assumed that Middle Woodland hunting bands, like Harold Hickerson's (1967) reconstruction of Ojibwa ones in early historical times, were patrilineal, exogamous clans. A simple change of residence rule would have produced a situation in which women remained in their natal communities, while men would have had to marry women from different ones. David Aberle (1970:221-222) has found statistical support for David Schneider's (1961:27) observation that isolated communities consisting of a matrilineal core and in-marrying spouses are extremely difficult to maintain. Such systems operate most easily in communities composed of more than one descent group or in monolineage communities that are located near each other. Also, if hunting remained of considerable importance, especially over the winter, it is unlikely that men would have acquiesced to such dispersal after marriage (Murdock 1949:213-214). This raises the alternative possibilities either that matrilineal communities quickly came to be composed of more than one descent group, as suggested by the two cemeteries at the Sackett site, or that the transition from patrilineal to matrilineal descent was more gradual than Whallon's study of pottery styles suggests. The stylistic analysis of male-produced Iroquoian artifacts, such as lithics, has not yet been undertaken and the material may not be sensitive enough to permit the testing of propositions about the transmission of such skills within particular communities that, in turn, might shed light on how local or heterogeneous in origin were the male inhabitants of these communities. Yet such studies are worth attempting as a counterpart to a more far-reaching analysis of the social implications of pottery designs.

There is clearly much to be learned about the development of social organization during the early Iroquoian period. Conclusions so far tend to be contradictory. Tentative indications of the prevalence of matrilocality in early times do not accord with theories that would correlate the development of this practice with marked dependence on horticulture, even if we were to assume that some crops were grown earlier in Middle Woodland times than is generally believed. This is especially so if we must take account of evidence that suggests that the Iroquoians may have become dependent on food crops only rather slowly during this period. There are also theoretical problems about how early matrilocal communities would have functioned. It must be remembered that our understanding of Iroquoian residence patterns, even in the historic period, is beset by many uncertainties and that the indices used to measure matrilocality in prehistoric times are not unambiguous. What is needed is a less stereotyped attitude towards the interpretation of Iroquoian social organization and a more comprehensive approach to using archaeological data to study this problem.

Whatever their patterns of marriage and residence were like, early Iroquoian villages were not isolated from one another, even though there is little evidence of long-distance trade at this time and they have been described as "self-sufficient and locally orientated [Ritchie 1965:293]." Wright (1966:53) has interpreted the emergence of a uniform Uren culture across Ontario at the end of this period (ca. A.D. 1300) as resulting from the conquest and partial assimilation of the Glen Meyer culture by the Pickering one. He has noted that Uren pottery combines many of the diagnostic features of both cultures, while male-manufactured items show greater similarity to Pickering. Other archaeologists do not accept this interpretation (White 1971; Noble 1975:50). It is possible that this homogenization resulted from marriage patterns that promoted the intervillage movement of both sexes, perhaps combined with an increasing population at this time. Fifty years later, pipes, which had hitherto been few in number and rather crude in Ontario, became abundant and began to occur in a variety of sophisticated shapes. Wright (1966:62-63) believes that these new types diffused into Ontario from the Oak Hill culture of New York State, where prototypes seem to have developed from the already more evolved pipe complex of the Owasco culture. Some of this contact may be related to the affinity, noted in historic times, between members of clans that were named after the same animal or bird, even when they belonged to different communities or tribes. It is not known when this cross cutting of clan and territorial affiliations began. It may already have been practiced during the Middle Woodland period.

LATER IROQUOIAN DEVELOPMENT

There is little doubt that by Uren-Oak Hill times the Iroquoian subsistence economy was established along essentially the same lines as in historic times. Women, children, and old people lived and worked year-around in or near agricultural villages, while men periodically went to hunt and fish in the surrounding forests. Yet this and subsequent periods witnessed major changes in Iroquoian social and political organization. Both in Ontario and New York State, houses at first grew longer, some reaching over 90 m. This suggests a marked increase in the size of extended families. Then, in late prehistoric times, houses seem to have grown shorter in both regions. While it has been suggested that the latter process reflected the breakdown of matrilineal family organization as a result of the fur trade (Tyyska and Hurley 1969), the trend seems to have begun too early for this to have been the initial cause (Tuck 1971: 221).

There is great need of a detailed study of social factors that relate to the layout and use of Iroquoian houses. There is much regional as well as temporal variation in house types. Tuck (1971: 209) notes that houses in the Onondaga Hill area tended to be longer than those found in other areas occupied by the proto-Onondaga. In Ontario, most longhouses remained round-ended. Ontario Iroquoian house plans either show clear evidence of sleeping platforms or lack such evidence entirely, although these houses were close to one another spatially and temporally and may even occur in the same village. Houses of unusual shapes are recorded from various periods (Channen and Clarke 1965). Differences have also been noted in construction techniques, locations of hearths and house entrances, presence or absence of storage cubicles at the ends of houses, and degree of emphasis on internal sweat baths (a subject that has only begun to be studied). The unusually large post molds associated with some historic Huron houses have been explained in terms of the introduction of iron axes (Tyyska 1969:76). This does not, however, account for the similar use of large posts by the Iroquois in prehistoric or very early protohistoric times. It remains to be discovered what sorts of patterns of behavior these differences represent and what local traditions some of them may signify.

Attempts have been made to determine empirically a ratio that would indicate the number of people who lived in a longhouse as a function of the area of its ground plan (Casselberry 1974). These studies have not, however, yielded results that are confirmed by other methods. Wright (1974:71) has more convincingly estimated the population of nine houses at the Nodwell site by determining the number of hearths associated with each and assuming that there were two families per hearth and eight people per family. His findings suggest that population densities in these houses varied from a hypothetical minimum of one person per 1.6 m^2 to a maximum of one person per 4.0 m^2. Wright also tentatively estimated the varying frequency of children in different longhouses according to the number of "juvenile" pots found in each.

It has been suggested that Alan McPherron's "trampling index," which measures the degree to which pottery has been fragmented by being broken underfoot, could be used to measure patterns of movement and the intensity of use of different portions of longhouses (Brose 1970:46-49). Sizeable portions of some longhouses do not contain hearths and apparently were not occupied by specific families. This and the observation that other houses were extended in length during their relatively brief period of occupation suggested to Brian Hayden (1979:23-24) that factors less predictable than membership in matrilineal extended families were determining membership in households. Determining the demography of longhouses and, by analyzing the distribution of artifacts, the uses to which each part of them was put is a vital prerequisite for reconstructing the nature of the extended families that lived in them. Archaeological data can yield more information about these topics than they have been made to do so far.

The maximum size of villages also tended to increase through time, some acquiring populations that have been estimated as high as 1500 people or more. Yet, Hayden (1979:8) has recently reminded us that communities do not increase in population automatically as more resources become available. Not all Iroquoian villages increased in size and it is clear that in historic times some Huron ones were deliberately opting not to do so (Trigger 1969:13-17). The larger a village was, the more quickly it depleted the fertility of nearby fields, sources of firewood, and some types of game in its immediate hinterland; hence the more often such communities had to be relocated. Tuck (1971:58) estimates that the small villages of early Iroquoian times might have been occupied for eighty years or more, whereas the large settlements of later times and their satellite communities had to be relocated in a fraction of that time. Both for chronological purposes and in order to understand social organization better, more accurate information is required concerning environmental factors as they relate to Iroquoian village size. For example, do middens show a gradual diminution in the bones of certain animals over time and is this process more marked in the case of large villages than of small ones?

Hayden (1979:184) argues that intertribal trade played a major role in the development of large Iroquoian settlements. He suggests that large communities assured the control of trading networks. This led to a concentration of wealth in such communities that attracted additional settlers to them. Nuclear families were eager to attach themselves to the households of successful traders. Yet, there is relatively little evidence of intervillage trade in prehistoric times and at present no evidence that large communities had disproportional access to exotic goods, although such evidence might be forthcoming in the future. Hence, there is little to support Hayden's proposal.

The traditional explanation of increasing village size is that it represents a reaction to the increasing threat of warfare. Larger village size is paralleled by growing emphasis on elaborate palisades, and the location of villages on sites that offered strong natural defenses and were remote from navigable streams. It is also paralleled by evidence of a growing emphasis on prisoner sacrifice, in the form of human bones, sometimes burned and hacked, in the village middens. These first appear during Owasco times in New York State and in Uren sites in Ontario. Various economic causes have been suggested for increasing warfare. The low population density, in relation to the total amount of fertile land that the Iroquoians could have worked in the lower Great Lakes region, seems to rule out pressure of that sort. Others have proposed that deer, which provided skins necessary for clothing, were the critical scarce resource (Gramly 1977).

A modified version of John Witthoft's (1959:32-36) theory of the origin of Iroquoian warfare suggests that it was an indirect response to the development of horticulture. As hunting became less important for subsistence, warfare, which had always been practiced to a limited degree in connection with blood feud, provided a substitute means for men to acquire personal prestige and establish a role for themselves in the political lives of their communities. The need for this prestige necessitated having enemies and stimulated the spiralling pattern of bloodshed that became an integral part of the Iroquoian way of life. In historic times, prisoner sacrifice was conceptualized as a sacrifice to the sun and to a deity associated with war and life-giving forces. It seems to represent a local reworking of ideas that were also prevalent in the southeastern United States and perhaps were ultimately of Mesoamerican origin. Such concepts were no doubt welcomed by the Iroquoians as an additional rational for waging war (Trigger 1976a:144-147).

Archaeologists have attempted to trace prehistoric patterns of warfare in the archaeological record by noting distributions of foreign-style pottery. It is frequently assumed that small to moderate amounts of such pottery occurring reciprocally in sites belonging to two different groups represent the capture and integration into these communities of female potters. Analyses undertaken to date have not employed sufficiently sensitive criteria to detect such movements among culturally similar groups living close to one another. The possibilities are also excluded, perhaps rather arbitrarily, that such patterns result from either intermarriage or long-distance trade. The first is thought unlikely because of the reluctance of Iroquoian women in historic times to leave their native villages. Trace element analysis has not been used to determine whether exotic pottery was made locally or not. The latter finding would rule out local manufacture by captive women. The best-studied case of possible warfare, using pottery as an index, is between some proto-Huron groups and the St. Lawrence Iroquoians. Although it has recently been suggested that this warfare arose as a result of the early fur trade (Ramsden 1977:291-293), the earliest evidence for it occurs on sites that are clearly prehistoric. Hence the unknown causes of this conflict antedate the fur trade. Interestingly, there is little evidence of this sort of warfare between the Huron and the Iroquois prior to the late sixteenth century. A tentative interpretation of late prehistoric warfare in southwestern Ontario has recently been based on a distributional study of shapes and flint sources of projectile points occurring on two clusters of sites (Fox 1980).

There is evidence that as villages increased in size, their layout was planned more carefully. Longhouses were aligned parallel to one another, in part to permit more of them to be located within a palisaded area (Noble 1969:19). There were also open spaces between the ends of longhouses, where the Huron disposed of garbage. Defensive considerations appear to have played a significant role in determining the internal layouts of villages (Pearce and Smith 1980).

There is little evidence so far to confirm that localized clans occupied different sections of communities. As we have already noted, three groupings of longhouses were differentiated at the Nodwell site on the basis of stylistic criteria, but the houses were not geographically contiguous. It is tempting to equate the three clusters of longhouses at the Garoga site with the three Mohawk clans: Bear, Wolf, and Turtle. This is all the more likely since, despite Lenig's theory that the Mohawk had separate clan territories (Ritchie and Funk 1973:332), ethnohistorical evidence clearly indicates that families belonging to all three clans lived in individual villages (Trigger 1976a:657; Fenton and Tooker 1978:467). However, at the present time no additional archaeological evidence is available with which to explore this problem further. There is also a problem of the degree to which patterns of ceramic contexts of manufacture and use are reflected in patterns of disposal, and how evidence relating to one pattern can be distinguished from that relating to another. It is hoped that research currently underway on material from the Draper and Benson sites in Ontario will help to clarify the nature of internal social patterning. Another problem to be investigated is whether or not as village size increased, the inclusion of matrilineages belonging to different clans reduced the frequency of village exogamy.

A related issue is the degree to which increases in the sizes of communities resulted from population expansion or from the merger of two or more previous villages. Tuck (1971:212) proposes that, around 1420, two small proto-Onondaga communities merged at the

Christopher site to form a new community that lasted into historic times. Unfortunately, we do not have enough information about settlement patterns or artifact distributions within the Christopher site and its two predecessors to know precisely how this merger occurred or how it affected the material culture of the communities involved. In Ontario, a series of village expansions has been traced at the Draper site, some of which appear to represent the incorporation of separate communities into the original site (Finlayson 1979). In the Trent Valley, there is evidence that what may have been a group of St. Lawrence Iroquoian refugees were allowed to settle in houses located outside the palisade at the Kirche site. By the time this community had relocated to the Coulter site (if this is, indeed, what happened) these refugees seem to have been incorporated into the main settlement (Ramsden 1979). The detailed analysis of artifacts from these and similar sites ought to reveal much about the social consequences of such merging, in particular how distinctive the different groups remained. It may also help to reveal how important a role was played by matrilocal residence.

Archaeologists have so far paid less attention to the process by which large villages split apart, although this is attested in the ethnohistorical record as being a not infrequent occurrence. We also have no reliable information about how people were adopted into villages or left them as households, nuclear families, and individuals, rather than as clan groups. These processes may explain part of the cultural homogenization that seems to characterize the historic Huron after they had settled in northern Simcoe County. Such studies will require, however, extremely detailed knowledge of site sequences, as well as of internal variation within sites.

Studies of reasons for increases in community size, when combined with a broader regional pattern of settlement, will provide data that are vital for understanding the role played by population expansion in the later development of Iroquoian culture. Larger villages have been interpreted as evidence of major overall increases in population. There is, however, evidence that at least some large communities resulted from the merging of small villages. If the total number of Iroquoian settlements grew smaller through time, this would indicate that the main trend was towards greater nucleation rather than one of massive population growth. In view of the importance that has been assigned to population increase as an explanation of culture change, studies of this problem are of far-reaching importance. It is noteworthy that, in historic times, Iroquoian families were small and women practiced birth-spacing methods resembling those generally associated with hunter-gatherer populations (Trigger 1969:64).

A specific demographic problem is whether or not the Iroquoian region was affected during the sixteenth century by the epidemics of European diseases that appear to have had a disastrous impact upon the indigenous cultures of the southeastern United States. Ruinous outbreaks of epidemics are recorded in the Chesapeake Bay area prior to 1570 (Quinn 1979, II:557). These might have spread north to the Iroquois by way of the Susquehannock. It is claimed that there is evidence of heightened mortality in Seneca cemeteries dating from the sixteenth century, but such evidence has not been noted (or, admittedly, looked for) in Huron ossuaries. A resolution of this problem, using various types of archaeological evidence, is important for understanding not only historic Iroquoian culture but also Iroquoian development in still earlier times.

The growth of larger communities probably necessitated the development of more complex mechanisms of political control. Forge (1972) suggests that, if communities with more than about 300 people are to function well, there must be internal segmentation and a village council on which these segments are represented by their spokesmen. It is also suggested that, if communities with populations exceeding about 1500 are to endure for more than a short period, some form of coercion must be at the disposal of authorities. This is to ensure that there will not be too great a delay in decisions of major importance being implemented (Heidenreich 1971: 129-134). Ethnohistorical evidence indicates that the Iroquoian village councils functioned in accord with Forge's generalization, but that Iroquoian society never passed the second threshold. The carrying out of all decisions still required individual assent. This may account for why, although Iroquoian villages often had populations exceeding 300 people, communities with more than 1500 inhabitants seem to have been rare and short-lived.

According to ethnohistorical evidence, one of the signs of village chiefship was the extra-long dwellings that were lived in by the war and peace chiefs and which also served as loci for public feasts and rituals. At the historic Warminster site, most European trade goods were found in two of the nine houses that were excavated, and in each of these the cluster of pits around one hearth contained far more European goods than did the rest. This has been interpreted as an indication of status differences within and between Huron households (Tyyska 1968). To my knowledge, no similar study has been undertaken of individual burials in Iroquois cemeteries in New York State.

It is also argued that religious curing societies, with memberships cutting across clan lines, played a major role in stabilizing

Iroquoian society as it grew more complex. Attention is now being paid to trying to identify artifacts that are associated with, or reflect, the existence of such societies, so that their antiquity can be established archaeologically (Tuck 1971:213; Latta 1971:125-126). The growing importance of other socially-integrative rituals, such as the Huron version of the Feast of the Dead, is also deserving of more detailed study from the archaeological record.

It has usually been assumed that the Iroquoian tribes, as they were known in historic times, are of considerable antiquity. Superficially, this view seems to be supported by MacNeish's (1952) reconstruction of Iroquoian prehistory, which culturally traces many of these groupings back into the Middle Woodland period. On the basis of his settlement data, Tuck (1971:214-216) has argued that the formation of the Onondaga tribe, as a political entity, occurred between A.D. 1450 and 1475. At that time, the two communities remaining in the Onondaga area, a large and a small one, relocated within two miles of each other. Tuck suggests that this event, which is indicative of a close and peaceful relationship between these settlements, marked the founding of the Onondaga tribe. Nevertheless, similarities in language and culture among a number of neighboring groups may have provided the basis of an Onondaga cultural identity in earlier times. Other New York State groups have not been analyzed in this manner and may not provide such obvious clues as to their political evolution.

In Ontario, the definition of tribal groups is made more difficult by much geographical relocation in prehistoric times. Because tribal identity had primarily a geographical basis, it may have been more fluid among the prehistoric Huron and Neutral peoples than it was among the Iroquois. Most prehistoric tribal groups probably embraced only the few villages that were located in any one small drainage system. Ramsden (1977:295-296) is correct when he states that it is dangerous to assume that the Huron tribes, as they were known in the seventeenth century, existed already even in the protohistoric period. It is also clear, however, that cultural differences between the various peoples who later composed the Huron and Neutral confederacies can be traced back at least as far as A.D. 1400.

The archaeological study of confederacies is even more challenging and beset with pitfalls than that of tribes. Yet the subject is of great theoretical importance in view of the unresolved controversy as to whether confederacies were or were not entirely a response to the trading of furs with Europeans along the east coast of North America in the sixteenth century. Iroquoian confederacies differed structurally from one another. The Iroquois one was a peace league involving five tribes, each of which continued to maintain its villages in its ancestral territory. The final expansion of the Huron confederacy, if not its initiation, was marked by all of its member communities relocating themselves in a small part of northern Simcoe County.

William Engelbrecht (1974) hypothesized that the increasing friendly contact resulting from the formation of the Iroquois confederacy would have produced an increase in the similarity of ceramics within its territory and increasing heterogeneity of pottery within individual sites. Yet this analysis failed either to define boundaries for the confederacy or to pinpoint a date for its formation. It did, however, indicate more widespread contact, which Engelbrecht believes can be accounted for by trade that extended beyond the borders of the confederacy. At least some of the increasing influence of Mohawk ceramic styles on those of the Oneida may also reflect the large amount of intermarriage between these two groups that is recorded as having followed the slaughter of a high percentage of Oneida males by the Huron and their allies in 1638 (Trigger 1976a: 560).

The settlement of all the Huron tribes in northern Simcoe County at the end of the sixteenth century has traditionally been interpreted as a retreat from Iroquois attacks (Heidenreich 1971: 88-90). More recently, it has been argued that this move was motivated by a desire to participate in the fur trade, which involved trading surplus corn for furs with the northern Algonquians and traveling to the St. Lawrence River by way of Georgian Bay and the Ottawa River in order to trade with the French. This trade compensated the Huron who moved north for the slightly shorter growing season and snowier winters that they encountered in Simcoe County (Trigger 1962). The closing of the upper St. Lawrence River as an artery of trade as a result of Iroquois attacks, rather than direct attacks on Huron villages, may have been the military reason for these Huron to shift northward. It is hoped that as more protohistoric sites are excavated, enough data pertaining to trade and warfare will be collected to permit the adequate testing of these hypotheses. There is already some indication that groups like the Petun may have moved north into their historic area of settlement in order to exploit the vast beaver swamps at the headwaters of the Grand River. There is no evidence of them living nearby until the protohistoric period, and the unusually high frequency of beaver bones and scrapers at the Sidey-Mackay site suggests that the processing of beaver pelts was an important activity at that time (Ramsden 1977: 274).

CONCLUSIONS

The northern Iroquoian cultures are of particular interest as a case study of relatively recent transition from hunting and gathering to horticulture in the temperate zone. Although there has been a long tradition of archaeological and ethnographic study of these peoples, many questions concerning their history and culture remain unanswered. Because the northern Iroquoian cultures were located in a part of North America that is experiencing continuing urban and industrial expansion, there is a need to work quickly and efficiently, if much vital archaeological information is not to be lost irretrievably. The most important progress affecting the recovery of these data in recent years has been associated with development of the settlement pattern approach.

Experience indicates that we are unlikely to resolve in a wholly convincing manner any problems relating to Iroquoian social and political organization by applying analytical techniques to bodies of data isolated from their broader contexts. Few problems can be understood on their own terms. Instead, they must be investigated in a holistic manner that takes account of the relationship of what is being investigated to the total patterns of Iroquoian cultures and their historical development. This type of approach is well-exemplified by David Clarke's (1972) provisional model of an Iron Age society, a study that implicitly criticizes the propensity of American New Archaeology to examine limited problems in isolation from their broader contexts. For example, many problems relating to the use of Iroquoian houses can be understood only in the context of total community patterns and the latter only in terms of regional patterns of exploitation and human competition. If the social organization of many sites is to be understood properly, their economic functions and the seasons they were occupied are going to have to be determined more meticulously than in the past. This will require collecting more detailed paleobotanical and paleozoological information than was formerly common. It will also require paying more attention to the production and use of artifacts, something that has long been unduly neglected by Iroquoian archaeologists. More exhaustive and disciplined research to determine who made Iroquoian pottery and how much of it was used is a vital prerequisite for any research that seeks to use pottery to infer social organization. Such studies will require the total excavation of at least some sites.

More detailed chronological information is also vital to explain social and political organization. The manner in which pottery attributes respond to growing intercommunity contact, and the patterns of marriage and residence that may be partly correlated with such changes, can perhaps best be resolved by examining what happens in situations where two or more small villages unite to produce a single large one. To be effective, however, such studies would have to consider what happens to the pottery as it is associated not only with these communities as a whole but, as far as possible, with every midden, household, and nuclear family area. This requires the total excavation or very extensive sampling of sites. The occupational history of individual settlements is also of considerable interest from a social and political viewpoint. Yet studying it requires establishing chronological sequences that are shorter than those of villages. Where such analysis is possible, it will increase our knowledge of changes in population, patterns of residence, and the effects of environmental exploitation by the community.

We have stressed the need for archaeologists to establish social and political facts archaeologically. This is the reverse of the once popular idea that, if prehistoric economies could be reconstructed using archaeological evidence, ethnographic analogies would suffice to extrapolate social and political organization without a further input of archaeological information. Besides unduly circumscribing the interpretative power of archaeology, that approach overestimated the reliability of an ethnological understanding of traditional native cultures in the Northeast. On the contrary, ethnological knowledge of the contact period is so troubled by unresolved problems that archaeology has an important role to play in learning more about it. This cautions archaeologists against passively adopting a direct historical approach. We do not, however, deny that archaeological findings will be of maximum value if interpretations concerning the prehistoric period flow smoothly into an understanding of the early historic period, as derived from a harmonious combination of archaeological and ethnohistorical data.

Perhaps the most important aspect of archaeologists attacking new problems is that what they seek to do cannot simply build upon past achievements. Instead, it requires them to study more thoroughly, and from new angles, even problems that they have long regarded as established components of their research programs. Learning more about prehistoric social and political organization challenges archaeologists to refine their chronologies, to excavate sites more completely, to study artifact distributions more carefully, and to reconstruct patterns of subsistence and exchange more zealously. Such activities require funding, concentration of effort, and commitment to single projects on a scale hitherto not seen in Northeastern archaeology. All of this, of necessity, limits the value of data that once seemed complete, as the reading of most old archaeological site reports readily testifies. In exchange, however, it not only extends the range of archaeological curiosity but also renews the foundations of the discipline.

ACKNOWLEDGEMENTS

Many of the controversial views expressed in this paper were discussed in detail with the following graduate students in a seminar on "Problems in the Prehistory of Eastern North America" (151-552B) held at McGill University during the spring term, 1980: David Denton, James B. Jamieson, Moira McCaffrey, David G. Smith, and Ronald J. Williamson. The seminar was also attended by Louise Charette. I wish to thank Mr. Jamieson and Mr. Smith for reading and commenting on a draft of this paper.

REFERENCES

Aberle, D.F.
  1968   Comments by David F. Aberle. In *New perspectives in archeology*, edited by S.R. and L.R. Binford, pp. 353-359. Aldine, Chicago.
  1970   Comments. In *Reconstructing prehistoric Pueblo societies*, edited by William A. Longacre, pp. 214-223. University of New Mexico Press, Albuquerque.
Beardsley, R.K., P. Holder, A.D. Krieger, B.J. Meggers, J.B. Rinaldo, and P. Kutsche
  1956   Functional and evolutionary implications of community patterning. Seminars in archaeology: 1955. *Society for American Archaeology Memoir* 11:129-155.
Bellhouse, D.R., and W.D. Finlayson
  1979   An empirical study of probability sampling designs. *Canadian Journal of Archaeology* 3:105-123.
Biggar, H.P. (editor)
  1922-36 *The works of Samuel de Champlain* (6 vols.). The Champlain Society, Toronto.
Boucher, P.
  1664   *Histoire véritable et naturelle des moeurs et productions de la Nouvelle France, vulgairement dite le Canada*. F. Lambert, Paris.
Bradley, R., and I. Hodder
  1979   British prehistory: An integrated view. *Man* 14:92-104.
Brose, D.S.
  1970   *The Summer Island site: A study of prehistoric cultural ecology and social organization in the northern Lake Michigan area*. Case Western Reserve Studies in Anthropology No. 1, Cleveland.
Brown, J.A. (editor)
  1971   *Approaches to the social dimensions of mortuary practices*. Memoirs of the Society for American Archaeology No. 25, Washington.

Byers, D.S.
  1961 Second comment on William Ritchie's "Iroquois archaeology and settlement patterns." In Symposium on Cherokee and Iroquois culture, edited by William Fenton and John Gulick. *Smithsonian Institution, Bureau of American Ethnology Bulletin* 180:47-50.
Casselberry, S.E.
  1974 Further refinement of formulae for determining population from floor area. *World Archaeology* 6:117-122.
Channen, E.R., and N.D. Clarke
  1965 *The Copeland site: A precontact Huron site in Simcoe County, Ontario.* National Museum of Canada, Anthropology Papers No. 8, Ottawa.
Clarke, D.L.
  1972 A provisional model of an Iron Age society and its settlement system. In *Models in archaeology*, edited by David L. Clarke, pp. 801-869. Methuen, London.
  1977 Spatial information in archaeology. In *Spatial archaeology*, edited by D.L. Clarke, pp. 1-32. Academic Press, New York.
  1979 *Analytical archaeologist: Collected papers of David L. Clarke*, edited by his colleagues. Academic Press, New York.
Cohen, M.N.
  1977 *The food crisis in prehistory: Overpopulation and the origins of agriculture.* Yale University Press, New Haven.
Cook, S.F., and R.F. Heizer
  1968 Relationships among houses, settlement areas, and population in aboriginal California. In *Settlement archaeology*, edited by K.C. Chang, pp. 79-116. National Press, Palo Alto.
Dunnell, R.C.
  1978 Archaeological potential of anthropological and scientific models of function. In *Archaeological essays in honor of Irving B. Rouse*, pp. 41-73. Mouton, The Hague.
Earle, T.
  1978 *Economic and social organization of a complex chiefdom: The Halelea district, Kaua'i, Hawaii.* Museum of Anthropology, University of Michigan Anthropological Papers No. 63, Ann Arbor.
Eggan, F.R.
  1966 *The American Indian: Perspectives for the study of social change.* Weidenfeld and Nicolson, London.
Ember, M.
  1973 An archaeological indicator of matrilocal versus patrilocal residence. *American Antiquity* 38:177-182.
Engelbrecht, W.
  1974 The Iroquois: Archaeological patterning on the tribal level. *World Archaeology* 6:52-65.
Finlayson, W.D.
  1977 *The Saugeen culture: A Middle Woodland manifestation in southwestern Ontario.* Archaeological Survey of Canada, Mercury Series No. 61, Ottawa.

1979   The 1975 and 1978 excavations at the Draper village site. *Newsletter, Museum of Indian Archaeology at the University of Western Ontario* 1(2):1-4.

Fitting, J.E., and C.D. Cleland
1969   Late prehistoric settlement patterns in the Upper Great Lakes. *Ethnohistory* 16:289-302.

Fitzgerald, W.R.
1979   The Hood Site: Longhouse burials in an historic Neutral village. *Ontario Archaeology* 32:43-60.

Forge, A.
1972   Normative factors in the settlement size of neolithic cultivators. In *Man, settlement and urbanism*, edited by P.J. Ucko, R. Tringham, and G.W. Dimbleby, pp. 363-376. Duckworth, London.

Fox, W.A.
1980   Of projectile points and politics. *Arch Notes, Newsletter of the Ontario Archaeological Society* 80-2:5-13.

Friedman, J., and M.J. Rowlands
1978   Notes towards an epigenetic model of the evolution of 'civilisation'. In *The evolution of social systems*, edited by J. Friedman and M.J. Rowlands, pp. 210-276. Duckworth, London.

Girouard, L.
1975   *Station 2, Pointe-aux-Buissons*. Les Cahiers du Patrimoine, Ministère des affaires culturelles, Québec.

Gramly, R.M.
1977   Deerskins and hunting territories: Competition for a scarce resource of the northeastern woodlands. *American Antiquity* 42:601-605.

Granger, J.E.
1978   Cache blades, chert and communication: A reappraisal of certain aspects of Meadowood phase and the concept of a burial cult in the Northeast. In Essays in Northeastern anthropology in memory of Marian E. White, edited by William Engelbrecht and D.K. Grayson, pp. 96-122. *Man in the Northeast, Occasional Papers in Northeastern Anthropology No. 5.*

Grassmann, T.
1969   *The Mohawk Indians and their valley*. Hugo Press, Schenectady.

Guemple, L.
1972   Eskimo band organization and the "dp camp" hypothesis. *Arctic Anthropology* 6:80-112.

Haviland, W.A.
1967   Stature at Tikal: Implications for ancient Maya demography and social organization. *American Antiquity* 32:316-325.

Hayden, B.
1976   Corporate groups and the late Iroquoian longhouse. *Ontario Archaeology* 28:3-16.

Hayden, B. (editor)
1979   *Settlement patterns of the Draper and White sites*. Department of Archaeology, Simon Fraser University Publication No. 6, Burnaby.

Heidenreich, C.E.
1971 *Huronia: A history and geography of the Huron Indians, 1600-1650.* McClelland Stewart, Toronto.

Hickerson, H.
1967 Some implications of the theory of the particularity, or "atomism", of northern Algonkians. *Current Anthropology* 8:313-343.

Hodder, I. (editor)
1978 *The spatial organization of culture.* Duckworth, London.

Horwath, S.
1979 A computerized study of Princess Point Complex ceramics: Some implications of late prehistoric social organization in Ontario. In The Princess Point Complex. *National Museum of Man, Archaeological Survey of Canada Mercury Series No.* 58:310-317.

Johnston, R.B.
1979 Notes on ossuary burial among the Ontario Iroquois. *Canadian Journal of Archaeology* 3:91-104.

JR = Thwaites, R.G. (editor)
1896-1901 *The Jesuit relations and allied documents: Travel and explorations of the Jesuit missionaries in New France, 1610-1791* (73 Vols.). Burrows, Cleveland (reprinted by Pageant, New York, 1959).

Kapches, M.
1976 The interment of infants of the Ontario Iroquois. *Ontario Archaeology* 27:29-39.

Kenyon, W.A.
1968 *The Miller site.* Royal Ontario Museum, Art and Archaeology, Occasional Paper No. 14, Toronto.
1979 The geometry of death: The Neutral Indian cemetery at Grimsby. *Rotunda* 12:27-31.

Lane, R.A., and A.J. Sublett
1972 Osteology of social organization: Residence patterns. *American Antiquity* 37:186-201.

Latta, M.A.
1971 Archaeology of the Penetang Peninsula. In *Palaeoecology and Ontario prehistory II,* edited by W.M. Hurley and C.E. Heidenreich, pp. 116-136. Department of Anthropology, University of Toronto, Research Report No. 2, Toronto.
1979 Great poker chip caper. *Arch Notes, Newsletter of the Ontario Archaeological Society* 79-6:15.

LeBlanc,S.
1971 An addition to Naroll's suggested floor area and settlement population relationship. *American Antiquity* 36(2):210-211.

Lee, R., and I. DeVore
1968 Problems in the study of hunters and gatherers. In *Man the hunter,* edited by R.B. Lee and I. DeVore, pp. 3-32. Aldine, Chicago.

MacNeish, R.S.
1952 Iroquois pottery types: A technique for the study of Iroquois prehistory. *National Museum of Canada Bulletin* 124.

Marois, R.
1978 Le gisement Beaumier: Essai sur l'évolution des décors de la céramique. *National Museum of Man, Archaeological Survey of Canada Mercury Series* 75.

Marx, K.
1964 *Precapitalist economic formations, with an introduction by Eric Hobsbawm.* Lawrence and Wishart, London.

McPherron, A.
1967 On the sociology of ceramics: Pottery style clustering, marital residence, and cultural adaptations of an Algonkian-Iroquoian border. In *Iroquois culture, history, and prehistory*, edited by Elisabeth Tooker, pp. 101-107. University of the State of New York, Albany.

Molto, J.E.
1979 Saugeen osteology: The evidence of the second cemetery at the Donaldson site. *Museum of Indian Archaeology at the University of Western Ontario Bulletin* 14 (London).

Murdock, G.P.
1949 *Social structure.* Macmillan, New York.

Naroll, R.
1962 Floor area and settlement population. *American Antiquity* 27(4): 587-589.

Noble, W.C.
1968 *Iroquois archaeology and the development of Iroquois social organization (1000-1650 A.D.): A study in culture change based on archaeology, ethnohistory, and ethnology.* Unpublished Ph.D. dissertation, University of Calgary, Calgary.
1969 Some social implications of the Iroquois "in situ" theory. *Ontario Archaeology* 13:16-28.
1975 Van Besien (AfHd-2): A study in Glen Meyer development. *Ontario Archaeology* 24:3-95.
1978 The Neutral Indians. In Essays in Northeastern anthropology in memory of Marian E. White, edited by William Engelbrecht and D.K. Grayson, pp. 152-164. *Man in the Northeast, Occasional Papers in Northeastern Anthropology No. 5.*
1979 Ontario Iroquois effigy pipes. *Canadian Journal of Archaeology* 3: 69-90.

Noble, W.C., and I.T. Kenyon
1972 Porteous (AgHb-1): A probable early Glen Meyer village in Brant County, Ontario. *Ontario Archaeology* 19:11-38.

Ossenberg, N.S.
1976 Within and between race distances in population studies based on discrete traits of the human skull. *American Journal of Physical Anthropology* 45:701-709.

Parker, A.C.
1922 The archaeological history of New York State. *New York State Museum Bulletins* 235-238.

Pearce, R.J.
   1978   Archaeological investigations of the Pickering phase in the Rice Lake area. *Ontario Archaeology* 29:17-24.
   1979   Excavations and reconstruction of the Lawson site. *Newsletter, Museum of Indian Archaeology at the University of Western Ontario* 1(3):1-4.
Pearce, R.J., and D.G. Smith
   1980   The longhouse and Iroquoian defensive strategy. Paper presented at the 13th annual meeting of the Canadian Archaeological Association, Saskatoon.
Pendergast, J.F.
   1975   An in-situ hypothesis to explain the origin of the St. Lawrence Iroquoians. *Ontario Archaeology* 25:47-55.
Quinn, D.B. (editor)
   1979   *New American world: A documentary history of North America to 1612* (5 vols.). Arno Press, New York.
Ramsden, P.G.
   1977   A refinement of some aspects of Huron ceramic analysis. *National Museum of Man, Archaeological Survey of Canada Mercury Series* 68.
   1979   Late Iroquoian occupations of south-central Ontario. *Current Anthropology* 20(3):597-598.
Renfrew, C., and K.L. Cooke (editors)
   1979   *Transformations: Mathematical approaches to culture change.* Academic Press, New York.
Richards, C.
   1967   Huron and Iroquois residence patterns 1600-1650. In *Iroquois culture, history, and prehistory,* edited by Elisabeth Tooker, pp. 51-56. University of the State of New York, Albany.
Ritchie, W.A.
   1944   The pre-Iroquoian occupations of New York State. *Rochester Museum of Arts and Sciences Memoir* 1.
   1956   Prehistoric settlement patterns in northeastern North America. In *Prehistoric settlement patterns in the New World,* edited by Gordon R. Willey, pp. 72-80. Viking Fund Publications in Anthropology 23, New York.
   1965   *The archaeology of New York State.* Natural History Press, Garden City, New York.
Ritchie, W.A., and R.E. Funk
   1973   Aboriginal settlement patterns in the Northeast. *New York State Museum and Science Service Memoir* 20.
Rogers, E.S.
   1967   The material culture of the Mistassini. *National Museum of Canada Bulletin* 218.
Sanders, W.T., J.R. Parsons, and R.S. Santley
   1979   *The basin of Mexico: Ecological processes in the evolution of a civilization.* Academic Press, New York.

Schneider, D.M.
  1961 The distinctive features of matrilineal descent groups. In *Matrilineal kinship*, edited by David M. Schneider and Kathleen Gough, pp. 1-29. University of California Press, Berkeley.
Service, E.R.
  1962 *Primitive social organization: An evolutionary perspective.* Random House, New York.
Smith, D.G., R.F. Williamson, R.D. Fecteau, and R.J. Pearce
  1979 The longhouse experiment: An experience in Iroquoian archaeology. Paper presented at the Ontario Archaeological Society Symposium, Toronto.
Smith, P.E.L.
  1972 Land-use, settlement patterns and subsistence agriculture: A demographic perspective. In *Man, settlement and urbanism*, edited by P.J. Ucko, R. Tringham, and J. Dimbleby, pp. 409-425. Duckworth, London.
Smith, W.M.
  1970 A re-appraisal of the Huron kinship system. *Anthropologica* 12: 191-206.
Snow, D.R.
  1977 Archeology and ethnohistory in eastern New York. In Current perspectives in northeastern archeology. *New York State Archeological Association Researches and Transactions* 17(1):107-112.
  1980 *The archaeology of New England.* Academic Press, New York.
Spence, M.W.
  1980 Exchange and the development of rank. Paper presented at the 45th annual meeting of the Society for American Archaeology, Philadelphia.
Spence, M.W., W.D. Finlayson, and R.H. Pihl
  1979 *Hopewell archaeology: The Chillicothe conference*, edited by D.S. Brose and N'omi Greber, pp. 155-121. Kent State University Press, Kent.
Steward, J.H.
  1955 *Theory of culture change: The methodology of multilinear evolution.* University of Illinois Press, Urbana.
Stothers, D.M.
  1977 The Princess Point complex. *National Museum of Man, Archaeological Survey of Canada Mercury Series* 58.
Thom, R.
  1975 *Structural stability and morphogenesis.* W.A. Benjamin, Reading, Massachusetts.
Trigger, B.G.
  1962 The historic location of the Hurons. *Ontario History* 54:137-148.
  1963 Settlement as an aspect of Iroquoian adaptation at the time of contact. *American Anthropologist* 65(1):86-101.
  1968 The determinants of settlement patterns. In *Settlement archaeology*, edited by K.C. Chang, pp. 53-78. National Press, Palo Alto.

1969 *The Huron: Farmers of the north.* Holt, Rinehart and Winston, New York.
1970 The strategy of Iroquoian prehistory. *Ontario Archaeology* 14:3-48.
1976a *The children of Aataentsic: A history of the Huron people to 1660* (2 vols.). McGill-Queen's University Press, Montreal.
1976b Inequality and communication in early civilizations. *Anthropologica* 18:27-52.
1978 Iroquoian matriliny. *Pennsylvania Archaeologist* 48(1-2):55-65.
1979 Sixteenth century Ontario: History, ethnohistory, and archaeology. *Ontario History* 71:205-223.
1980 Archaeology and the image of the American Indian. *American Antiquity* 45(4):662-676.
1981 Webster vs. Champlain. *American Antiquity* 46(2):420-421.
Trigger, B.G., and I. Longworth (editors)
1974 Political systems. *World Archaeology* 6, No. 1.
Trigger, B.G., L. Yaffe, M. Diksic, J.-L. Galinier, H. Marshall, and J.F. Pendergast
1980 Trace-element analysis of Iroquoian pottery. *Canadian Journal of Archaeology* 4:in press.
Tringham, R.
1978 Experimentation, ethnoarchaeology, and the leapfrogs in archaeological methodology. In *Explorations in ethnoarchaeology,* edited by Richard A. Gould, pp. 169-199. University of New Mexico Press, Albuquerque.
Trubowitz, N.
1977 A statistical examination of the social structure of Frontenac Island. In Current perspectives in northeastern archeology. *New York State Archeological Association Researches and Transactions* 17(1):123-147.
Tuck, J.A.
1971 *Onondaga Iroquois prehistory: A study in settlement archaeology.* Syracuse University Press, Syracuse.
1976 *Ancient people of Port aux Choix: The excavation of an Archaic Indian cemetery in Newfoundland.* Memorial University of Newfoundland, Newfoundland Social and Economic Studies No. 17, St. John's.
1977 A look at Laurentian. In Current perspectives in northeastern archeology. *New York State Archeological Association Researches and Transactions* 17(1):31-40.
1978 Archaic burial ceremonialism in the "Far Northeast". In Essays in Northeastern anthropology in memory of Marian E. White, edited by William Engelbrecht and D.K. Grayson, pp. 67-77. *Man in the Northeast, Occasional Papers in Northeastern Anthropology No. 5.*
Tyyska, A.E.
1968 Settlement patterns at Cahiague. Unpublished report submitted to the Archaeological and Historic Sites Board of the Province of Ontario.
1969 Archaeology of the Penetang Peninsula. In *Palaeoecology and Ontario prehistory,* edited by W.M. Hurley and C.E. Heidenreich, pp. 61-88. Department of Anthropology, University of Toronto, Research Report No. 1, Toronto.

Tyyska, A.E., and W.M. Hurley
    1969   Maurice village and the Huron Bear. Paper presented at the 2nd
           annual meeting of the Canadian Archaeological Association, Toronto.
Webster, G.S.
    1979   Deer hides and tribal confederacies: An appraisal of Gramly's hypoth-
           esis. *American Antiquity* 44(4):816-820.
Whallon, R., Jr.
    1968   Investigations of late prehistoric social organization in New York
           State. In *New perspectives in archeology*, edited by S.R. Binford and
           L.R. Binford, pp. 223-244. Aldine, Chicago.
White, M.E.
    1963   Settlement pattern change and the development of horticulture in
           the New York-Ontario area. *Pennsylvania Archaeologist* 33(1-2):1-12.
    1971   Review of the Bennett site. *American Antiquity* 36(2):222-223.
Williamson, R.F.
    1979   *The Robin Hood site: A study of functional variability in Iroquoian
           settlement patterns.* M.A. thesis, McGill University, Montreal.
    1980   The Kelly site: Report on the 1979 excavations. Unpublished report
           to the Lower Thames Valley Conservation Authority.
Witthoft, J.
    1959   Ancestry of the Susquehannocks. In *Susquehannock miscellany*,
           edited by J. Witthoft and W.F. Kinsey, III, pp. 19-60. The Pennsylvania
           Historical and Museum Commission, Harrisburg.
Woolfrey, S., P. Chitwood, and N. Wagner
    1976   Who made the pipes? A study of the decorative motifs on Middleport
           pipe and pottery collections. *Ontario Archaeology* 27:3-11.
Wright, J.V.
    1965   A regional examination of Ojibwa culture history. *Anthropologica* 7:
           189-227.
    1966   The Ontario Iroquois tradition. *National Museum of Canada Bulletin*
           210.
    1972   *Ontario prehistory: An eleven-thousand year archaeological outline.*
           National Museums of Canada, Ottawa.
    1974   The Nodwell site. *National Museum of Man, Archaeological Survey of
           Canada Mercury Series No. 22.*
    n.d.   The cultural continuity of the northern Iroquoian-speaking peoples.
           Unpublished manuscript in the author's possession.
Wright, J.V., and J.E. Anderson
    1963   The Donaldson site. *National Museum of Canada Bulletin* 184.
    1969   The Bennett site. *National Museum of Canada Bulletin* 229.
Wright, M.J.
    1978   Excavation at the Glen Meyer Reid site, Long Point, Lake Erie.
           Ontario Archaeology 29:25-32.
Wrong, G.M. (editor)
    1939   *The long journey to the country of the Hurons.* The Champlain
           Society, Toronto.

2

PALEOENVIRONMENTAL RECONSTRUCTION
IN THE NORTHEAST: THE ART OF
MULTIDISCIPLINARY SCIENCE

DENA F.DINCAUZE
*University of Massachusetts
at Amherst*

Paleoenvironmental reconstruction in the service of North American prehistoric archaeology had early and successful beginnings in the Northeast. The relationship of lower sea levels to archaeological sites was an early interest in New England (Crosby 1903; Willoughby 1927; Delabarre 1925). Frederick Johnson set enviable standards for interdisciplinary research when he assembled a team of specialists to study the Boylston Street fishweir in 1939 (Johnson 1942).

My task here is to review the current state of the art in the Northeast and to consider the potential of paleoenvironmental reconstruction for future research contributions to archaeological data and theory. In fact, this paper reflects only the state of the art represented in the literature up to about mid-1979. The future is, of course, underway now. Much fine work, currently being done or recently completed and unpublished at the moment, will be referred to here only in passing, if at all. Of some, I am unaware; for the rest, I await with interest the publication of the research results.

Throughout this paper my perspective is that of a cultural ecologist. I am explicitly concerned here with human societies in their natural environments. By purposely eschewing engagement with the complexities of social environments, I imply no denigration of the latter's importance to human beings. It is simply not the topic of *this* paper. It is my conviction that well formulated cultural ecological work can immeasurably strengthen and support efforts to understand what is purely cultural, or human, in human lifestyles.

This paper does not offer a summary of methods. Rather, it considers why archaeologists study past environments, what kinds of data are available to them in that undertaking, and recent trends in paleoenvironmental studies. The geographical focus is limited to northeastern North America, here narrowly defined as the area including, and east of, Pennsylvania, New York, southeastern Ontario, and Quebec.

THE IMPORTANCE OF ENVIRONMENTAL DATA

To the uninitiated, "paleoenvironmental reconstruction" sounds like an esoteric pursuit, more esoteric, even, than traditional archaeology. To the initiate, it is an expensive undertaking, requiring much staff time and extensive laboratory facilities. It can never re-create for us real environmental amenities. Why, then, do it?

It is not enough to say that archaeologists need to place their sites in context; that answer merely drives the question one step deeper. The answer must be that the evaluative description of ancient environments provides the archaeologist with data crucial to the full achievement of the archaeological (ultimately the scientific and humanistic) value of the human behavioral relics studied. That leaves us with the need to justify archaeology. Because my topic is paleo-environments, not archaeology, the justification will begin with a discussion of some major questions that paleoenvironmental reconstruction in the service of archaeology can help answer. These questions derive from three interrelated but analytically separable topics: (1) the relationships between climate and cultural changes, (2) human responses to short-term and long-term change, and (3) human and ecosystem interactions.

RELATIONSHIPS BETWEEN CLIMATIC AND CULTURAL CHANGES

The existence of a systemic relationship between any human culture and its natural environment is a major tenet of ecological anthropology (Hardesty 1977). Of all the components of environment, climate is least equivocally an independent variable at the system scale, although the past three centuries of industrialization may constitute an exception to this generalization (SMIC 1971). From these postulates we derive the question, To what extent is cultural stability dependent upon climate? Or, to put the case in a more familiar way, Does climatic change cause cultural change? These questions have been salient in the archaeology of the Northeast for at least twenty-five years (see Chapter 3). Archaeologists working in the middle and high latitudes can scarcely avoid them, and indeed do recognize that their field situations offer excellent "laboratory" conditions for investigating them.

The past fifteen years have seen a number of syntheses in which major trends in the cultural record of the Northeast are interpreted within a framework of late-glacial and Holocene climatic changes (Ritchie 1969a, 1969b; Fitzhugh 1972; Salwen 1975; Funk and Rippeteau 1977; Chapdelaine 1978; inter alia). While most researchers recognize clearly the mediating role of biotic assemblages in the climate-culture relationship, many still succumb in publication to the simplification of a climatic periodization chart to summarize the historical dynamics. The result is an unexamined implication of a short cause and effect chain. It is often unclear whether independent evidence or theoretical convenience define the cultural and climatic synchronies so displayed.

Actually, the situation is much more complex, not only in the realities of the natural world but also in the methodologies and formal logic of science. There are at least two crucial methodological sources of confusion. The first is the problem of unit scales employed in correlation studies and causal hypotheses; incongruence of scale between posited interacting variables can invalidate arguments. The second is the problem of measurement—finding a validly *independent* measuring device in order to define change rates and relative chronologies. It is axiomatic that any postulated cause must occur prior to its effect. To measure relative time in two distinct domains, we need, ideally, a measuring device totally independent of both. Unfortunately, radiocarbon dating does not meet that standard. It is known that both ^{14}C production *and* climate vary with changes in the intensity of geomagnetism (Wollin et al. 1971; Ralph and Michael 1974). Geomagnetic fluctuations result in the secular variations in ^{14}C production, which in turn cause the phenomenon of "lumped" dates. A number of discrete samples may give the same calculated date, although their actual ages may range over a period of centuries (Stuiver 1971; Ralph et al. 1973). The result may be a distortion of the time scale and the production of artificial synchronies between climatic and cultural change, synchronies which are in effect artifacts of the measuring technique. Since inherent technical error may be on the scale of centuries, caution is advisable when historical causation is the issue. Finer methods of chronological calibration are required. We may need to develop them in the field, by refinements of excavation techniques, including the meticulous recovery of associations among diverse data classes.

The scale problem can be attacked by both improved logic and better data. Obviously, the impact of any climatic change on culture will vary with the structure and kinds of biotic resources through which it is mediated. In general, the impacts will be more directly transferred and most strongly felt when the biotic resources are low in diversity, unpredictable, and fragile (the products of short food chains), as classically displayed in the Arctic. Under those conditions, cultural response to climatic change may be expected to be strong and nearly immediate. However, the expression of the response can take many forms, so that its representation in the archaeological record may well be equivocal. It may be impossible to distinguish responses to climatic change expressed via strategy changes from similar responses to environmental changes of nonclimatic origin. This is McGhee's point exactly, when he warns that systemic models of culture change in the Arctic may be imputing change to variables at the wrong scale—climate instead of, for instance, weather or disease (McGhee 1976, 1978). His unfashionable championship of historical particularism should not blind systematists to the genuine problems of scale incongruities in the data adduced for these culture change explanations.

The scale problem is a pervasive one. Researchers and theoreticians in evolutionary biology (S. J. Gould 1980), anthropology (Renfrew 1978), ecology (Wright 1976a; M. B. Davis 1976), and climatology (Hare 1976; Kutzbach 1976) are developing remarkably convergent models of dynamic change. Without opening the question of independence among all these fields, we can still be impressed with the similarities in the models. Systemic changes are seen as occurring discontinuously, with rapid episodes of change and adjustment interrupting periods of relative equilibrium. If change in one system is even partly dependent upon change in another, episodes of dynamic adjustment between systems should be, at some scale, serial rather than sychronous. Identification and isolation of the appropriate scale is a severe theoretical and methodological challenge.

Techniques for paleoenvironmental interpretations are not yet as refined as they need to be for application to anthropological problems. Most of them work within the scales of geological time; it has never been claimed that the cultures of Homo sapiens adjust to environments at such majestic rates. Improvements in anthropological explanations will ultimately require (1) improved models of culture change with explications of mechanisms by which cultures adapt to new conditions, (2) greatly refined techniques for identifying environmental changes, (3) independent chronological measurements, and (4) more closely reasoned arguments involving a greatly expanded inventory of relevant variables (Barry et al. 1977) and regional rather than site-specific research emphases.

HUMAN RESPONSES TO SHORT-TERM AND LONG-TERM CHANGES

While ultimately related to the previous problem, this one focuses securely on the dynamics of change—the causes, effects, and risks incurred. We want answers to the question, What social and biological responses to short-term and long-term changes in the natural environment can we identify in the archaeological record? Merely asking this question brings us closer to the fundamental humanity of ancient peoples, to their worries, their failures, and their successes in the business of survival. To the extent that we can, repeatedly, answer the question, we may expect to achieve understanding and knowledge of immediate and future value for social planning. If we can produce from archaeological studies models of dynamic response, we can understand, and perhaps manage better, our options in the face of changes ranging from a cooling global climate to critical shortages of fuel. At the very least, a better understanding of past responses to change can give us insights to the specific risks incurred by imposed or internally generated changes.

William Fitzhugh is perhaps the first archaeologist to explicitly address the question of short-term responses in the Northeastern data. He recognized a decade ago that the subarctic zone was an excellent laboratory for studying these phenomena (Fitzhugh 1972). In the middle and high latitudes, significant environmental changes occur in both short-term and long-term scales. The importance to human populations of these disequilibria, long assumed, has rarely been studied closely. Choosing an ecotone in the subarctic, where change is easily visible and systemic variables are relatively few in number, Fitzhugh modeled a variety of human responses, and elucidated specific examples of them (Fitzhugh 1972).

The short-term changes that can be assumed to have challenged northeastern peoples in the past are, on the whole, still with us. Some are potentially visible in the archaeological and paleoenvironmental records; we do not know yet the limits of these records (Hecht et al. 1979). Weather phenomena, as opposed to larger-scale climate, lead the list, with floods, drought, icy winters, open winters, and cold summers posing obvious challenges, even threats, to human populations (see Chapter 3). The severity of the challenge will vary with the nature and structure of the human adaptation involved. Clearly, floods are more threatening to townspeople on floodplains than to seasonally transient hunter-gatherers; icy winters are a greater threat to caribou hunters than to farmers with adequate crop storage. Other potential short-term dangers include plant and animal epidemic diseases, infestations such as spruce budworm or the algal red tides which make shellfish poisonous, boom-and-bust cycles among small animal populations, and migratory route oscillations of large game. Changes in the natural environment can also be initiated by human action. Local overkill of seasonally concentrated or territorially circumscribed game animals are obvious examples which, however, will be difficult if not impossible to perceive archaeologically.

Environmental changes on long-term scales are those most typically considered in the literature. Climatic changes ranging from glacial oscillations to temperature regimes on the order of 1000 years duration have dominated research. Changes in floral and faunal assemblages are typically explained by reference to climatic changes or, conversely and sometimes simultaneously, used to infer the direction and degree of climatic changes. More recently, paleoenvironmental studies have focused on such agents of biotic change as inter- and intraspecific competition, habitat expansion and shifts, soils development, changes in hydrology and landforms, and other such variables only indirectly related to climate. To these must be added perturbations introduced by the activities of human populations, a species whose dominance is unprecedentedly pervasive.

The response options available to human populations vary between the short-term and long-term scales. In all, however, there are risks as well as opportunities and we may expect the record, appropriately exploited, to show us a gradient between successes and failures, with the risks more clearly exposed toward the failure end. Strategies appropriate to short-term changes, whether harmful or beneficial, include group fission or fusion, intensified trade, emigration or immigration. Short-term catastrophies can provoke demographic oscillations. We can expect strategies applied to short-term changes to be, at least initially, conservative, with reversion toward a former state typically occurring as the environment itself recovers. Long-term changes, however, are by definition not reversible within the life span of individuals or even of several generations. Therefore, strategies will probably change cumulatively, to the extent that they are successful, and will involve major reorganization of resource procurement, of settlement patterns, and of territory or range. Changes in demography and gene pools can be expected if the environmental changes are of significant magnitude.

HUMAN AND ECOSYSTEM INTERACTIONS

The ecological consequences of the nest-fouling propensities of the human species have been too long unrecognized or ignored. In our twentieth-century arrogance, we may denigrate or dismiss the significance of environmental impact by nonindustrialized peoples, or even by our own agricultural predecessors. As social scientists, archaeologists have a fruitful field of inquiry into the extent and significance of human effects on ecosystems, and the feedback loops so engendered (e.g. Thorbahn and Mrozowski 1979). It is of more than academic interest that we achieve a realistic and sophisticated appreciation of human roles, past and present, in the environment. How have human communities affected northeastern ecosystems, and how have resultant changes affected them in turn?

Evidence of human manipulation of environmental variables is the basis for the archaeological record. To the extent that no human impression is made on the environment, there is no archaeological record. The opportunities for studying the consequences of such manipulation are therefore pervasive, although they have been little exploited in the Northeast. For example, people cut trees and make forest clearings to create shelter and living space and to make garden plots. Such clearings have the effect of locally reversing biotic succession. Reversed succession and the creation of edge habitats results in locally enriched biotic diversity, which may directly benefit people and their prey (cf. Linares 1976). The cleared area proper eventually suffers soil depletion if used repeatedly to raise harvested crops, or it may have its soil enriched excessively by concentrations of organic debris in living areas. In either case, the locale eventually becomes unsuited for continued occupation or use and is abandoned, unless expensive efforts are made to restore its productive balance. This cycle is not necessarily relevant only to farmers; we do not know the environmental costs of hunter-gatherer habitation or exploitation areas. Fires of human origin exaggerate the natural fire burden on biotic communities; the effects for humans can be either beneficial or deleterious, depending on the effects on the habitat of major game species (Fitzhugh 1972; Day 1953).

Local extirpation of game animals, edible plants, and accessible firewood is known or can be expected to have occurred in the past. The importance of such events in entailing mobility among hunter-gatherers needs to be considered before we can adequately discuss degrees of sedentism among foragers (Gramly and Gwynn 1979), and the same questions are relevant for understanding the mobility of northeastern farming peoples. Granted that enforced mobility imposes an energy burden on a human group, better understanding of the causes of mobility will permit more realistic assessments of the costs of various adaptive strategies.

I have elsewhere presented a model of Late Archaic subsistence strategies and demographic changes that implies the possibility of internally-generated resource crises (Dincauze 1980). The model builds on evidence for Late Archaic population growth and site distributions, which are seen as manifestations of a systemic relationship involving increasingly intensive exploitation of edible foods, constricting territories, and rising population densities. Expansion of intensive exploitation into fragile marginal habitats may have caused local resource failure, which might have been magnified as people fell back into habitats already occupied at equilibrium densities. The crisis is inferred from the relative scarcity of Early Woodland sites in comparison to Late Archaic ones, even when appropriate statistical adjustments are made to equalize time durations. At present, there are no subsistence data sufficiently rigorous or abundant to test the implications of the model.

In European archaeology, human-environmental interactions have been investigated repeatedly and in some detail by marshalling evidence from soils history and pollen studies. Cycles of forest clearance by farmers, abandonment, and regeneration of fields, show clearly in these data. In northeastern North America, European clearance and the subsequent adjustment of the floral environment has been identified in Connecticut (Brugam 1978) and elsewhere (Davis and Norton 1978). Aboriginal farming, on the other hand, has proven notoriously difficult to detect. The fact that the major crop plants were insect-pollinated rather than wind-pollinated results in their minimal appearance in natural pollen traps, but does not explain why forest clearance activities have been so rarely observed. The situation might be rectified if some attention were directed to choosing pollen study locations in terms of their spatial relationship to likely prehistoric farming areas. In the Northeast, aboriginal farming has been recognized in one pollen spectrum (McAndrews 1976) and land clearance appears evident in another (Anderson and Webb 1980), demonstrating the feasibility of present methods and indicating the potential for expanded study.

TECHNIQUES AND DATA SOURCES

The tool kit for use in paleoenvironmental reconstruction keeps expanding, with concurrent expansion of the applicable data base and of the reliability and refinement of the results. The American Northeast in the sense employed here imposes on researchers its own particular set of limitations and opportunities. Even a glance at a slim text such as *An Introduction to Environmental Archaeology* (Evans 1978) exposes the inquirer to a wider range of techniques than have been, or could ever be, used in the Northeast. However, we have available a promising diversity of data and techniques for the description and interpretation of paleoenvironments, and recent studies are demonstrating their power. The following discussion will be organized mainly around data classes, with techniques referenced where applicable. The exception is the first section, where the computer stars. Citations to literature are selected mainly for their comprehensiveness and recency, so that they can serve as guides for those venturing further.

COMPUTER MODELING

Atmospheric modeling is a special case of paleoclimatology, which draws upon and integrates a wide range of data from other disciplines. Data on atmospheric, oceanic, and terrestrial variables and interrelationships are used in computer simulations which are then manipulated to derive descriptions of conditions at different states. The first major result of the multi-institutional and multidisciplinary undertaking called "CLIMAP" was a map of boundary conditions during the peak of the last glacial period, 18,000 B.P. (CLIMAP 1976). The method is still in its infancy, with data often inadequate to model complexity even on continental scales. Evaluations of the results to date (Williams 1978; Heath 1979) indicate cautious optimism for eventual production of powerful and accurate models. At present, it is recognized that different models for the full-glacial state give somewhat different results because of varying emphases and disparate values for critical boundary conditions. Essential agreement has been achieved among the models in predicting a full-glacial atmosphere cooler and drier than that of the present, with the northern hemisphere jet stream "strengthened and shifted south [Williams 1978]." The potential for these models to predict past climatic states is exciting. Ongoing empirical investigations are refining the data on boundary conditions, variables, and correlations (Peterson et al. 1979). The results will be highly significant for paleoenvironmental students of all disciplines.

An equivalent triumph has been achieved by a group of Yale University foresters who have built a computer model which "reproduces the major dynamic characteristics of a forest community, such as competition among individuals and changes in the species composition of a forest with time and climate [Botkin and Miller

1974:451]." We look forward to the day when, supplied with a few well-defined boundary conditions from a regional paleoenvironmental study, we can set the computers running to model the coeval atmospheric circulation, forest state, and maybe even the animal consumers. Given the resolution of our data just now, that happy day seems still far off.

ISOTOPE RATIOS

Studies involving proportions of oxygen and carbon isotopes in organic or inorganic materials are making important contributions to environmental reconstructions. Their use is likely to increase, hence their mention here, although they have seen few applications in the Northeast, none of which are primarily archaeological.

Isotopes of oxygen (^{18}O and ^{16}O) in water bodies vary in their ratios with the water temperature (other variables assumed constant for each particular case). They are incorporated into the calcium carbonate of molluscan shells at the same ratio as in the water in which the organisms live. The isotopic ratios then can be read to reflect the water temperatures during the animals' lifespans. During continental glaciations, ^{16}O is preferentially locked up in glacial ice, so that the proportion of ^{18}O in sea water rises relative to interstadials. Oceanographers, therefore, can distinguish relatively colder from warmer climatic phases by analysis of organic carbonates even without calculating temperature transfer functions.

Oxygen isotope measures thus contribute to paleoclimatic reconstructions with local, regional, and global relevance. Oceanographers use them to indicate changes from glacial to interglacial periods, and to support and amplify faunal indicators of paleotemperature fluctuations (Ruddiman and McIntyre 1973, 1977; Hillaire-Marcel 1977; Occhietti and Hillaire-Marcel 1977). Paleolimnologists use them in studies of ancient lacustrine environments, reading paleotemperatures from carbonaceous faunal remains or inorganic carbonate concretions. The special problem of high latitude environments for such studies are presented clearly by Hillaire-Marcel (1977). Glaciologists use oxygen isotopes to reconstruct hemispheric climatic fluctuations from ice cores (Dansgaard et al. 1969), thus bypassing biological processes. Archaeologists in turn use the derived climatic and environmental data to understand the contexts of archaeological sites and human adaptive strategies (Fitzhugh 1972). The methods are applicable directly to molluscan fauna in middens as well, when information on seasonality or paleotemperature curves for local water bodies are sought (Shackleton 1973).

Isotopes of carbon in organic materals can be analyzed for information about such disparate matters as atmospheric conditions (temperature and humidity) and diets. Studies that archaeologists use only indirectly have related carbon isotope ratios to the climatic fluctuations which correlate with secular changes in ^{14}C production (Occhietti and Hillaire-Marcel 1977; Denton and Karlén 1973), and to magnetic field changes which may cause the two former variables (Bucha et al. 1970; Ralph and Michael 1974). Isotopic fractionation in tropical grasses makes possible carbon isotope studies of the relative amounts of maize in the diets of temperate-latitude populations, since the ratios can be recovered from skeletal elements of the consumers (Vogel and van der Merwa 1977; Bender et al. 1981). This research method, still being perfected, has exciting promise for Northeastern archaeology, where tangible remains of tropical cultigens are so rarely recovered (Bumsted 1980; Chapter 7, this volume).

LANDFORMS

Geomorphology is here considered as the study of landforms and sea levels. This probably does not closely coincide with what geomorphologists see themselves doing, but is convenient for our purpose (Gladfelter 1977). Geomorphologists have been intimately involved in archaeology from the beginnings of the latter discipline; even the recognition of tells as artifacts depends upon geomorphological concepts. Northeastern archaeologists have benefited from, and are increasingly active partners in, a variety of geomorphological field studies.

Archaeologists have depended upon glacial geologists for information about the chronology of glacial retreat, for which the direct evidence comes from studies of morainal fronts. Such research has implications for hemispheric climate (Denton and Karlén 1973) and regional climate and weather, especially during the waning of the Wisconsinan ice sheets and in the Neoglacial period (Connally and Sirkin 1970; Borns and Calkin 1977; Ives 1978). Morainal studies have contributed directly to understanding Paleo-Indian environments in the Hudson Valley (Funk et al. 1970; Connally and Sirkin 1970; Connally 1970) and in Nova Scotia (MacDonald 1968).

Prehistoric archaeology began in Pleistocene river and lake terraces in France and England and the geomorphology of such situations remains an important aspect of multidisciplinary studies, extending into near-recent times. Mutuality in data exchange may be high in these circumstances, although not in every study. Geomorphologists provide context and limiting dates for archaeological sites on river and lake terraces, and may help with a detailed study of the nature of incorporation of site materials in sediments. In favorable circumstances, and especially for holocene landforms, archaeologists may contribute crucially important chronological data, at a scale of refinement which geomorphologists can rarely exceed, or even meet. Examples of such cooperation and data sharing include studies of lake terraces in interior Quebec (McAndrews and Samson 1977) and central Maine (University of Maine, Orono, work in progress), as well as river terraces in the Merrimack and Connecticut river valleys (Dincauze 1976; Moir 1975; University of Massachusetts, Amherst, work in progress).

Raised marine beaches are another class of landforms where geological and archaeological studies have a long history of cooperation, extending from Africa to Scandinavia in the Old World but confined mainly to high latitudes and post-Wisconsinan time in the New. Marine terraces have provided fundamental chronological and environmental data for studies of prehistoric human populations in Labrador (Fitzhugh 1972; Tuck and McGhee 1975), Nova Scotia (MacDonald 1968), Quebec and Vermont, where the Champlain Sea conditioned the earliest occupations (Benmouyal 1978; Ritchie 1953; Loring 1980).

The relationships between present and ancient seacoasts and archaeological sites have long fascinated archaeologists and geologists in the Northeast (Crosby 1903; Delabarre 1925; Johnson 1942; Salwen 1965; H. Kraft 1977; Edwards and Merrill 1977; J. Kraft 1977; Dincauze 1972, 1973). Cooperation on this subject is increasing, as both parties realize the rewards of their interdependence. The range and wealth of environmental data that can be obtained from coastal middens and associated with coeval shore features and landforms is only beginning to be exploited to its potential. For instance, knowledge of ancient estuarine environments, with evolutionary and adaptive significance to marine biologists, climatologists and archaeologists, is likely to be gained principally through cooperative studies focusing on ancient coastal middens, whether now emergent or submerged.

Archaeologists have eagerly consumed information supplied by other disciplines on Pleistocene sea levels and the environments of the continental shelves (Curray 1965; Milliman and Emery 1968; Edwards and Emery 1977; Emery et al. 1967; Dillon and Oldale 1978). The available data have been incorporated into models of human adaptations (e.g. Dincauze and Mulholland 1977; Salwen 1962, 1965) which have been subjected to rapid obsolescence as knowledge of the offshore environments grows, and concepts of sea level fluctuations mature (Blackwelder et al. 1979; Oldale and O'Hara 1980). The most ambitious applications of these data have been made in predictive studies of human occupations on the continental shelf, undertaken for purposes of resource management by the Bureau of Land Management, U.S. Department of the Interior (Gagliano 1977; Roberts 1979b).

Other potential areas for archaeological use of geomorphological data exist. As examples, we may cite studies of dune progression, periglacial features, and local mass wasting. These have been applied to archaeological studies elsewhere but not yet to any significant extent in the Northeast.

SEDIMENTS

Archaeological applications of sediment study techniques have long since proven their worth in Europe; they are slowly becoming accepted and being applied in North America (e.g. Davidson and Shackley 1978; Hassan 1978; Shackley 1975). In the Northeast, the techniques have to date been rarely applied, and even less often reported. There are three classes of deposits in which archaeological materials are typically found: subaerial, subaqueous, and speleological. Although sedimentological techniques may vary somewhat among them, all can offer significant information about the origin, mode of deposition, and subsequent history of site sediments. The sediments, rather than being a passive element of geography, bear testimony to the processes of the site's incorporation into its immediate environment. Understanding of a site's paleoenvironment begins with the matrix, and to the extent that enclosing sediments are unstudied the environment will remain unknown.

Subaerial deposits are the matrix of the typical archaeological site. They may be developed in place by the weathering of parent material or, as is typical in New England, be left on the ground after wind transport (Hartshorn 1965; Colby et al. 1953). Whatever their origin, surficial sediments have undergone chemical changes by the action of plants, animals and precipitated water, and have experienced mechanical disturbance by a great variety of biological and geological agents (Strauss 1978; Wood and Johnson 1978). They have received increments of opaline silica (phytoliths) from decaying plants, and of a variety of other materials displaced and transported by human and animal activities. Interpretation of the sediments can provide invaluable insights into all these processes. The application of sedimentological studies to open sites in the Northeast has little history, but it clearly has a future. A simple granulometric analysis of the terrace deposits enclosing the Neville site in New Hampshire was critical for the proper interpretation of the site's history (Dincauze 1976:15, 23). Only a single soil monolith was available from the totally destroyed site; its analysis indicated eloquently what a richness of environmental and cultural detail could have been extracted from the intact site. At the Whipple site in southern New Hampshire, paleostratigraphic techniques were applied during excavation (Curran 1979); sedimentological analyses have aided significantly in understanding both the history and subsequent modifications of the deposits, and will contribute to the environmental reconstruction.

Freshwater and marine deposits less often form the matrix of archaeological sites. When they do, as in river terraces, their analysis can bring additional dimensions of information to the environmental inquiry. In addition to providing information of the sort derived from study of subaerial deposits, water-borne sediments can inform about hydrological variables as well. The study of water-borne sediments was crucial to the interpretation of the complex Shawnee-Minisink site in Pennsylvania (Foss 1977; McNett et al. 1977). Problems of funding and personnel availability have limited the development of such studies in the Northeast, where preliminary work has been done by investigators from SUNY Oneonta, University of Connecticut, University of Massachusetts at Amherst, and the University of Maine at Orono.

Cave deposits are not typical of the archaeology of northeastern North America, but when they are involved the results can be spectacular, providing the analyses are appropriate. Solution caves in limestone are rare features in the Northeast, where rock shelters of erosional or depositional origin are more typical. However, the special environments of all caves and shelters leave evidence in the sediments accumulating on their floors and, given the essential uniqueness and boundedness of each case, the interpretation of floor deposits is worth every possible effort. Sedimentological analyses can inform about the sources of sediments, the conditions under which they were separated from parent material, transported, laid down, and subsequently disturbed. Sedimentological analyses were not a major concern of the excavators of Sheep Rock Shelter in Pennsylvania (Michels and Smith 1967). The excavation of the Meadowcroft Shelter, however, incorporated sedimentological concerns from the beginning, with extremely informative results (Adovasio et al. 1977). The presence of a sedimentologist during the excavation of the enigmatic Dutchess Quarry Cave in southeastern New York would have significantly reduced the indeterminacies of that fascinating situation. A close study of the sediments might have directly clarified the relationship of the early artifacts and bones to the late-glacial outwash and lake deposits, obviating the need for geomorphological interpretation from outside (Funk et al. 1970; Connally 1970). Additional climatological information might have been retrieved through study of the upper strata.

The full realization of the paleoenvironmental information in a site entails field involvement of a sedimentologist or, at a minimum, of an archaeologist trained in appropriate sedimentological techniques. Given the scarcity of specialists within the Northeast, archaeologists may have to take the compromise route and acquire the skills themselves.

SOILS

The U.S. Department of Agriculture defines soils as "natural bodies on the earth's surface . . . supporting or capable of supporting plants out-of-doors [USDA 1975:1]." In this present discussion, soils will be defined as biochemically and physically modified sediments, whether subaerial or buried (paleosols). With this definition we focus on analytical techniques and soil properties distinct from those discussed under the previous heading (sediments).

The use of soils studies for archaeological paleoenvironmental reconstruction is not so well developed in the New World as in the Old, where paleosols especially have been aggressively exploited for their environmental data potential (Butzer 1971; Limbrey 1975). In northeastern North America, particularly, the current interest in soils has tended to center upon techniques for site location (Eidt 1973; P. Thomas 1974; Dincauze 1979) or for intrasite mapping and behavioral analyses (Eidt 1977; Heidenreich and Navratil 1973; Heidenreich and Konrad 1973; Dincauze 1976).

The paleoenvironmental data inherent in soils, particularly buried soils, relate to conditions of soil formation—factors such as climate and vegetation which, acting on particular sediments in specific geographical situations, produce a given type of soil. The archaeologist wishing to utilize such information to broaden and strengthen paleoenvironmental reconstructions must understand that the study of soil genesis is still in its infancy. The USDA warns that "Because the genesis of a soil cannot be observed or measured, pedologists may have widely differing opinions about it . . . [USDA 1975:10]." Canadian pedologists are more sanguine, and even deign to use interpretations of genesis as elements in their soil taxonomy (CSSC 1978:16). We can expect, therefore, that Canadians may be more willing to risk statements about environmental factors in soils genesis than are their southern colleagues.

Soils surveys, and the publication of soils maps, are far from complete in either Canada or the United States. Where survey publications are available, especially those produced since the mid-1950s, archaeologists have a very useful tool for preliminary paleoenvironmental estimates. Progress has been steady, and the more recent the publication, the more detail it is likely to yield. The soils taxonomies employed in the United States and Canada differ somewhat because of divergent applications and intellectual histories. They may be compared within limits (USDA 1975, chap. 21; CSSC 1978, chap. 15). For the archaeologist, the important thing is that similar ranges of information are provided. The U.S. taxonomy tends to emphasize management applications, so that archaeological uses, particularly paleoenvironmental interpretations, may require some redefinition with attendant loss of precision. The stronger Canadian reliance on genetic and environmental factors in soils taxonomy should be a boon to archaeologists.

Modern soils maps, especially those at scales near 1:20,000, mapped onto aerial photos, have some direct environmental applications for archaeological studies. Archaeologists at the University of Massachusetts at Amherst have used the maps to derive approximate measures of environmental diversity in site-catchment areas. The descriptive data accompanying the maps include information on modern temperature and precipitation regimes, the physical, chemical and structural properties of the soil mapping units, the distribution and local (county in the U.S.) acreage of the units, and their habitat potential for both flora and fauna. The habitat potential provides a rough approximation of recent past wildlife communities, and can be extended somewhat by application of the ecological principles which constrain the details of seral succession. The rough estimates which result are productive sources of test implications for seeking hard data on past local environments.

Interaction in the field between pedologists and archaeologists is fervently recommended. Archaeologists have a great deal to learn about the matrices of their sites, and pedologists can enlarge their horizons. University of Massachusetts archaeologists have been in the field with both geologists and soils scientists who have misinterpreted extreme anthropogenic soils (extensive black-earth middens), calling them "raised bog soils." Cooperative communication is mutually beneficial.

MICROBOTANY

Pollen analysis, that familiar tool of paleoenvironmental reconstruction, has metamorphosed in the last decade, becoming at once a more complex and demanding discipline, and a more informative, refined, and reliable data source. The number of practitioners in the Northeast has grown at a most gratifying rate; reports from the region are now a regular feature of the literature.

The introduction of direct-counting methods (Absolute Pollen Influx and Absolute Pollen Deposition rates) for the description of pollen spectra promises a revolution in the precision of analyses, and should make the pollen studies applicable to a wide range of environmental modeling efforts (M. B. Davis 1969a, 1969b, 1976; M. B. Davis et al. 1973; R. Davis et al. 1975; Bernabo and Webb 1977; Ogden 1977). The new methods have brought their own challenging problems to replace those associated with the traditional percentage diagrams; some of these are briefly explicated in a pithy article by Paul Colinvaux (1978). Research has proliferated in innovative new directions as palynologists come to grips with the possibilities and problems of the new approaches. The resultant studies of modern pollen rain and of palynological evidence of species competition are of immediate relevance to biogeographers and of theoretical importance to paleoenvironmentalists and modelers (Davis and Webb 1975; Watts 1973; Ogden 1977).

Recent research in glaciated North America has opened new perspectives on postglacial recolonization by plants (and by implication, animals), revising some traditional concepts such as latitudinal shifts of communities, and revealing the complexities of the interactions of variables such as species migration rates, competitive advantages, soils development, relative insolation, temperature, precipitation, geographical barriers and distance from refugia (Bernabo and Webb 1977; M. B. Davis 1976; Hare 1976; R. Davis et al. 1979; Wright 1976a, 1976b; Mott 1977; Richard 1977). Studies currently under way in the region will provide data of a quality and abundance unprecedented, and unmatched, outside of northwestern Europe.

The challenge now is for archaeologists to understand and appropriately exploit the situation, using the available data to best advantage and collaborating creatively in the development and application of more data as needed. It has been typical for archaeologists to use palynological data for regional environmental reconstruction to the extent that they were available. In the past decade, truly interdisciplinary research has been initiated, which puts palynologists in the field with archaeologists, collecting data directly applicable to archaeological problems (Fitzhugh 1975; Jordan 1975;

McAndrews and Samson 1977; Curran 1979). Derivation of pollen from site soils has been attempted less often; conditions for preservation vary through a range of special situations (King et al. 1975). Success cannot be taken for granted (Dincauze 1976; McBride 1978), but the effort is always worthwhile and the occasional rewards are sweet (Holmes 1980).

Another kind of microbotanical remains, phytoliths, can be expected to occur in archaeological soils. Phytoliths are casts of opaline silica which form in and between the cells of plants; they remain after the organic matter decays. Interpretive techniques are still too poorly developed to derive more than very coarse environmental indications from the totality of phytolith shapes present in soils (Carbone 1977). However, domesticated maize produces a characteristic form (Pearsall 1977) which is being diligently sought in the soils of sites of appropriate ages (a liberal interpretation of possibilities is recommended).

MACROBOTANY

Macrobotanical remains are not routinely recovered from northeastern archaeological sites. Preservation factors such as permafrost, dry cold, dry caves, and waterlogged sites are unevenly and thinly distributed in the region. Charred remains, the most usual form of discernible plant materials, pose special problems of recovery that are not always successfully solved. The introduction of flotation techniques (Struever 1968) and their recent elaboration has improved the situation greatly (McBride 1978). Archaeologists now expect to recover charred seeds and nuts, at least, and can do so by dry screening as well as flotation in many instances. The result has been a rapid increase in the amount of floral remains recovered from sites without, however, intensive exploitation of the environmental data inherent in such remains. Systematic study of floral remains at regional or even local scales, along either synchronic or diachronic dimensions, has not been attempted. Nor have the ethnobotanical aspects of the data been seriously considered, in spite of the insights such analyses offer for consideration of human manipulation of environmental variables (Ford 1979). Food remains are generally listed when recovered, even if the imputation of food status depends solely on the edibility of the materials. The seasonal implications of plant remains in middens or pits are rarely ignored; occasionally the analysis is intensive and demanding (P. Thomas 1975). Climatological data are less reliably exploited. Plant materials used for fuel typically remain unidentified.

In the Arctic, where wood may survive in either exposed or permafrost contexts, some studies have applied growth ring analyses for climatological inferences (Fritts 1976). The distribution of driftwood on high arctic beaches and terraces, and dead trees beyond the modern tree line have been interpreted paleoclimatically, indicating, respectively, seas relatively free of sea ice part of the year, and growing seasons longer than those of the present.

Russell Barber has called attention to the unexploited information to be derived by carefully controlled studies of disjunct plant distributions; his conclusion that Late Archaic peoples may have introduced wild onions to southern Ontario is unexpected and challenging in suggesting purposefully modified environments at an early date (Barber 1977). Plant materials recovered from Pennsylvania caves (Michels and Smith 1967; Adovasio et al. 1977) could yield more environmental data than have been wrung from them to date. Phytogeographic and· paleotemperature data possibly relevant to Paleo-Indian environments have recently been reported from a remarkable lake-bed deposit in northeastern Vermont (Miller and Thompson 1979). For macrobotanical studies in the Northeast, all is potential (Dimbleby 1967).

FAUNA

The extraordinary variety of environmental data to be derived from faunal remains, at the scales of region or site, has not been well exploited by northeastern archaeologists. A large body of multidisciplinary literature exists, available now, to enhance the definition of regional reconstructions. For example, limnological studies constitute a rich source of biological, as well as chemical and climatological, data that has not yet been used to advantage by archaeologists. The literatures of oceanography, paleontology, biogeography and ecology are more familiar; archaeologists and archaeological data have contributed to, as well as benefitted from, the last three categories.

Oceanographers and limnologists deal routinely with the climatological and environmental implications of populations of foraminifera and plankton, producing results with immediate applicability to archaeological problems involving regional paleoenvironments (Balsam and Heusser 1976; Bartlett and Molinsky 1972; Hillaire-Marcel 1977; Ruddiman and McIntyre 1977; Root 1978b). Vertebrate paleontologists have been at pains to discuss the relevance of their research findings to archaeologists (Guilday 1967; Whitmore et al. 1967; Harrington 1977). Biogeography, especially of fish and small animals, offers unrealized potential for insights into the recolonization of glaciated country and subsequent Holocene changes in ranges that affected the game available for human consumption (Andrews 1972; Cronin 1977; Deevey 1949; Dadswell 1974; Wagner 1970). Insect studies promise refinements of paleotemperature concepts (Schwert and Morgan 1980). The biogeographical literature is growing robustly; reliance on static descriptive summaries of precontact biota (e.g. Dice 1943) is no longer necessary or appropriate (see Chapter 3). It is now possible to base paleoenvironmental reconstructions of faunal resources partly on direct data, and to incorporate such data into models of regional climates, rather than depending exclusively on pollen studies for speculative reconstructions. Initial archaeological applications of this data base to ecological modeling have indicated that many time-honored concepts of human adaptation patterns and predation strategies must be revised (Brown and Cleland 1969; Finison 1978; Loring 1980; Dincauze 1980).

Faunal remains recovered from archaeological sites present opportunities for environmental reconstructions at more intimate scales. The classic studies in the Northeast have tended to emphasize food animals as contributors to diet and indicators of seasonality (Ritchie 1969b; Snow 1972; Bourque 1973; Perlman 1976). Fish, shellfish, birds and game animals have received the bulk of the archaeologists' attention. It is useful to recall in this context that all these categories of faunal remains were brought to the pits, middens, and living floors and discarded there by human agency. Their environmental relevance is to local, but not precisely site-specific, habitats. Smaller fauna, especially those like burrowing rodents and terrestrial molluscs, bear witness to the intimate environment of the site itself. The techniques of site-specific faunal analysis are available in a number of publications (Chaplin 1971; Bonnichsen and Sanger 1978; inter alia).

Coordination of research between archaeologists and trained zoologists has been rare. Typically, archaeologists have either shipped out bones and shells for specialist identification and interpretation after the field season, or have developed zooarchaeological skills themselves (Bourque et al. 1978). In the first case, limited expertise is gained at the expense of genuine mutuality of benefit from the research and with the loss of integration of results in the final report. In the second case, integration is achieved, but only a restricted range of research questions is brought to the data, and there is the loss of those spontaneous insights that can develop easily in truly cooperative research. It is not clear yet whether the promise of zooarchaeology, as a technical specialty for archaeologists, can be realized in the context of reduced financing for archaeological research staffs. Efforts to involve zoologists directly in mutually interesting and mutually beneficial research seem more worthwhile than ever. The unparalleled "time capsules" that archaeological sites represent should fascinate biogeographers, paleontologists, and ecologists.

INTEGRATION AND COORDINATION

A few years ago, Karl Butzer lamented the failure of environmental studies in archaeology to achieve successful interdisciplinary integration (Butzer 1975). He observed that archaeologists had failed their own goals by assuming too much of the burden of integration themselves, therefore not fully coordinating their research methods and results with those of their collaborators, and by erring in one of two possible directions, either toward excessive empiricism or excessive theoreticality. In the former case, an excess of empiricism leads to fragmented research results and reports integrated only by binding glue and book covers. In the latter case, there may be unbridged gaps between theoretically-defined goals and the project's data base. In the Northeast, excessive empiricism has typically prevailed; the second situation is a danger we are just beginning to confront.

Recently, the ingenuity of Northeastern archaeologists was tested by the federal Bureau of Land Management (BLM). The BLM, about to grant oil-drilling leases on the eastern continental shelf, needed to estimate potential impacts on cultural resources on the shelf. The Institute for Conservation Archaeology of Harvard University was selected to meet the challenge, providing data and management guidance to the BLM. In the near-total absence of data on prehistoric resources on the shelf, ICA chose to approach the problem by assembling an interdisciplinary team of researchers to develop models for human use of the formerly dry areas of the shelf. The familiar team of archaeologists, geologists, oceanographers, and paleoclimatologists was augmented by a theoretical ecologist, and a commitment was made to use foraging strategy models as devices to integrate the data from the several disciplines. The result was a body of environmental data that was selected for, among other criteria, its relevance to the modeling of food-gathering strategies and spatial distributions of both human groups and their principal faunal and floral resources (Moir 1979). Archaeologists, with the patient guidance of the ecologist, assumed responsibility for integrating the data by means of modeled expectations (Root 1978b; Barber 1979). With the descriptive data and theoretical predictions in hand, it was possible to make some satisfactorily concrete statements about areas of archaeological sensitivity off shore, to suggest within broad limits what might be encountered in them, and to devise explicit research designs for testing the predictions and gathering field data (Roberts 1979a). The result sets new standards for the integration of environmental data and archaeological goals.

The experience of working on this relatively successful project provided an opportunity to reconsider some of the strengths and weaknesses of interdisciplinary coordination. Butzer's (1975) call for broader training in the natural sciences for archaeologists needs to be strongly reiterated (see also Newman and Salwen 1977). There is no available substitute for an archaeologist's working familiarity with the basic theory, methods, potential and limitations of the several disciplines from which he draws his collaborators. This familiarity requires time, effort, and exposure on the part of the archaeologist. Wide reading in the natural sciences, an essential beginning, is not enough. It must be amplified by collegiality, involving a sharing of ideas and data with a problem focus. Team teaching is an ideal way to develop this, but is not a widely available option. Multidisciplinary research institutes, such as the Institute for Quaternary Research at the University of Maine, Orono, are an excellent context in which such collegiality can develop and mutual understanding can mature.

Collegiality is probably the only effective means to alleviate the constraints imposed by interdisciplinary information lags. In any profession, it is recognized that publication delays of about two years intervene between the completion of a research project and the appearance of a report. The delay can, of course, be much greater. Personal contacts and presentations at meetings bridge the gap for the working professional. The archaeologist reading across disciplinary boundaries is heavily dependent, for referral to sources, on citations and indexes, a dependence which extends the delay between publication and reading. We too often forget this and proceed as if the current journals represent the state of the art. The situation may even be exaggerated grotesquely when the archaeologist embraces, or continues to employ, concepts already obsolete in other disciplines (Dincauze 1978).

The pervasive problem of scale manifests itself so subtly in interdisciplinary research that it can be overlooked unless collaboration and communication are very effective. For example, geologists and archaeologists both view stratigraphy from similar bodies of theory; in practice, the scale of relevant units may be completely incompatible, and the observable processes may be of very different orders of magnitude. Less obvious, in the literature and in discussion, are the equally incompatible spatial scales of traditional palynological reconstructions and the data requirements of archaeologists trying to understand the realities of human adaptation to patchy environments. The latter's need for precision on a site-catchment scale can be met neither by the generalities of regional summaries nor the particularism of bog-margin reconstructions. Considerable creativity, and a good understanding of inherent limitations of data and theory, are needed to avoid the pitfalls. They are, furthermore, needed on both sides of the disciplinary boundary (see Chapter 3).

It probably needs no emphasis that the success of the continental shelf interdisciplinary project is a perceived, not empirically demonstrated, success. However, at that subjective level, it surpasses other projects completed to date. A number of ambitious northeastern collaborative efforts are still underway, or at any rate, not yet fully reported. Their potential for successful integration cannot yet be evaluated, but they have raised expectations. Among these must be counted the studies of human occupancy of the Delaware coast (Thomas et al. 1975; J. Kraft 1977), the Meadowcroft investigations in Pennsylvania (Adovasio et al. 1977), the Munsungan Lake project in central Maine (R. Bonnichsen, director), and the investigation of the Paleo-Indian Whipple site and its environs in New Hampshire (Curran 1979).

THE ADVANTAGES OF MODELING

Models are tools which help us to think more creatively and more precisely. They do this by artificially simplifying multivariate realities so that only those variables judged to be essential to a problem are manipulated during the search for a solution. The evaluations of relevance are made according to rules of logic and evidence, the rules being, so far as possible, explicit. The resulting clarity is gained at some expense; however, logically constructed models permit the researcher to identify and incorporate those variables which his basic assumptions implicate as critical (Levins 1966; Maynard-Smith 1978). The logical clarity of models is an unparalleled advantage in the creation of hypotheses and the deduction of test implications (see Chapter 4).

A model is thus a useful tool and a conceptual compromise. "All models are both true and false. [They] leave out a lot and are in that sense false, incomplete, inadequate. Unlike the scientific hypothesis, a model is not verifiable directly by experiment. The validation of a model is not that it is 'true' but that it generates good testable hypotheses relevant to important problems [Levins 1966: 430]." Here I wish to briefly consider two kinds of models—analogue models and theoretical models.

Analogue models are elaborated by means of logical rules or mathematical equations from assumed equivalencies between observable data states and hypothetical ones. They are, in a sense, formal expressions of the Principle of Uniformitarianism. Analogue models are effective devices for integrating, exploiting, and expanding data sets from separate but related disciplines. Archaeologists employ ethnographic data as analogue models for prehistoric situations (Yellen 1977; Funk 1972). Dendrochronologists and palynologists relate contemporary tree rings or pollen rain to modern climatic data to calculate calibration (transfer) functions which permit them to infer climate from older tree rings and pollen spectra (Fritts 1976; Webb and Clark 1977). Climatologists use modern meteorological data to build simulations which can model past climates (CLIMAP 1976).

Thoughtful experience with such models has demonstrated their inherent limitations and drawbacks, which derive from the difficulties of (1) selecting appropriate variables, (2) dealing with interactions among variables in the diachronic dimension, and (3) avoiding circularity between initial assumptions and the results (Wobst 1978; Webb and Clark 1977; Williams 1978; Heath 1979). Analogue models in archaeology have additional liabilities. By their very nature they are biased toward parameters dominant under present conditions. Furthermore, as products of synchronic analyses, they tend to imply static conditions. Their application alone, unsupplemented by other kinds of models and theory, cannot expand our knowledge, but only replicate it by extrapolation into the past (Binford 1967; R Gould 1980). Nevertheless, the heuristic utility of analogue models, and their perfectability given maturing theory and refined data, assure them of a creative role in interdisciplinary research.

The experience gained on the continental shelf project indicates an equally bright prospect for the employment of theoretical models. Ecological theory, especially, is promising because it offers hope of applicability to both natural and cultural data. Foraging strategy models are based on evolutionary ecology and on economic theory which derives originally from the social sciences (MacArthur and Pianka 1966; Joachim 1976; Pyke et al. 1977). Their application to anthropological problems has produced new insights into the mechanics of human adaptation (Winterhalder 1977; Joachim 1976; Root 1978a). This body of theory has been criticized, among other things, for being unquantifiable (Lewontin 1978); its usefulness in biology is limited because of that. Levins has made a persuasive case for the employment of qualitative parameters in ecological modeling

(Levins 1966). Foraging models work well with only qualitative variables, and their strengths in this mode are particularly helpful for archaeological and paleoenvironmental applications, where quantification is only coarse or relative at best. It probably bears repeating that qualitative models borrowed from the life sciences will help anthropologists to think about only those environmental and ecological variables which human communities share with the natural world. The broad range of social and cultural variables which imbue human behavior are beyond the reach of these models, although they may be eloquently implicated as residual factors in well-designed studies.

Ethnographic analogies have enjoyed a long life span in northeastern archaeology for lack of alternative models. Refined paleoenvironmental data and ecological theory now provide some alternatives (Dincauze 1980). As an example, consider the Paleo-Indian case. It has been traditional in northeastern archaeology to imagine fluted-point-using peoples moving in tundra landscapes in dogged pursuit of large game (Witthoft 1952; Funk 1972). In only one case has the requisite paleoenvironmental work been done to demonstrate the existence of tundra conditions coeval with the archaeological occupation of a site (MacDonald 1968). This single case near the northern limits of the available territory (Debert) has by implication validated the use, in more southerly latitudes, of analogies derived from barren-ground hunters of the ethnographic record.

If we relax the tundra assumption and look closely at the data presently available to us, we see a different picture (Curran and Dincauze 1977). Evidence for human occupation of the region earlier than 11,000 years ago is still controversial; it will not be used in this discussion, which therefore does not apply to any pre-11,000 occupations. There are now enough dated pollen spectra from the Northeast to demonstrate that tundra conditions had been superceded by open spruce forest throughout most of the region by 11,000 years ago ("forest-tundra" of R. Davis et al. 1979). At Rogers Lake, Connecticut, the spruce-park pollen zone begins ca. 12,000 B.P. (M. B. Davis 1969b). At New Hampton Bog in southeastern New York, spruce vegetation was established by 12,850 B.P. (Connally and Sirkin 1970). Berry Pond in the Berkshire hills of Massachusetts showed "open boreal forest" succeeding treeless tundra by 11,500 B.P. (Whitehead 1979). Tundra had given way to forest-tundra at Moulton Pond in central coastal Maine by ca. 10,300 (R. Davis et al. 1975). At Boundary Pond on the Maine-Quebec border just west of the divide, there was a spruce pollen maximum at 11,200 B.P., and closed forest conditions with northern deciduous species included were established by 10,000 B.P.; the spruce trees are thought to have come "from the southeast along valleys through the mountains . . . [Mott 1977:148]." In the Champlain Lowland to the west, Richard sees significant retardation of forest communities, because of the late glacial marine inundation of the basin. Even so, open spruce-woodland was established in the southern part of the basin in the eleventh millennium B.P. (Richard 1977:171). It would appear that Paleo-Indians had to move close to the wasting ice sheet or into high mountains before they would be confronted with open tundra conditions (see Curran and Dincauze 1977 and Sanger et al. 1977 for additional dates).

The spruce parkland environment which was typical of the Northeast in the eleventh millennium was diversifying in the south, as both coniferous and deciduous species moved in. Climatic control of biota would have been clinal, weakest in the south. The implication is for unstable habitats of low predictability; in areas close to tundra conditions, the diversity and productivity would also have been relatively low. "Work on the joint evolution of habitat selection and niche breadth, on the role of productivity of the environment, and on food-getting procedures all converge in supporting the theorem that environmental uncertainty leads to increased niche breadth [generalizing strategy] while certain but diverse environments lead to specialization [Levins 1966:426-7]." We cannot escape the conclusion that Paleo-Indian peoples were far more likely to have been generalist foragers than specialists on big game (Curran 1979; Eisenberg 1978; Dincauze 1980). Generalists in an uncertain environment must have at least the capability for mobility. Mobile generalists are unlikely to burden themselves with a highly diversified and specialized tool kit. It is more plausible that Paleo-Indians equipped themselves with multipurpose tools, than that they would have devoted energy and resources to developing an Eskimo-like range of special purpose tools. This is a testable proposition, presently untested.

With these boundary conditions, we might expect that Paleo-Indian peoples left behind a diversity of site types, scattered through the available range of habitats (Eisenberg 1978). However, there is not likely to be tight correspondence between site size and habitat types, as people may converge for many different reasons, ranging from high resource uncertainty (Hamilton and Watt 1970; Root 1978a) to local abundance (Moore and Root 1979). Furthermore, it is not to be assumed that tool kits will covary in any patterned manner with either site size or habitat type. If the tool kits were generalized for efficient transportation, then lithic artifacts were likely to be similar wherever they were discarded. The possibility of specialization in artifacts of perishable materials seems high, but unknowable from the present data base (Lacy 1979). It is likely that the variations in lithic inventories we perceive from site to site were conditioned by factors unrelated to task applications per se—factors like distance to source of good stone, numbers of people in the group, length of stay, etc.

A model such as this has a number of explicit implications for testable hypotheses involving the interaction of human behavior and environmental variables. Some will entail the collection of environmental data of kinds, or of degrees of resolution, previously neglected, such as information on the full range of biotic and mineral resources available to occupants of the site. The model encourages research integrating environmental and cultural factors more closely than has been done, and in that direction lies significant explanation.

Modeling is not a panacea for all our difficulties. It imposes heavy requirements for clarity of logic and comprehensiveness of deduction, and gives us at best partial solutions and better formulated questions. What models can certainly do is move us out of the stalemate of unproductive analogies and toward that fruitful integration of cultural and environmental data which alone can facilitate the testing of our ecological theory.

TRENDS IN PALEOENVIRONMENTAL INTERPRETATION

Within the past decade, paleoenvironmentalists in all the major disciplines, climatology, geology, biology, and oceanography, have thoroughly revised traditional ideas about Quaternary environments. The revision began earlier with the realization that there were considerably more than four major glacial periods. Chronological studies in deep-sea cores show that the glacial stadials were longer, by about an order of magnitude, than the warm-to-temperate interstadials. These data reversed ideas about "normal" and "abnormal" climates within the Quaternary, with far-reaching implications for guiding concepts of biogeography and biological evolution. This background is conveniently and clearly summarized by M. B. Davis and H. E. Wright, Jr. in two papers from a 1974 symposium (M. B. Davis 1976; Wright 1976a).

Instability is the key concept for students of Quaternary environments—climatic and biotic instability must be understood as the norm, especially on the time scale of the Holocene. Evidence mounts to demonstrate Quaternary climatic instability in both long-term and short-term cycles, which are overlain by stochastic variations, which in turn may be locally catastrophic (Hare 1976; Lorenz 1976; Kutzbach 1976; Hecht et al. 1979). Biotic instability followed, based fundamentally on responses to climatic variation and further complicated by interspecific and intraspecific competition, changes in available land surface caused by glacial and marine movements, soils development, and adaptations to latitudinally distinct insolation values encountered during migrations (Hare 1976; Balsam and Heusser 1976; M. B. Davis 1976; Wright 1976a; Horn 1974; Watts 1973; Weins 1976). All of this has special significance for the glaciated areas of North America. "Although the present interglacial interval is nearly over, the flora . . . is far from equilibrium. . . . Modern species evolved during an epoch characterized by climatic and floristic instability; presumably they are adapted for successful penetration of closed communities in order to survive the rapid environmental changes that have characterized the Pleistocene [M. B. Davis 1976:13]."

The rates of change vary from one environmental system to another—atmospheric circulation, oceanic circulation, floral and faunal population structures; responses to environmental perturbations are determined for each by inherent mechanisms and appropriate rates. It is not enough to think of change as constant. What we have to deal with are the dynamics of variable and discontinuous rates of systemic change. The fact of different response rates means that there are lags, even in direct causal sequences, and the magnitude of the lags may be as important to system dynamics as the inherent rates of change (Wright 1976a, 1976b). Researchers have identified some of these. "The mounting evidence that the recovery of [postglacial] temperature was very rapid implies . . . that for much of the period 11,000-6,000 B.P. the biomes probably lagged behind the thermal climate [Hare 1976:515]." "Comparison of marine and terrestrial paleoclimatic indicators from marine cores off Chesapeake Bay indicates that terrestrial climatic changes occurred after similar changes in the oceans. . . . Sea surface temperatures warmed some two thousand years earlier [than] the transition from a boreal to temperate forest [Balsam and Heusser 1976:138]."

A crucial result of the new insights and understanding is that the old analogies that have served as stock in trade for paleoenvironmental reconstruction must be conceded obsolete. Biogeographers no longer talk of whole communities shifting north and south in response to climatic changes. Rather, the need is to look at species migration rates and the unique mixing and overlaps that their interactions produced (Brown and Cleland 1969; M. B. Davis 1976; Bernabo and Webb 1977). The task of the paleoclimatologist is similarly complicated by this awareness: "There seems . . . to be no *simple* fact of climatic history to be learned from our scattered knowledge of the history of the biomes. The widely held view that one should base oneself on ecosystem analogs rather than on the history of individual species, is at least open to challenge. For, if biomes are shifted into regions of differing radiation climate the ecosystem functions are necessarily different, even where the composition and structure of the biome appear little changed—which is probably not the case for late Pleistocene and Holocene fossil assemblages [Hare 1976:515]."

Among the last of the old standbys to go may be the habit of comparing northeastern American postglacial climatic history with that of northwestern Europe. When palynology and paleoclimatology were in their infancies, it was convenient and defensible to use the northwest European pollen history "zones" as if they directly represented climatic intervals, and as if those climatic intervals had hemisphere-wide, or at least pan-Atlantic, validity. Crucial to any assumption of equivalence are at least three questions, which have either been answered in the negative or remain open. Do changes in pollen spectra reflect mainly, and directly, climatic changes? Are changes in pollen spectra synchronous across the hemisphere? Are the *qualities* of climatic/biotic changes equivalent on both sides of the Atlantic? Recent palynology has demonstrated that pollen spectra respond to both local and regional climates, and reflect as well historical accidents of species migration rates and routes, soils development, and local drainage changes as well as more pervasive but unpredictable phenomena such as species competition. The causes of particular pollen spectra are vigorously multivariant. Climate is only part of the story, and may act only as a more or less limiting factor.

With the answer to the first question a clear negative, the synchrony of pollen zones is cast into doubt. The situation is obviously more complicated than concepts of time-transgressive communities imply; the variables controlling species presence and absence are many, and may, in sum, appear quite arbitrary in their effects at any given place. It is, therefore, not fully defensible to assume synchrony in episodes of climatic change on the basis of inferred climatic controls on pollen assemblages.

This leads directly to the complications of the third question, which remain unresolved. On the basis of recent advances in meteorology and in paleoclimatology, it appears increasingly unlikely that even the large-scale climate and weather patterns downwind of a major continental mass can be expected to resemble closely those to the lee of an ocean. Conceding both to be generically "temperate" does not suit our purposes, when we wish to understand ecological systems. It seems fundamentally misleading to employ such terms as "Atlantic" or "Boreal" to climatic episodes, however inferred, of northeastern North America.

ARCHAEOLOGICAL APPLICATIONS

The implications of all this for archaeologists are demanding; we must be prepared to control a larger set of environmental variables whenever we undertake reconstruction, and we must do so on generally finer scales than we have been accustomed to do. At the very least, we must not confound regional-scale data with site-catchment reconstruction, or site-specific data with regional conclusions. For example, the familiar outlines of northeastern Late Archaic cultural adaptation, delineated against an assumed stable environment, quickly blur and metamorphose in the newly revealed context of spatial and temporal diversity. The assumption of tradition-specific adaptive strategies which were spatially repetitive, internally coherent and mutually contrastive (Ritchie 1969a; Funk 1976; Dincauze 1974) can no longer be supported. Instead, we must try to control strategy variation on the scale of site as well as season (Cordell and Plog 1979), and expect temporal change in addition, in patterns far more complex than the time-transgressive ones so far formulated.

The now classic confrontation of strategy models regarding shellfish exploitation on the New England coasts illustrated the stakes involved here. Ritchie on Martha's Vineyard and Snow in Maine exposed sequences of shellfish species in coastal middens. They both explained the serial changes by invoking cultural choices and technological change—purely cultural factors (Ritchie 1969b; Snow 1972). Braun, approaching the same problem from an ecological perspective and with the advantage of additional data on marine conditions, was able to show that the sequence of species changes could be accounted for by successional sequences in substrate and marine current changes (Braun 1974). Consequently, he had no residuals requiring uniquely cultural explanations, and might have concluded that people were acting economically, that is, optimizing return rates on available resources.

MULTIDISCIPLINARY CONVERGENCES

It is exciting to watch the theory and data of the disparate disciplines involved in paleoenvironmental reconstruction converging toward new insights. With some familiar old concepts abandoned, some previously discounted ideas reinstated, the reconstructed paleoenvironments of the Northeast currently look quite different from those we have become used to. A number of disciplinary convergences are fundamentally revising the map of the ice-age coast of northeastern North America.

Geomorphologists working in Labrador and the Maritimes have concluded that the Laurentide ice sheet probably did not cover the entire continental shelf during the last glacial period. Instead, small glacial tongues or discontinuous alpine glaciers fringed the mainland, leaving exposed terrestrial environments seaward on the shelf (Grant 1977; Ives 1978).

Oceanographers here supplied some fascinating support for this idea of exposed continental shelves. Submarine cores from the Labrador Shelf indicate the presence of sedge-shrub tundra from as early as 21,000 B.P., uninterrupted by ice advance, and seasonally open water along the coast (Vilks and Mudie 1978). Cores from the surface of seamounts south of Newfoundland also show no grounded ice there during the last glacial period (Alam and Piper 1977). Recalculations of sea level rise on the shelf off South Carolina were interpreted to mean that previous estimates of sea levels after 20,000 B.P. may have been exaggeratedly low, and that "substantially less ice was present from 17,000 to 10,000 years B.P." than had been believed (Blackwelder et al. 1979). These data are occasionally in conflict with the results of other studies, and the conclusions cannot be considered definitive now.

The implications for biogeography are exciting. Ives noted in his 1978 article that old theories of biological refugia on the northeastern emergent shelves should now be reconsidered. The work of Dadswell (1974), Cronin (1977), and Wagner (1970) on aquatic fauna in the St. Lawrence lowland and adjacent waters indicates that a very diverse fauna was available to colonize meltwater bodies and the early marine transgression; assemblages of plankton, crustacea, molluscs, and bony fishes were not far from the ice front. Some research now underway is suggestive of the presence of temperate reptilian and fresh-water fauna on the shelf and perhaps Georges Bank throughout the glacial episode (Smith 1980). Reptiles don't live alone; we can expect further work to reveal a variety of faunal and floral species on the shelves, available for early recolonization to the west and north. Habitats congenial to temperate-adapted reptiles should have suited human beings very well. Reasonably easy access to and from the mainland, at least occasionally, is also implied.

The import of these new ideas for human paleogeography remains to be determined. Old generalities are giving way to exciting new concepts of diversity and dynamism in Quaternary environments. If we pay attention, stay involved, and contribute our share of the data and problems in this field, we can expect to find the history of human adaptations in the Northeast becoming an unexpectedly fascinating and rewarding study. The opportunity for making significant contributions to cultural ecological theory also seems close at hand.

ACKNOWLEDGEMENTS

    In undertaking this multifaceted review, I have relied on and have benefited beyond estimation from the interest, encouragement, and support of a number of colleagues, students, and friends. Direct and indirect contributions to this paper have been made by Raymond S. Bradley, M. Pamela Bumsted, John R. Cross, Marylou Curran, Joseph H. Hartshorn, Elizabeth A. Little, Stephen Loring, James A. Moore, William A. Patterson, Michael E. Roberts, Dolores Root, Douglas G. Smith, and H. Martin Wobst. None of the above reviewed the manuscript, and all are thereby completely absolved from any complicity in whatever errors of fact, interpretation, or judgement inhere in the text. A half-year sabbatical leave granted by the University of Massachusetts at Amherst made possible the review of current literature on which this article is based.

REFERENCES

Adovasio, J.M., J.D. Gunn, J. Donahue, and R. Stuckenrath
    1977   Progress report on the Meadowcroft Rockshelter—a 16,000 year chronicle. In Amerinds and their paleoenvironments in northeastern North America. *Annals of the New York Academy of Sciences* 288: 137-159.
Alam, M., and D.J. Piper
    1977   Pre-Wisconsin stratigraphy and paleoclimates off Atlantic Canada, and its bearing on glaciation in Québec. *Géographie physique et Quaternaire* 31(1-2):15-22.
Anderson, P., and T. Webb, III
    1980   Two short cores from the Greenwich Cove area, Rhode Island. Abstract, Northeast Anthropological Association, 20th annual meeting, Amherst, Massachusetts.
Andrews, J.T.
    1972   Recent and fossil growth rates of marine bivalves, Canadian arctic, and Late-Quaternary arctic marine environments. *Paleogeography, Paleoclimatology, Paleoecology* 11:157-176.
Balsam, W.L., and L.E. Heusser
    1976   Direct correlation of sea surface paleotemperatures, deep circulation and terrestrial paleoclimates: Foraminiferal and palynological evidence from 2 cores off Chesapeake Bay. *Marine Geology* 21:121-147.
Barber, R.J.
    1977   Disjunct plant distributions and archaeological interpretation. *Man in the Northeast* 13:103-107.

1979   Archaeology and paleontology. In *Summary and analysis of cultural resource information on the continental shelf from the Bay of Fundy to Cape Hatteras*, edited by Michael Roberts, Vol. 2. Institute for Conservation Archaeology, Peabody Museum, Harvard University.

Barry, R.G., W.H. Arundale, J.T. Andrews, S. Bradley, and H. Nichols
1977   Environmental change and cultural change in the eastern Canadian arctic during the last 5000 years. *Arctic and Alpine Research* 9(2): 193-210.

Bartlett, G.A., and L. Molinsky
1972   Foraminifera and the Holocene history of the Gulf of St. Lawrence. *Canadian Journal of Earth Sciences* 9:1204-1215.

Bender, M.H., D.A. Baerreis, and R.L. Steventon
1981   Further light on carbon isotopes and Hopewell agriculture. *American Antiquity* 46(2):346-353.

Benmouyal, J.
1978   La Gaspésie. In Images de la préhistoire du Québec, compiled by Claude Chapdelaine. *Recherches amérindiennes au Québec* 7(1-2): 55-61.

Bernabo, J.C., and T. Webb, III
1977   Changing patterns in the Holocene pollen record of northeastern North America: A mapped summary. *Quaternary Research* 8:64-96.

Binford, L.R.
1967   Smudge pits and hide smoking: The use of analogy in archaeological reasoning. *American Antiquity* 32(1):1-12.

Blackwelder, B.W., O.H. Pilkey, and J.D. Howard
1979   Late Wisconsinan sea levels on the southeast U.S. Atlantic shelf based on in-place shoreline indicators. *Science* 204:618-620.

Bonnichsen, R., and D. Sanger
1978   Integrating faunal analysis. *Canadian Journal of Archaeology* 1:109-133.

Borns, H.W., Jr., and P.E. Calkin
1977   Quaternary glaciation, west-central Maine. *Geological Society of America Bulletin* 88:1773-1784.

Botkin, D.B., and R.S. Miller
1974   Complex ecosystems: Models and predictions. *American Scientist* 62(4):449-453.

Bourque, B.J.
1973   Aboriginal settlement and subsistence on the Maine coast. *Man in the Northeast* 6:3-20.

Bourque, B.J., K. Morris, and A. Spiess
1978   Determining the season of death of mammal teeth from archaeological sites: A new sectioning technique. *Science* 199(4328):530-531.

Braun, D.P.
1974   Explanatory models for the evolution of coastal adaptation in prehistoric eastern New England. *American Antiquity* 39(4):582-596.

Brown, J.A., and C.E. Cleland
  1969 The late glacial and early postglacial faunal resources in midwestern biomes newly opened to human adaptations. In The Quaternary of Illinois. *College of Agriculture, Special Publications* 14:14-122. University of Illinois, Urbana.

Brugam, R.B.
  1978 Pollen indicators of land-use change in southern Connecticut. *Quaternary Research* 9:349-362.

Bucha, V., R.E. Taylor, R.M. Berger, and E.W. Haury
  1970 Geomagnetic intensity: Changes during the past 3000 years in the western hemisphere. *Science* 168:111-114.

Bumsted, M.P.
  1980 The potential of stable carbon isotopes in bioarchaeological anthropology. In Biocultural adaptation: Comprehensive approaches to skeletal analyses, edited by Debra L. Martin and M. Pamela Bumsted. *Research Reports* (in press), Department of Anthropology, University of Massachusetts, Amherst.

Butzer, K.W.
  1971 *Environment and archaeology* (2nd ed.). Aldine-Atherton, Chicago.
  1975 The ecological approach to archaeology: Are we really trying? *American Antiquity* 40(1):106-111.

Carbone, V.A.
  1977 Phtoliths as paleoecological indicators. In Amerinds and their paleoenvironments in northeastern North America. *Annals of the New York Academy of Sciences* 288:194-205.

Chapdelaine, C. (compiler)
  1978 Images de la prehistoire du Quebec. *Recherches amerindiennes au Quebec* VII (1-2).

Chaplin, R.E.
  1971 *The study of animal bones from archaeological sites.* Seminar Press, New York.

CLIMAP
  1976 The surface of the ice-age earth. *Science* 191:1131-1144.

Colby, W.C., M.A. Light, and T.A. Bertinuson
  1953 The influence of wind-blown material on the soils of Massachusetts. *Soil Science Society Proceedings* 1953:395-399.

Colinvaux, P.A.
  1978 On the use of the word "absolute" in pollen statistics. *Quaternary Research* 9:132-133.

Connally, G.G.
  1970 Discussion: Caribou and Paleo-Indian in New York State: A presumed association. *American Journal of Science* 269:314-315.

Connally, G.G., and L.A. Sirkin
  1970 Late glacial history of the upper Wallkill Valley, New York. *Geological Society of America Bulletin* 81(11):3297-3305.

Cordell, L., and F. Plog
  1979 Escaping the confines of normative thought: A reevaluation of Puebloan prehistory. *American Antiquity* 44(3):405-429.

Cronin, T.
  1977 Late-Wisconsin marine environments of the Champlain Valley (New York, Quebec). *Quaternary Research* 7:238-253.
Crosby, W.D.
  1903 A study of the geology of the Charles River estuary and the formation of Boston Harbor. Report of the Committee on Charles River Dam, Appendix 7:345-369.
CSSC = Canada Soil Survey Committee, Subcommittee on Soil Classification
  1978 The Canadian system of soil classification. *Canadian Department of Agriculture Publication* 1646. Supply and Services Canada, Ottawa.
Curran, M.L.
  1979 Studying human adaptation at a Paleo-Indian site: A preliminary report. In Ecological anthropology of the middle Connecticut River valley, edited by Robert Paynter. *Research Reports* 18, Department of Anthropology, University of Massachusetts, Amherst.
Curran, M.L., and D.F. Dincauze
  1977 Paleoindians and paleo-lakes: New data from the Connecticut drainage. In Amerinds and their paleoenvironments in northeastern North America. *Annals of the New York Academy of Sciences* 288:333-348.
Curray, J.R.
  1965 Late Quaternary history, continental shelves of the United States. In *The Quaternary of the United States*, edited by H.E. Wright, Jr. and D. Frey, pp. 723-735. Princeton University Press.
Dadswell, M.
  1974 Distribution, ecology and postglacial dispersal of certain crustaceans and fishes in eastern North America. *Publications de zoologie* 11. National Museum of Canada, Ottawa.
Dansgaard, W., S.J. Johnson, J. Møller, and C.C. Langway, Jr.
  1969 One thousand centuries of climatic record from Camp Century on the Greenland ice sheet. *Science* 166:377-381.
Davidson, D.A., and M.L. Shackley (editors)
  1978 *Geoarchaeology: Earth sciences and the past.* Duckworth and Co., London.
Davis, M.B.
  1969a Palynological and environmental history during the Quaternary period. *American Scientist* 57(3):317-332.
  1969b Climatic changes in southern Connecticut recorded by pollen deposition at Rogers Lake. *Ecology* 50:409-422.
  1976 Pleistocene biogeography of temperate deciduous forests. *Geoscience and Man* 13:13-26.
Davis, M.B., L.B. Brubaker, and T. Webb, III
  1973 Calibration of absolute pollen influx. In *Quaternary plant ecology*, edited by H.J.B. Birks and R.G. West, pp. 9-27. Blackwell Scientific Publications, Oxford.
Davis, R.B., T.E. Bradstreet, and H.W. Borns, Jr.
  1979 Reply to R.J. Mott (1977) regarding an early postglacial boreal forest in New England and adjacent Canadian areas. *Geographie Physique et Quaternaire* 33(1):113-115.

Davis, R.B., T.E. Bradstreet, R. Stuckenrath, Jr., and H.W. Borns, Jr.
  1975   Vegetation and associated environments during the past 14,000 years near Moulton Pond, Maine. *Quaternary Research* 5(3):435-466.
Davis, R.B., and S.A. Norton
  1978   Paleolimnologic studies of human impact on lakes in the United States, with emphasis on recent research in New England. *Polskie Archiwum Hydrobiologe* 25(1-2):99-115.
Davis, R.B., and T. Webb, III
  1975   The contemporary distribution of pollen in eastern North America: A comparison with the vegetation. *Quaternary Research* 5:395-434.
Day, G.M.
  1953   The Indian as an ecological factor in the northeastern forest. *Ecology* 34:329-346.
Deevey, E.S., Jr.
  1949   Biogeography of the Pleistocene, Part I. Europe and North America. *Geological Society of America Bulletin* 60:1315-1416.
Delabarre, E.B.
  1925   A possible pre-Algonkian culture in southeastern Massachusetts. *American Anthropologist* 27:359-369.
Denton, G.N., and W. Karlén
  1973   Holocene climatic variations—their pattern and possible cause. *Journal of Quaternary Research* 3(2):155-205.
Dice, L.R.
  1943   *The biotic provinces of North America.* University of Michigan Press, Ann Arbor.
Dillon, W.P., and R.N. Oldale
  1978   Late Quaternary sea-level curves: Reinterpretation based on glacio-tectonic influence. *Geology* 6:56-60.
Dimbleby, G.W.
  1967   *Plants and archaeology.* John Baker, London.
Dincauze, D.F.
  1972   The Atlantic phase: A Late Archaic culture in Massachusetts. *Man in the Northeast* 4:40-61.
  1973   Prehistoric occupation of the Charles River Estuary. *Archaeological Society of Connecticut Bulletin* 38:25-39.
  1974   An introduction to archaeology in the greater Boston area. *Archaeology of Eastern North America* 2:39-66.
  1976   The Neville site: 8000 years at Amoskeag. *Peabody Museum Monographs No. 4.* Peabody Museum, Harvard University.
  1978   "Common sense" and scientific insight. *Archaeology of Eastern North America* 6:83-87.
  1979   Teaching prehistoric archaeological survey in the Northeast. In Essays in Northeastern Anthropology in Memory of Marian E. White, edited by W.E. Englebrecht and D.K. Grayson. *Man in the Northeast, Occasional Publications in Northeastern Anthropology No.* 5:22-40.

1980   Research priorities in northeastern archaeology. In Proceedings of the conference on northeastern archaeology, edited by James A. Moore. *Research Reports* 19:29-48. Department of Anthropology, University of Massachusetts, Amherst.

Dincauze, D.F., and M.T. Mulholland
1977   Early and Middle Archaic site distributions and habitats in southern New England. In Amerinds and their paleoenvironments in northeastern North America. *Annals of the New York Academy of Sciences* 288:439-456.

Edwards, R.L., and K.O. Emery
1977   Man on the continental shelf. In Amerinds and their paleoenvironments in northeastern North America. *Annals of the New York Academy of Sciences* 288:245-256.

Edwards, R.L., and A.S. Merrill
1977   A reconstruction of the continental shelf areas of eastern North America for the times 9,500 B.P. and 12,500 B.P. *Archaeology of Eastern North America* 5:1-43.

Eidt, R.C.
1973   A rapid chemical field test for archaeological surveying. *American Antiquity* 38(2):206-210.
1977   Detection and examination of anthrosols by phosphate analysis. *Science* 197:1327-1333.

Eisenberg, L.
1978   Paleo-Indian settlement pattern in the Hudson and Delaware river drainages. *Man in the Northeast, Occasional Publications in Northeastern Anthropology No. 4.*

Emery, K.O., R.L. Wigley, A.S. Bartlett, M. Rubin, and E.S. Barghoorn
1967   Freshwater peat on the continental shelf. *Science* 158:1301-1307.

Evans, J.G.
1978   *An introduction to environmental archaeology.* Cornell University Press, Ithaca.

Finison, K.
1978   Hypotheses about late-Wisconsin ungulate fauna in the Northeast and Paleo-Indian adaptations with an example from the Wallkill Valley. Paper for Anthropology 529, Department of Anthropology, University of Massachusetts, Amherst.

Fitzhugh, W.W.
1972   Environmental archaeology and cultural systems in Hamilton Inlet, Labrador: A survey of the central Labrador coast from 3000 B.C. to the present. *Smithsonian Contributions to Anthropology* 16.
1975   A Maritime Archaic sequence from Hamilton Inlet, Labrador. *Arctic Anthropology* 12:117-138.

Ford, R.I.
1979   Paleoethnobotany in American archaeology. In *Advances in Archaeological Method and Theory* 2:285-336, edited by M.B. Schiffer. Academic Press, New York.

Foss, J.E.
1977   The pedological record at several Paleoindian sites in the Northeast. In Amerinds and their paleoenvironments in northeastern North America. *Annals of the New York Academy of Sciences* 288:234-244.
Fritts, H.
1976   *Tree rings and climate.* Academic Press, New York.
Funk, R.E.
1972   Early man in the Northeast and the late-glacial environment. *Man in the Northeast* 4:7-39.
1976   Recent contributions to Hudson valley prehistory. *New York State Museum and Science Service Memoir* 22.
Funk, R.E., D.W. Fisher, and E.M. Reilly, Jr.
1970   Caribou and Paleo-Indian in New York State: A presumed association. *American Journal of Science* 268:181-186.
Funk, R.E., and B.E. Rippeteau
1977   Adaptation, continuity and change in Upper Susquehanna prehistory. *Man in the Northeast, Occasional Publications in Northeastern Anthropology No. 3.*
Gagliano, S.M. (editor)
1977   *Cultural resources evaluation of the northern Gulf of Mexico continental shelf.* U.S. Department of the Interior, Washington.
Gladfelter, B.G.
1977   Geoarchaeology: The geomorphologist and archaeology. *American Antiquity* 42(4):519-538.
Gould, R.A.
1980   *Living archaeology.* Cambridge University Press, Cambridge.
Gould, S.J.
1980   Is a new and general theory of evolution emerging? *Paleobiology,* in press.
Gramly, R.M., and G. Gwynn
1979   Two Late Woodland sites on Long Island Sound. *Bulletin of the Massachusetts Archaeological Society* 40:5-19.
Grant, D.R.
1977   Glacial style and ice limits, the Quaternary stratigraphic record, and changes of land and ocean level in the Atlantic Provinces, Canada. *Géographic physique et Quaternaire* 31(3-4):247-260.
Guilday, J.E.
1967   The climatic significance of the Hosterman's pit local fauna, Centre County, Pennsylvania. *American Antiquity* 32(2):231-232.
Hamilton, W.J., III, and K.E.F. Watt
1970   Refuging. *Annual Review of Ecology and Systematics* 1:263-285.
Hardesty, D.
1977   *Ecological anthropology.* John Wiley, New York.
Hare, K.F.
1976   Late Pleistocene and Holocene climates: Some persistent problems. *Quaternary Research* 6:507-517.

Harrington, C.R.
1977   Marine mammals in the Champlain Sea and the Great Lakes. In Amerinds and their paleoenvironments in northeastern North America. *Annals of the New York Academy of Sciences* 288:508-537.

Hartshorn, J.H.
1965   Late-glacial and postglacial eolian activity in southern New England. Abstracts of the 7th congress, p. 196. International Association for Quaternary Research, Boulder, Colorado.

Hassan, F.
1978   Sediments in archaeology: Methods and implications for paleoenvironmental and cultural analysis. *Journal of Field Archaeology* 5:197-213.

Heath, G.R.
1979   Simulations of a glacial paleoclimate by three different atmospheric general circulation models. *Palaeogeography, Palaeoclimatology, Palaeoecology* 26:291-303.

Hecht, A.D., R. Barry, H. Fritts, J. Imbrie, J. Kutzbach, and J.M. Mitchell
1979   Paleoclimatic research: Status and opportunities. *Quaternary Research* 12:6-17.

Heidenreich, C.E., and V.A. Konrad
1973   Soil analysis at the Robitaille site. Part II: A method useful in determining the location of longhouse patterns. *Ontario Archaeology* 20: 33-62.

Heidenreich, C.E., and S. Navratil
1973   Soil analysis at the Robitaille site. Part I: Determining the perimeter of the village. *Ontario Archaeology* 20:25-32.

Hillaire-Marcel, C.
1977   Les isotopes du carbone et de l'oxygène dans les mere postglaciaires du Québec. *Géographie physique et Quaternaire* 31(1-2):81-106.

Holmes, R.D.
1980   Pollen as an environmental indicator at the Shea site east, Belchertown. Paper presented at the 20th annual meeting, Northeast Anthropological Association, Amherst, Massachusetts.

Horn, H.S.
1974   The ecology of secondary succession. *Annual Review of Ecology and Systematics* 5:25-37.

Ives, J.D.
1978   The maximum extent of the Laurentide ice sheet along the east coast of North America during the last glaciation. *Arctic* 31:24-53.

Jochim, M.A.
1976   *Hunter-gatherer subsistence and settlement: A predictive model.* Academic Press, New York.

Johnson, F. (editor)
1942   The Boylston Street fishweir. *Papers of the Robert S. Peabody Foundation for Archaeology No. 2.*

Jordan, R.H.
1975   Pollen diagrams from Hamilton Inlet, central Labrador, and their implications for the northern Maritime Archaic. *Arctic Anthropology* 12:92-116.

King, J.E., W.E. Klippel, and R. Duffield
1975 Pollen preservation and archaeology in eastern North America. *American Antiquity* 40(2):180-190.
Kraft, H.C.
1977 The Paleo-Indian sites at Port Mobil, Staten Island. In Current perspectives in northeastern archeology. *New York State Archeological Association Researches and Transactions* 17(1):1-19.
Kraft, J.C.
1977 Late Quaternary paleogeographic changes in the coastal environments of Delaware, middle Atlantic bight, related to archaeological settings. In Amerinds and their paleoenvironments in northeastern North America. *Annals of the New York Academy of Sciences* 288:35-69.
Kutzbach, J.E.
1976 The nature of climate and climatic variations. *Quaternary Research* 6:471-480.
Lacy, D.
1979 In quest of a Paleoindian bone-tool industry: The missing dimension in the Northeast. Paper for Anthropology 529, Department of Anthropology, University of Massachusetts, Amherst.
Levins, R.
1966 The strategy of model building in population biology. *American Scientist* 54(4):421-431.
Lewontin, R.C.
1978 Fitness, survival and optimality. In *Analysis of ecological systems,* edited by D.H. Horn, R. Mitchell, and G.R. Stairs. Ohio State University Press, Columbus.
Limbrey, S.
1975 *Soil science and archaeology.* Academic Press, London.
Linares, O.
1976 "Garden hunting" in the American tropics. *Human Ecology* 4:331-349.
Lorenz, E.N.
1976 Nondeterministic theories of climatic change. *Quaternary Research* 6:495-506.
Loring, S.
1978 PaleoIndian manifestations in Vermont. Paper for Anthropology 529, Department of Anthropology, University of Massachusetts, Amherst.
MacArthur, R.H., and E.R. Rianka
1966 On optimal use of a patchy environment. *American Naturalist* 100:603-609.
MacDonald, G.F.
1968 Debert: A Paleo-Indian site in central Nova Scotia. *National Museum of Canada Anthropological Paper* 16.
Maynard-Smith, J.
1978 Optimization theory in evolution. *Annual Review of Ecology and Systematics* 9:31-56.

McAndrews, J.H.
1976   Fossil history of man's impact on the Canadian flora: An example from southern Ontario. *Canadian Botanical Association Bulletin Supplement* 9(1):1-6.
McAndrews, J.H., and G. Samson
1977   Analyse pollinique et implications archéologiques et géomorphologiques, Lac de la Hutte Sauvage (Mushuau Nipi), Nouvesu-Québec. *Géographie physique et Quaternaire* 31(1-2):177-183.
McBride, K.A.
1978   Archaic subsistence in the lower Connecticut River valley: Evidence from Woodchuck Knoll. *Man in the Northeast* 15-16:124-132.
McGhee, R.
1976   Paleoeskimo occupations of Central and High Arctic Canada. *Society for American Archaeology Memoir* 31:15-39.
1978   Discussion of "Holocene peopling of the New World" by William B. Workman. *American Quaternary Association Abstracts* 1978:149-152.
McNett, C.W., Jr., B.A. McMillan, and S.B. Marshall
1977   The Shawnee-Minisink site. In Amerinds and their paleoenvironments in northeastern North America. *Annals of the New York Academy of Sciences* 288:282-296.
Michels, J., and I.F. Smith
1967   *Archaeological investigations of Sheep Rock shelter, Huntingdon County, Pennsylvania* (2 Vols.). Department of Anthropology, Pennsylvania State University.
Miller, N.G., and G.G. Thompson
1979   Boreal and western North American plants in the late Pleistocene of Vermont. *Journal of the Arnold Arboretum* 60:167-218.
Milliman, J.D., and K.O. Emery
1968   Sea levels during the past 35,000 years. *Science* 162:1121-1123.
Moir, R.
1975   The surficial geology of Hadley and its relationship to the Connecticut Valley archaeological research project. Manuscript on file, Department of Anthropology, University of Massachusetts, Amherst.
1979   Physical Environment. *Summary and analysis of cultural resource information on the Continental Shelf from the Bay of Fundy to Cape Hatteras*, Vol. 1, edited by Michael Roberts. Institute for Conservation Archaeology, Peabody Museum, Harvard University.
Moore, J.A., and D. Root
1979   Anadromous fish, stream ranking and settlement. In Ecological Anthropology of the Middle Connecticut River Valley, edited by Robert Paynter. *Research Reports* 18:27-44. Department of Anthropology, University of Massachusetts, Amherst.
Mott, R.J.
1977   Late-Pleistocene and Holocene palynology in southeastern Québec. *Géographie physique et Quaternaire* 31(1-2):139-149.

Newman, W.S., and B. Salwen
   1977   Introduction. In Amerinds and their paleoenvironments in north-eastern North America. *Annals of the New York Academy of Sciences* 288:1-2.
Occhietti, S., and C. Hillaire-Marcel
   1977   Chronologie ^{14}C des événements paléogéographiques du Québec depuis 14,000 ans. *Géographie physique et Quaternaire* 31(1-2):123-133.
Ogden, J.G.
   1977   Pollen analysis: State of the art. *Géographie physique et Quaternaire* 31(1-2):151-159.
Oldale, R.N., and C.J. O'Hara
   1980   New Radiocarbon dates from the inner Continental Shelf off south-eastern Massachusetts and a local sea-level-rise curve for the past 12,000 years. *Geology* 8:102-106.
Pearsall, D.M.
   1977   Phytolith analysis of archeological soils: Evidence for maize cultivation in formative Ecuador. *Science* 199:177-178.
Perlman, S.M.
   1976   Optimum diet models and prehistoric hunter-gatherers: A test on Martha's Vineyard. Ph.D. dissertation, University of Massachusetts, Amherst.
Peterson, G.M., T. Webb, III, J.E. Kutzbach, T. van der Hammen, T.A. Wijmstra, and F.A. Street
   1979   The continental record of environmental conditions at 18,000 yr. B.P.: An initial evaluation. *Quaternary Research* 12:47-82.
Pyke, G.H., H.R. Pulliam, and E.L. Charnov
   1977   Optimal foraging: A selective review of theory and tests. *The Quarterly Review of Biology* 52:137-154.
Ralph, E.K., and H.N. Michael
   1974   Twenty-five years of radiocarbon dating. *American Scientist* 62(5): 553-560.
Ralph, E.K., H.N. Michael, and M.C. Han
   1973   Radiocarbon dates and reality. *MASCA Newsletter* 9:1-20.
Renfrew, C.
   1978   Trajectory discontinuity and morphogenesis: The implications of catastrophe theory for archaeology. *American Antiquity* 43(2):203-222.
Richard, P.
   1977   Végétation tardiglaciaire au Québec méridional et implications paléo-climatiques. *Géographie physique et Quaternaire* 31(1-2):161-176.
Ritchie, W.A.
   1953   A probable Paleo-Indian site in Vermont. *American Antiquity* 18(3): 249-258.
   1969a   *The archaeology of New York State* (2nd ed.). Natural History Press, Garden City, New York.
   1969b   *The archaeology of Martha's Vineyard.* Natural History Press, Garden City, New York.

Roberts, M.
   1979 Management. *Summary and analysis of cultural resource information on the continental shelf from the Bay of Fundy to Cape Hatteras,* Vol. 4. Institute for Conservation Archaeology, Peabody Museum, Harvard University.

Roberts, M. (editor)
   1979 *Summary and analysis of cultural resource information on the continental shelf from the Bay of Fundy to Cape Hatteras* (4 Vols.). Institute for Conservation Archaeology, Peabody Museum, Harvard University.

Root, D.
   1978a Hunter-gatherer social organization and utilization of varying environments. Paper presented at the 43rd annual meeting, Society for American Archaeology, Tucson, Arizona.
   1978b Predictive model of prehistoric subsistence and settlement systems on the outer continental shelf. MS on file, Department of Anthropology, University of Massachusetts, Amherst.

Ruddiman, W.F., and A. McIntyre
   1973 Time-transgressive deglacial retreat of polar water from the North Atlantic. *Quaternary Research* 3:117-130.
   1977 Late Quaternary surface oceans kinematics and climatic change in the high-latitude North Atlantic. *Journal of Geophysical Research* 82: 3877-3887.

Salwen, B.
   1962 Sea levels and archaeology in the Long Island Sound area. *American Antiquity* 28(1):46-55.
   1965 *Sea levels and the Archaic archaeology of the northeast coast of the United States.* Ph.D. dissertation, Department of Anthropology, Columbia University. University Microfilms No. 65-13,990, Ann Arbor.
   1975 Post-glacial environments and cultural change in the Hudson river basin. *Man in the Northeast* 10:43-70.

Sanger, D., R.B. Davis, R.G. MacKay, and H.W. Borns, Jr.
   1977 The Hirundo archaeological project—An interdisciplinary approach to central Maine prehistory. In Amerinds and their paleoenvironments in northeastern North America. *Annals of the New York Academy of Sciences* 288:457-471.

Schwert, D.P., and A.V. Morgan
   1980 Paleoenvironmental implications of a late glacial insect assemblage from northwestern New York. *Quaternary Research* 13:93-110.

Shackleton, N.J.
   1973 Oxygen isotope analysis as a means of determining season of occupation of prehistoric midden sites. *Archaeometry* 15:133-141.

Shackley, M.L.
   1975 *Archaeological sediments: A survey of analytical methods.* John Wiley and Sons, New York.

SMIC = Study of Man's Impact on Climate
    1971   Inadvertent climate modification. Report of the study of man's impact on climate. Massachusetts Institute of Technology Press, Cambridge.
Smith, D.G.
    1980   Relict and disjunct animal distribution in southern New England: Evidence for an isolated glacial refugium on George's Bank. MS in preparation, Museum of Zoology, University of Massachusetts, Amherst.
Snow, D.R.
    1972   Rising sea level and prehistoric cultural ecology in northern New England. *American Antiquity* 37(2):211-221.
Strauss, Alan E.
    1978   Nature's transformations and other pitfalls: Toward a better understanding of post-occupational changes in archaeological site morphology in the Northeast. Part I: Vegetation. *Bulletin of the Massachusetts Archaeological Society* 39:47-64.
Struever, S.
    1968   Flotation techniques for the recovery of small-scale archaeological remains. *American Antiquity* 33(3):353-362.
Stuiver, M.
    1971   Evidence for the variation of atmospheric C^{14} content in the late Quaternary. In *The Late Cenozoic Glacial Ages*, edited by K. Turekian, pp. 57-70. Yale University Press, New Haven.
Thomas, P.A.
    1974   Archaeological and historical impact statement, Montague nuclear power station. Northeast Utilities Corp.
    1975   A response to "Pit excavation techniques at the Faucett site". *Man in the Northeast* 10:74-78.
Thomas, R.A., D.R. Griffith, C.L. Wise, and R.E. Artusy, Jr.
    1975   Environmental adaptation on Delaware's coastal plain. *Archaeology of Eastern North America* 3:35-90.
Thorbahn, P., and S. Mrozowski
    1979   Ecological dynamics and rural New England historical sites. In *Ecological anthropology of the middle Connecticut River valley*, edited by Robert Paynter. *Research Reports* 18:129-140. Department of Anthropology, University of Massachusetts, Amherst.
Tuck, J.A., and R. McGhee
    1975   An Archaic sequence from the Strait of Belle Isle, Labrador. *National Museum of Man, Archaeological Survey of Canada Mercury Series No. 34.*
USDA = United States Department of Agriculture
    1975   Soil taxonomy: A basic system of soil classification for making and interpreting soil surveys. *USDA Handbook* 436, Washington.
Vilks, G., and P.J. Mudie
    1978   Early deglaciation of the Labrador shelf. *Science* 202:1181-1183.

Vogel, J.C., and N.J. van der Merwe
1977 Isotopic evidence for early maize cultivation in New York. *American Antiquity* 42(2):238-242.
Wagner, F.J.E.
1970 Faunas of the Pleistocene Champlain Sea. *Geological Survey of Canada Bulletin* 181:1-104.
Watts, W.A.
1973 Rates of change and stability in vegetation in the perspective of long periods of time. In *Quaternary plant ecology*, edited by H.J.B. Birks and R.G. West, pp. 195-206. Blackwell Scientific Publications, Oxford.
Webb, T., III, and D.R. Clark
1977 Calibrating micropaleontological data in climatic terms: A critical review. In Amerinds and their paleoenvironments in northeastern North America. *Annals of the New York Academy of Sciences* 288: 93-118.
Whitehead, D.R.
1979 Late-glacial and postglacial vegetational history of the Berkshires, western Massachusetts. *Quaternary Research* 12:333-357.
Whitmore, F.C., Jr., K.O. Emery, H.B.S. Cooke, and D.J.P. Swift
1967 Elephant teeth from the Atlantic continental shelf. *Science* 156:1477-1481.
Wiens, J.A.
1976 Population responses to patchy environments. *Annual Review of Ecology and Systematics* 7:81-120.
Williams, J.
1978 A brief comparison of model simulations of glacial period maximum atmospheric circulation. *Palaeogeography, Palaeoclimatology, Palaeoecology* 25:191-198.
Willoughby, C.C.
1927 An ancient Indian fish weir. *American Anthropologist* 29:105-108.
Winterhalder, B.P.
1977 Foraging strategy adaptations of the boreal forest Cree. Ph.D. dissertation, Cornell University, Ithaca.
Witthoft, J.
1952 A Paleo-Indian site in eastern Pennsylvania: An early hunting culture. *American Philosophical Society Proceedings* 96(4):464-495.
Wobst, H.M.
1978 The archaeo-ethnology of hunter-gatherers or the tyranny of the ethnographic record in archaeology. *American Antiquity* 43(2): 303-309.
Wollin, G., D.B. Ericson, W.B.F. Ryan, and J.H. Foster
1971 Magnetism of the earth and climatic changes. *Earth and Planetary Science Letters* 12:175-183. North Holland Publishing Company.
Wood, W.R., and D.L. Johnson
1978 A survey of disturbance processes in archaeological site formation. In *Advances in archaeological method and theory* I:315-381, edited by M.B. Schiffer. Academic Press, New York.

Wright, H.E., Jr.
  1976a Pleistocene ecology—some current problems. *Geoscience and Man* 13: 1-12.
  1976b The dynamic nature of Holocene vegetation. *Quaternary Research* 6: 581-596.
Yellen, J.E.
  1977 *Archaeological approaches to the present: Models for reconstructing the past.* Academic Press, New York.

3

APPROACHES TO CULTURAL ADAPTATION
IN THE NORTHEAST

DEAN R. SNOW
*State University of New York
at Albany*

Adaptation is another one of those topics of archaeological inquiry in which we seem to know just enough to make ourselves dangerous. A review of past efforts in the topic reveals a record of both real accomplishment and self-deception, and the future seems at this moment to hold more of both. Yet the archaeological data base that has been so arduously compiled over recent decades either is or is nearly sufficiently developed to allow us to do much better with the analysis of prehistoric adaptation than that. My purpose here, therefore, is to note the approaches that have been taken in the recent past, point out what seem to me to be generally unrecognized misunderstandings and shortcomings in these approaches, and on that basis plot a course for worth-while future research.

When discussing prehistoric adaptation we usually mean cultural adaptation to the physical environment, and I use the term in that restricted sense. The effects of and the evidence for such adaptation can be detected in the technological, social, economic and/or ideological subsystems of cultural systems, although archaeologists are usually able to observe the first of these more directly than the others. Largely for this reason, archaeologists have tended to maintain a materialist bias, and a readiness to accept adaptation to a changing environment as an explanation for culture change, as evidenced by archaeological remains. Indeed, archaeologists have seized upon this approach with astonishing alacrity considering the poor quality of our understanding of past environments and their evolutions. A few examples from recent literature will clarify this point.

I had thought that archaeologists had given up discussing prehistoric adaptation in the Northeast in terms of Dice's (1943) biotic provinces. I have strongly criticized this practice in the past (Snow 1977:433), and I intended to avoid mentioning it again here. However, I have seen continued use of biotic provinces as bounded containers of cultural systems dating back as far as the Early Archaic (e.g. J. Wright 1978). I am compelled to repeat my argument that Dice created his biotic provinces as grossly abstract expository units, not as heuristic tools for prehistorians. His "outline of the biotic provinces of North America is offered frankly as an experiment in classifying the major ecologic divisions of the continent [Dice 1943:7]." It may be that the provinces and their boundaries have no current reality except in the most general sense, and it is most unlikely that they can be projected very far into the past. Constituents and associations have evolved over time, and boundaries, to the extent that they were ever more than vague transitions, have shifted as well (see Chapter 2). Any discussion of prehistoric adaptation solely in terms of Dice's biotic provinces is a waste of time (see also Rhoades 1978).

Another problem area has been the too facile use of tentatively defined climatic episodes as explanations of prehistoric adaptation. Some initial attempts to show such connections seem cautious enough (Griffin 1960), but there has been a band-wagon effect over the last two decades that has led to some uncritical applications. The altithermal maximum, which Antevs originally proposed for western North America, provides a good example. Many archaeologists assumed that the peak was continental, but there is no strong evidence for it in the Northeast (M. Davis 1965:397). The midwestern drought of the 1930s had little significant effect in the Northeast, and it is quite possible that "the trend toward warmer, drier climate 8000 years ago in the Midwest may have been accompanied by little significant changes in the Northeast [H. Wright 1971:459]." Yet the Northeast archaeological literature is littered with attempts to use the altithermal peak as an environmental explanation of cultural changes that occurred anywhere within several centuries of it. In recent years "hypsithermal" has come to be heard more frequently than "altithermal" in these contexts, but there has been little improvement in archaeological application. My point is that while we may have a coincidence of climate change and culture change from time to time in prehistory (and even that is not certain), we have almost no notion of the mechanisms through which climate change led to environmental change that in turn led to culture change.

Without an understanding of those mechanisms we have what might be an association, but we have nothing at all approaching explanation.

Fitting (1978:44), in a contribution to the new *Handbook of North American Indians*, attempts to improve upon earlier efforts by sketching 1300 years of prehistory against a succession of climatic episodes proposed by Baerreis and Bryson (1965). The first of these is the Hopewell or Sub-Atlantic episode, which lasted from 300 B.C. to A.D. 300. It is described variously as either mild or severe, with either greater rainfall or a different distribution of rainfall, with no indication of precisely how it might have been different. This was followed by the Scandic episode, which lasted until A.D. 800 or 900 and which is also described as having been either milder or cooler, drier or wetter, depending upon season. The only agreement seems to be that the episode was different from the preceding one and that adapting cultural systems must therefore have been placed in some stress. The Neo-Atlantic period, which followed and lasted until A.D. 1300 is generally agreed to have been warmer or otherwise favorable for horticulture on the very good grounds that it was a period in which horticulture expanded dramatically in the Northeast. But even this is no explanation because there is no completely independent assessment of the episode by paleoclimatologists, a case of petitio principii in which we are invited to beg the question by assuming that which we should be trying to prove. A cool and dry Pacific episode is supposed to have followed between A.D. 1300 and 1450 with a return to the Neo-Atlantic around 1450. After claiming that the remainder of his discussion would "be developed against this background," Fitting (1978:44) in fact has the good sense not to mention it again. Instead, he honestly admits that we really have little idea how climate and cultural adaptation are connected with statements such as "the nature of the change in adaptive patterns and the cultural dynamics that mark the so-called decline in the Late Woodland period are not clear [Fitting 1978:52]."

Wendland and Bryson (1974) provide us with a rare and almost unique example of the correlation of climatic and cultural episodes. They plotted over 800 radiocarbon dates associated with pollen maxima and minima, sea level maxima and minima, and top and bottom surfaces of peat beds. This sample was drawn from a worldwide inventory of dates, and the results yielded synchronous environmental discontinuities in time that in turn allowed the definition of climatic episodes along the lines already described. Against this they plotted some 3700 radiocarbon dates associated with 155 cultural continua around the world. What they found was a broad tendency for discontinuities in cultural continua to follow soon after climatic discontinuities, and therefore a broad indication of climatic impact on human culture history. It is not clear how fluctuations in isotopic ratios that have been so widely discussed in recent years may have compacted radiocarbon dates from time to time and thereby possibly produced spurious clusterings. For the present, at least, Wendland and Bryson appear to have found a genuine association. However, both climate and culture are shown by them to be associated in only the most general and broad way. Their work leaves us still far from any ability to discuss specific cases.

If we cannot relate cultural adaptation directly to climatic episodes, then it may be possible to relate it in a more direct way to the physical environment. Through palynology and related disciplines we have almost direct access to prehistoric environments. For the most part, hypotheses concerning the climates that combined with edaphic variables to produce those environments depend upon extrapolation from what we know about modern analogues of the environments, not upon independent climatological data. It makes little sense to reconstruct environments on the basis of deep sea cores and meteorological guesswork, when palynologists can now do the same thing with more compelling accuracy. I have found the work of Margaret Davis (1965, 1967, 1969), Ronald Davis (Davis et al. 1975), and Thompson Webb III (Bernabo and Webb 1977; Webb and McAndrews 1976; Davis and Webb 1975) to be particularly useful. Clearly the approaches to environmental reconstruction proposed by Dincauze (see Chapter 2) are necessary prerequisites to any valid assessment of cultural adaptation. Yet as she points out, palynology remains a blunt instrument, and fundamental issues within the discipline are still hotly debated (see for example Davis et al. 1979). Even if we succeed in doing our jobs as anthropologists, we must be prepared to reassess cultural adaptation in the Northeast as palynologists define and redefine the extinct environments to which those cultural systems were constantly adapting.

SOME LESSONS OF HISTORY

It is appropriate at this point to indulge in a little ethnographic analogy as a means to clarify epistemological limits. As we shall see, some basic operating assumptions emerge from examples of the impact of changing climate and environment on historic cultural systems. One example can be drawn from the climatic episode that occurred roughly in the five-century period between A.D. 800 and 1300. This was a period during which northern regions experienced climatic amelioration. Growing seasons lengthened and regions where they had been previously too short to accommodate agriculture became attractive to farmers. This combined with other factors to attract Norse settlers to Iceland and even Greenland. I suspect that it had something to do with the spread of Laurentian Iroquois down the St. Lawrence Valley as well. Wendland and Bryson (1974:21) note that this was also a time when the Mill Creek culture flourished in northwestern Iowa. Toward the end of the episode, however, growing seasons shortened to their earlier levels once again, the Norse had to abandon attempts to farm in Greenland. The tall grass prairie and galley forest of northwest Iowa reverted to steppe, with consequent adaptive changes in Mill Creek culture. It is interesting that these examples, and most others I have been able to find, involve agriculturalists or horticulturalists adapting to environments that are marginal insofar as farming is concerned. For most parts of the world generally and most parts of the Northeast in particular, the effects of the episode either directly, in terms of altered growing seasons, or indirectly, by way of changes in habitat, seem to have been relatively minor. The history of Europe around this time is filled with widespread change, but climate and its effect upon the physical environment was only one of many factors, and probably a relatively unimportant one at that. The points that emerge from this series of examples are that subtle climatic and consequent environmental change affects regional cultural adaptations primarily at their margins, has greater impact on agriculturalists than nonagriculturalists, and must always be considered along with other factors as part of an ecological system.

Another example from the historical record is the Little Ice Age. I have read estimates of the beginning of this episode that vary from A.D. 1250 to 1650, a range of 400 years. Similarly, estimates of its end vary from A.D. 1720 to 1900, a range of 180 years. Certainly much of the disagreement has to do with the criteria selected, but the point remains that if we have this much trouble assessing an historic episode as well documented as this one is, it must be clear that the use of hypothesized prehistoric episodes of the same sort to explain changes in cultural systems necessarily involves a substantial amount of self-deception. Once again, as was the case with the previous example, there is little if any evidence that the Little Ice Age was anything like a dominant factor in the histories of the evolving cultural systems of the period.

There is, however, one event of the Little Ice Age that stands out and is particularly informative. In 1816 many parts of the world experienced a year without a summer. In New England it snowed in June, and there were killing frosts every month. Maize and some other crops were nearly wiped out. However, wheat, rye, and some garden vegetables did better than usual (Stommel and Stommel 1979).

Overall, however, the effects were severe, and there was considerable stress on the system as surplus was drawn down and emergency re-distribution measures were taken. The event, which was apparently caused by the horrendous 1815 volcanic eruption of Mount Tambora in Indonesia, cannot be detected in temperature averages for the nineteenth century, and had no lasting effect on the pollen rain that could be detected by future palynologists either. Yet it could have had a disastrous and permanent effect on marginal horticultural communities such as those of the prehistoric Northeast. Figure 3.1 shows temperatures for the Lake George region for sixteen months beginning with January 1977 and ending with April 1978. The figure shows the record for two winters and a summer. Average tempera-tures are shown as smooth waves through time, the upper line indi-cating average daily highs and the lower line average daily lows. Plotted against these are actual daily highs and lows for the period. Note that while there is a greater range between average highs and lows in the summer than in the winter, actual readings for the sample period indicate that the daily weather is much more erratic and un-predictable in the winter than in the summer. Thus winter in this area is not only the leanest part of the year, it is the time of the year when people are faced with the greatest environmental uncertainty. The winter of 1976-77 was one in which western New York sustained record snowfall, and the winter of 1979-80 was one in which the Northeast received much less snow than normal. Even more extreme variations are possible as the summer of 1816 shows, and I know of no palynological technique that allows us to detect it. It seems likely that such extremely rare events have been more important than long-term trends in affecting cultural adaptation, and we have only archae-ological means to detect them.

DISCONTINUITY THEORY

A community may be well adapted for centuries, but face convulsive change or even extinction in the course of one or a few years of very unusual conditions. Funk and Rippeteau (1977:34-37) have noted just this sort of pattern in their study of adaptation, continuity and change in the Susquehanna drainage (see also Chapter 2). Over and over they found evidence of periods of stability sepa-rated by sharp discontinuities. I see no reason to suspect that what they report is imaginary. Rather, I think it likely that the discontinu-ities they report, as well as many others we can point to in the Northeast sequences, are quite real and result from brief but dra-matic readaptations. In most cases we should predict that cultural

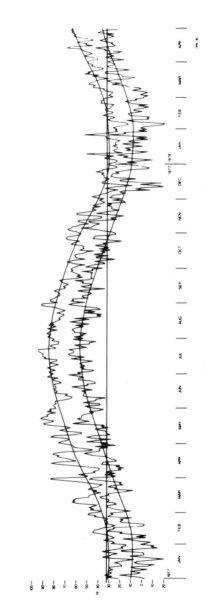

Figure 3.1. Temperatures in the Lake George region over a sixteen-month period. Smooth curves show average daily highs and lows for a thirty-year period, and the straight line marks the freezing point.

systems under unusual stress would experience that stress most strongly at their margins, and that readaptation often occurred first and most strongly there, the marginal developments later becoming more generally adopted. The process is analogous to some forms of biological speciation in which rapid evolution at the margin of a population's distribution followed by expansion of the new form and replacement of the old one leaves a record of abrupt discontinuity over most of the range of the original population. We should expect too that cultural systems occasionally collapsed completely and were replaced by systems expanding from adjacent areas. This, of course, is where we need the talents of demographers and osteologists (see Chapters 5 and 7), and where we must also rigorously apply Rouse's (1958) migration criteria.

Put simply, it matters little what the averages are if you cannot hold out until next year. This is known somewhat more elegantly as Liebig's Law of the Minimum, which holds that growth or survival is limited by the minimum availability of any single necessary factor rather than by the availability of all necessary factors. Thus any cultural adaptation is implicitly betting on security over the long term, implicitly counting on the rarity of extreme stress, and implicitly banking on quick readaptation if the worst should occur. General environmental trends such as climatic episodes are important to us not in and of themselves as some archaeological syntheses suggest, but to the extent that they increase or decrease the frequencies of such rare catastrophes.

My examples point out an interesting contrast between horticulturalists and hunter-gatherers. For hunter-gatherers, the most dangerous part of the year is late winter, when the meager surplus is drawn down and unusual weather can ruin hunting. Winter cycles are therefore the most important ones to examine when one tries to assess the chances of systemic failure in hunter-gatherer adaptations in the Northeast. For horticulturalists, however, the summer cycle is more important, for they depend upon productive growing seasons over the long term. This adaptation has several advantages over any hunter-gatherer adaptation. For one, horticulturalists can bank large surplus stores that will allow them to get through one or even a series of disastrous growing seasons. Another advantage is that they can always fall back on diversified hunter-gatherer techniques for survival in the short term. Although the game populations could not sustain relatively high populations of desperate horticulturalists over the long term in the Northeast, they were adequate for intensive short-term purposes. Indeed, we can think of hunter-gatherer techniques as a kind of unemployment insurance for late prehistoric Northeast horticulturalists, and that insurance functioned to reduce the frequency of systemic collapse.

In the Northeast, winter is the period during which hunter-gatherer subsistence systems are under maximum stress. Although they are hard to use, historical data on winters for our region shed some light on long-term cycles of maximum stress (Ludlum 1966, 1968). We have spotty data beginning in 1604 and gradually more complete data down to the present, a span approaching four centuries. Leaving aside for the moment the very important differences between what a hunter-gatherer might regard as a severe winter, and what early European colonists regarded as severe, we can identify about a dozen winters that began early, ended late, were unusually cold, and generally impressed observers as being almost uniquely severe. Such winters are usually used as comparisons for each other even by untrained observers. Thus in the winter of 1779-80, older people agreed that they had seen nothing like it since 1740-41. In 1820-21, people that were young in 1780 would make the same kind of comparison.

It is very hard to identify unusually severe winters because of the range of independent variables and the difficulty of assessing cumulative effects. For example, there are winters such as 1740-41 that are very severe and during which very cold temperatures are reached. However, there are also winters such as 1753-54 in which record cold is experienced but which overall appear to have been mild. Similarly, a winter in which snow arrives early and remains well into April can be either mild or severe depending upon what happens in between. Further, the cumulative effects of a sequence of many small snow storms are difficult to assess in comparison to a single large one. Many other combinations of temperature and precipitation conditions can be illustrated, with the conclusion that there is no objective way (or perhaps too many objective ways) to assess the severity of a winter. Since we are short on objective data for all but the last century anyway, we are forced to rely upon the subjective observations of those that lived through the most severe winters of the last four centuries.

Table 3.1 lists the dozen winters which a consensus of historical sources indicates were extremely severe. In one instance the cycle was only a period of fifteen years, and the longest period between severe episodes was forty-three years. The average period is about thirty-four years. Given the life expectancy of people in pre-industrial societies, many people would experience only one such winter. Indeed, a person born in the summer of 1698 and living eighty years would have experienced only one such winter, that of 1740-41. Some people died too young to experience such a winter at all, and only the truly unlucky lived long enough to experience three. It is fair to say that when such a winter occurred, there were usually a few older people around that remembered a previous one to which it could be compared. This is certainly not the kind of regular and frequent phenomenon that hunter-gatherers would be likely to anticipate fully. Certainly birth spacing, the maintenance of buffer zones, the tendency to live far below the carrying capacity of the environment for most of the year, and food storage all helped people to deal with the stress of severe winters, but it would be an over-statement to call this planning. Ludlum (1966:39) concludes that in the eighteenth century there were, in addition to two extremely severe winters, eight that were very severe, sixteen that were severe, forty-nine normal winters, and twenty-five very mild ones. Given these frequencies, it is likely that hunter-gatherer populations would regularly plan for a severe winter, allow if possible for the very severe winter that came along every dozen years or so, but not view the coming of an extremely severe winter as a real possibility. Looked at objectively, and considering all the information and planning options open to hunter-gatherers, this is not at all an irrational approach for them to take.

Table 3.1. Severe winters and the periods separating them.

WINTER	PERIOD
1604-05	
	36
1641-42	
	39
1680-81	
	17
1697-98	
	43
1740-41	
	39
1779-80	
	41
1820-21	
	15
1835-36	
	25
1860-61	
	38
1898-99	
	41
1939-40	
	37
1976-77	

To return to a point mentioned earlier, it is clear that what strikes a sedentary horticultural community as a severe winter is probably different from one that seems severe to a hunter-gatherer population. Champlain lost nearly half his comrades to scurvy and starvation during the long deep winter of 1604-05. Yet he describes the advantage the Indians took of the deep snow, in which the moose were easy prey for the hunters. Late in the winter the Indians brought meat to the exhausted and starving French. Yet two years later, during a winter described by Champlain as less severe than the previous ones, the Indians experienced famine and were forced to dig for shellfish. The reason was that the winter was mild and rainy, so there was too little snow for hunting (Grant 1907:55, 110).

There are other factors that affect hunter-gatherers and horticulturalists differently. Knight (1965:34) notes that for the northern Algonquians, "personal histories and parish records indicate that in the past, cases of starvation occurred most frequently in the early spring, when breakup restricted and immobilized hunting groups for three to four weeks. Indeed, immobilization is clearly recognized by local people as the major factor in cases of starvation." So we see evidence that mobility is vital to the survival of hunter-gatherers, and that they know it. A cold and prolonged but snowless winter, in which earth and water froze to unusual depths, could prolong the spring breakup, and thereby prolong immobility as well.

Despite the problem that winters that seem severe to us may not have seemed so to hunter-gatherers, the cyclicity of Table 3.1 and the cyclicity of other possible weather combinations recorded for the last four centuries all suggest that a given hunter-gatherer subsistence system would probably undergo severe stress on the order of every few decades, as opposed to every few years or every few centuries. We can safely presume that even with a cycle of three or four decades there were permutations of severity, such that only occasionally would a population fail to survive the extreme stress. After all, even catastrophe has a range of effects.

There is also the possibility that northern hunters suffered from the effects of periodic drops in animal populations. The bands of eastern Canada depended upon woodland caribou, moose, beaver, and bear during the winter. They resorted to snaring hares when the larger game animals were unavailable (Jenness 1955:265-286). Moose, like most other large game, do not seem to rise and fall in numbers in a periodic cycle, presumably because their life spans and gestation periods do not make them susceptible to such fluctuations. In both Maritime provinces and on Isle Royale there was a low ebb in the moose population between 1935 and 1937 as measured by the number of moose taken by hunters (Peterson 1955:209-213). But this apparent coincident decline in independent populations may well have been only a decline in the kill brought on by unfavorable hunting conditions. Hares, however, like some other rapidly reproducing northern species, are subject to periodic fluctuations. The amplitude of the fluctuation is greatest where food chains and buffer species are few, and environmental conditions are simpler and harsher. In such areas the peak hare population can be 3400 times larger than its minimum, whereas in the United States the variation is on the order of only 20:1 or 25:1. The period of the cycle is six to thirteen years, the mode being nine or ten years (Banfield 1974:82). Thus when an extremely severe winter makes the hunting of large game impossible, there is one chance in nine or ten that hares will not be available as an emergency food. The point of this additional permutation is that it suggests that widespread failure of both the primary subsistence system and emergency backup options is something that is apt to happen to hunter-gatherers in the Northeast once every few centuries. This is not an event that can be anticipated and forestalled by prudence in a preindustrial, nonliterate society. Just as important as the rarity of such an event is its apparent inevitability. Perhaps most important for present purposes is that a period of a few centuries is of the same scale as most established archaeological periods, each separated by apparent discontinuities. This is further confirmation that such discontinuities are real and not just the consequences of archaeological imagination. In short, our knowledge of hunter-gatherer adaptation in the Northeast predicts the kind of chronological periodization that archaeology has produced, and confirms that cycles of adaptation and established periods of prehistory are not operating at different scales.

Wendland and Bryson (1974) have confirmed the statistical significance of major discontinuities in prehistoric sequences at a scale similar to that just described. I have already noted that their analysis is based on a worldwide sample of radiocarbon dates. They carry the analysis a step or two further by identifying significant globally synchronous discontinuities and then matching them to globally synchronous environmental discontinuities. Although this has the superficial appearance of environmental determinism, in light of factors just discussed it would not be accurate to say that changes in climate caused cultural discontinuities to occur. Rather, broad and subtle changes in climate appear to have repeatedly increased chances that established adaptations would collapse catastrophically. In other words, long-term climatic changes may do nothing more than change the odds a little bit, but given the nature of hunter-gatherer adaptation, that is enough.

The issues discussed above incidentally parallel current debate in biological evolution, in which many paleontologists are coming to view the episodic character of the geological record as real rather than as the product of uneven sampling. Like paleontologists, archaeologists will find it difficult to operationalize the principles I have discussed. The scale at which Wendland and Bryson (1974) have worked is too coarse for our purposes, and it remains unlikely that we will find adequate independent evidence of the very short-term episodes of extreme environmental stress that I have proposed would account for many major discontinuities in the archaeological record. However, I have outlined a theory suggested by archaeological and ethnological evidence, and have cited archaeological data that support the theory. This procedure is methodologically sound (see Chapter 4), and the theory will serve so long as data cannot be found to invalidate it.

The theory I have outlined requires that we allow for the reality of discontinuities, by giving up our bias in favor of mean radiocarbon dates for archaeological phases. For example, the mean of several radiocarbon dates for the Meadowood phase in New York is around 800 B.C. (Snow 1980:257). If Meadowood were simply an arbitrarily selected node in a smoothly evolving continuum, we should expect future radiocarbon dates to distribute normally around this mean. If, on the other hand, Meadowood represents an episode of stable adaptation separated by discontinuities from its predecessor and successor phases, future radiocarbon dates should distribute randomly, not normally, between the dates of those discontinuities. I have discussed, and I urge that archaeologists abandon, the practice of discarding or discrediting radiocarbon age determinations that do not fall near enough to a predicted mean. Indeed, radiocarbon dates at the extremes of phase ranges are the most important ones we have for studying discontinuities in the record. We need to focus attention on archaeological components producing dates near discontinuities, and study such sites in the context of fine-grained environmental reconstructions. Such an approach will do much to explain the periodization of local sequences, and will help clarify the differences between stable adaptive systems.

DEMOGRAPHY AND ADAPTATION

Prehistoric hunter-gatherers appear to have maintained stable populations by birth spacing, a consequence of the need for families, particularly mothers, to manage the burden of small children. Failure to do so would result in the birth of additional infants before older siblings could shift for themselves, an impossible burden that would

have fallen squarely on the nuclear family. Early agricultural communities did not have to meet the demands of mobility by spacing
births, and the responsibility for care of additional children was more
broadly distributed within the community. Mortality may have remained the same as earlier, but natality increased dramatically. This
has been intensified in nonindustrial societies in recent decades by
campaigns to reduce mortality, while in industrialized societies the
incentive to space births has been reimposed. In the latter case the
incentives have to do with the financial and other burdens connected
with the education and socialization of children, burdens that tend
once again to fall upon the nuclear family. In this regard, Dumond
(1975) argues that the nuclear family in modern industrial society is
more like a prehistoric hunter-gatherer family than either is like the
families of preindustrial agricultural societies.

Table 3.2. Annual age-specific natality rates per 1000 women
(after Dumond 1975:716).

Age (yrs.)	1	2	3	4	5	6
15 to 19	300	250	200	200	150	100
20 to 24	400	350	350	300	300	250
25 to 29	500	400	350	300	250	250
30 to 34	400	350	300	250	200	200
35 to 39	350	250	250	200	150	150
40 to 44	250	200	200	150	100	50
over 44	11	9	8	7	6	5

To be more specific, Table 3.2 shows a series of hypothetical
natality schedules, the highest (1) based on data from twentieth century Hutterites, and the lowest (6) deemed the lowest possible rate
needed by hunter-gatherers to maintain a stable population (after
Dumond 1975:716). In each cell we see the number of births per
1000 women. For example, rate 5 calls for 250 births per 1000
women in the 25-29 age range per year, equivalent to a spacing of a
birth every four years for each of these women. We can couple these
natality rates with a series of hypothetical mortality rates that cover
the range for preindustrial communities. These survivorship curves
can be simplified and identified by the life expectancy at birth presumed by each of them. The very high mortality reflected in a life
expectancy of 13 years is probably about that experienced by Homo
erectus, while a life expectancy of 35 years is about that of preindustrial European agriculturalists. Table 3.3 (after Dumond 1975:

717) shows that when reproductive rates are calculated from the four mortality rates expressed as life expectancies at birth, and the six natality rates outlined in Table 3.2, a wide range of possible rates is generated. High mortality and low natality produce a rate that falls below the replacement rate of 1.00. Low mortality and high natality produce a rate much higher than that required for the maintenance of a stable population. Table 3.3 shows that hunter-gatherers with a life expectancy at birth of only 21 years could maintain a stable population with a natality rate of type 5, the sort of rate one would expect of a population in which women spaced births for the sake of mobility. These same people could increase their reproductive rate rather easily by simply reducing birth spacing, something I predict would occur if favorable conditions arose. Such conditions could be produced by such things as extended episodes of improved environmental conditions, sudden access to territory not occupied by other people, or technological innovation. The last would include the shift to horticulture and sedentism in the Northeast.

Table 3.3. Net reproductive rates from 6 natality rates and 4 mortality rates (after Dumond 1975:717).

Mortality rates (life expectancies)	Natality rates					
	1	2	3	4	5	6
13	1.05	0.87	0.78	0.69	0.58	0.50
21	1.89	1.56	1.39	1.21	1.02	0.88
25	2.25	1.86	1.65	1.45	1.21	1.05
35	2.81	2.70	2.41	2.11	1.75	1.52

Dumond argues against population pressure and in favor of stability amongst hunter-gatherers at levels far below maximum carrying capacity of the environment. The key is the need for women in these conditions to maintain their mobility. The generalization also relates to the point I made earlier regarding the tendency for population sizes to be determined by the maximum that could be supported under the most restrictive circumstances they customarily experience. In the Northeast, this is the largest population density a given region can support through a severe winter. Maintenance of a stable hunter-gatherer population at a level substantially below the theoretical carrying capacity of the environment is a sensible strategy and one that in the past worked well over the long term. Nevertheless, it remained vulnerable to rare collapse. Such a collapse need happen only once for it to occasion major subsistence readaptations, or even local or regional population extinctions followed by expansions of survivor populations into vacated areas.

Despite the very serious difficulties that we know attend efforts to determine the population sizes of societies when first contacted by European explorers (McArthur 1970), I have argued that reasonably accurate estimates for the Northeast around A.D. 1600 can be made (Snow 1980:31-42). Table 3.4 shows my estimates of native populations in New England and eastern New York around that time. The densities for the hunter-gatherers in the north are consistently about a tenth those of the horticulturalists of the south in this region. The catastrophe of the seventeenth century came in the form of European diseases, and these populations suffered reductions that reached 95% mortality in some of the drainages listed.

The figures in Table 3.4 provide us with a numerical basis for studying prehistoric adaptation in the Northeast. We can further advance our understanding of adaptation and cultural ecology generally by bringing economic principles to bear on specific issues. Rapport and Turner (1977) have shown that analyses developed for economics often work well when applied to predator-prey and other relationships in animal ecology. It stands to reason that they should apply at least as well in human ecology. For example, as the abundance of preferred prey types in a particular habitat declines, a generalist strategy becomes more profitable to the predator. In Cleland's (1976) terms, this amounts to a shift from a focal adaptation to a diffuse one. For nonhuman predators, this is because of the increased costs in time and energy needed to exploit the preferred prey, and the principle holds even for simple life forms. Clearly we do not need to concern ourselves excessively regarding the role of rational thought amongst hunter-gatherers if this is the case.

Another principle borrowed from economics leads to the observation that any predator (human included) will maximize its net energy gain by taking the amount of prey that will yield the greatest difference between energy gained (income) and energy expended (cost). Perhaps more useful to us is the general economic theory of refuging systems, wherein the relationships between the size of a defended territory and the resources available are examined along with settlement and resource patterns in time and space. This theory has been able to account for the field observation that as the centralized population of predators increases the foraging territory is less likely to be defended. The approach has value for the study of hunter-gatherer territoriality and changes that accompany a shift to settled life.

Table 3.4. Drainage divisions of aboriginal New England, A.D. 1600: Areas, cultures, and enumeration (Snow 1980:33).

Drainage	Area (km^2)	Culture	Estimated population	Density per 100 km^2
St. John	59,000	Maliseet	7,200	12
St. Croix	3,000	Passamaquoddy	400	12
Penobscot	26,000	Eastern Abenaki	3,200	12
Kennebec	18,000	Eastern Abenaki	5,300	29
Androscoggin	10,000	Eastern Abenaki	2,600	26
Presumpscot	6,000	Eastern Abenaki	800	13
Upper Merrimack	9,000	Western Abenaki	2,000	22
Upper Connecticut	17,000	Western Abenaki	3,800	22
Champlain	19,000	Western Abenaki	4,200	22
Lower Merrimack	8,000	Massachusett	15,500	193
Southeastern New England	11,000	Massachusett ^{a}	21,200	193
Thames and eastern Long Island	5,000	Mohegan-Pequot	13,300	266
Middle Connecticut	8,000	Pocumtuck	15,200	190
Lower Connecticut and central Long Island	13,000	Quiripi-Unquachog	24,700	190
Middle and upper Hudson	17,000	Mahican	5,300	31
Mohawk	10,000	Mohawk	9,000-11,300	90-113
Lower Hudson	17,000	Munsee	15,300-32,300	90-190
Upper Delaware	10,000	Munsee	9,000-19,000	90-190
Totals	266,000		158,000-187,300	

^{a} Includes Narragansett.

It is also the case that analyses of reproduction and optimal foraging can be stated as ecological markets, which turn out to have structures that parallel models of economic markets. Viewed as consumers, hunter-gatherers assess cost in terms of energy. They take advantage of situations in which resources become abundant and the costs of obtaining them decline. Again, market principles operate in the ecological systems of nonhuman (and presumably nonrational) communities, so there is no reason to stipulate an intellectual or ideological component, so long as the entire range of resources and the scheduling of their uses are known in detail. Unfortunately, we rarely if ever know such things in sufficient detail, and cultural interventions such as food preservation and storage are at work in even the most rudimentary hunter-gatherer systems. Consequently, as a practical matter we can never set aside the intellectual or ideological component in dealing with human ecological markets without risking oversimplification and implicitly opting for environmental determinism. The market analogy works only so long as we use it only as a general guide and do not treat cultural factors as a residual in our analyses.

Finally, economists have something to tell us about the role of uncertainty and how we can adjust for it in our analyses. I have already argued that hunter-gatherers cannot predict their future opportunities with any certainty. They may be able to guess best-case and worst-case limits, but even these are uncertain. This appears to account for the failure of hunter-gatherers to optimize resources in many specific instances. Satisficing behavior, rather than optimizing behavior has been discussed by other anthropologists, and fits well with the other features of hunter-gatherer subsistence systems. I can only add that what may appear to us to be satisficing behavior may in fact be optimizing behavior in the eyes of a hunter-gatherer. It makes no sense to optimize exploitation of a resource if a lack of adequate storage and transportation is likely to cause most of it to spoil or be abandoned. In other words, hunter-gatherers may well be optimizing by avoiding wasted effort in the very situations in which we may perceive them to be engaging in satisficing behavior. A useful corollary concept is that of threshold behavior, which accounts for the failure of a community to exploit a resource until it reaches some threshold of abundance. The costs of acquiring information about the resource and gearing up to exploit it are sufficiently high to compel this behavior. Until the profit to be gained from changing over to another resource is clearly greater than the profit to be gained by continuing current practices, a band of hunter-gatherers is not likely to make the switch. Such a switch can involve movement of a camp, deployment of task groups, manufacture of tools, or any of several other costly steps. Failure to appreciate this principle has led to several controversies in Northeast archaeology, perhaps most notable the one surrounding the prehistoric importance of shell-fishing (Snow 1980:178-182).

THE DISJUNCTION OF THEORY AND PRACTICE

Much has been said and written regarding adaptation or change in prehistoric subsistence systems in recent years. Studies in ethnoarchaeology have refined the use of analogy, and various complex models have been developed for these data alone or in conjunction with linear programing, game theory, and other theoretical models. The difficulties have been many, and not always appreciated by the authors of these constructs. In general, both linear programing and game theory demand data in quantities and at scales not available in archaeology, and are consequently not fully applicable. They serve mainly to raise the sophistication of our thinking, but yield few results that we could not otherwise obtain by simpler inspection. For example, Reidhead (1980) draws upon data from the Ohio Valley and uses a linear programing model to show that there was an adaptive advantage in the replacement of hunting and gathering by horticulture in that area. It may be that this approach will eventually lead us to discover things that we do not already know, but for now it is difficult to predict that archaeological data will ever permit this kind of model to produce new insights.

Jochim (1976) covers main issues quite well in his review of ecological approaches in archaeology. The problem is again that although we keep approaching the issues we only rarely come to grips with them at a practical level. Formalization seems often to elude us simply because we have too few data and too little trust in what we do have to allow us to perform rigorous tests. Jochim's effort to model hunter-gatherer subsistence draws upon an imposing data base, the Round Lake Ojibwa data being directly relevant for our purposes. Yet even here he deals with adaptation normatively, and we get little feel for the ways in which extraordinary stresses might bring about change. Even more difficult, of course, is the transference of the model into prehistoric context.

Much the same can be said regarding approaches to demographic archaeology as summarized by Hassan (1978). Hassan hands us imposing and powerful formulas for dealing with relations between resources, area, population density, and so on, but at its present state of development our archaeological data base will allow us to make honest use of only a small part of them.

Similar criticisms can be raised regarding the use of a systems approach to archaeological problems (see Chapter 4). Spaulding (1973) long ago noted that archaeologists have made no real use at all of general systems theory, that we probably could not do so if we wanted to, and that he saw no future for archaeologists in a theory that could barely cope with the complexities of slime mold. Salmon has echoed that opinion. She does not "expect either general systems theory or mathematical systems theory to provide . . . a developed theory that could be adapted to archaeology, or even with much specific help in constructing an archaeological theory. Even Flannery's work, often cited as a model of work done under systems theory guidelines, makes no real use of concepts that are unavailable outside of systems theory, let alone any general principles or laws unique to systems theory [Salmon 1978:182]." Trigger (1979:246) wonders "Can archaeologists ever quantify enough variables sufficiently for the validity of the approach to be tested objectively or must it be applied at best metaphorically?"

Coombs (1980) discusses Naskapi-Montagnais adaptations in terms of game theory. He discusses Bayes strategies, which can parallel the focal adaptions I mentioned earlier, and makes useful points regarding the nature of their pay-offs. Put simply, a minimax strategy maximizes minimum pay-offs and a Bayes strategy maximizes average pay-offs. The focal adaptation of Naskapi caribou hunters turns out to have been a Bayes strategy in the language of game theory. It was more susceptible to failure than the more diffuse minimax strategy of the Montagnais, and collapsed catastrophically in 1916. Despite the elegance of his restatement of Fitzhugh's (1972) earlier discussion of the case, it appears that once again the data have not allowed a sophisticated new approach to really tell us anything we did not already know.

Earle (1980) presents another model of subsistence change in which the relationships between cost and maximum yield in various subsistence strategies are discussed with uncommon clarity. He simplifies his model by assuming that "the primary objective of all procurement strategies under investigation is their caloric yield [Earle 1980:3]." He thereby wisely avoids discussion of other nutritional requirements, which probably did not figure importantly in many prehistoric contexts, and lie beyond the empirical grasp of contemporary field archaeology in any case. Certainly, nutritional deficiencies apart from simple caloric shortfalls were not significant in the prehistoric Northeast. To the extent that we know them, all prehistoric diets in our region contained sufficient amounts of essential nutrients to make nutritional diseases unimportant. The single exception could be scurvy, which is caused by a deficiency of vitamin C (ascorbic acid). Yet the historical record shows that although early European explorers in the Northeast often died of scurvy, the Indians of the region knew a quick and easy remedy for it. Cartier's men suffered horribly from scurvy, and he assumed that the illness he observed among the Indians was the same disease. But it seems likely that what the Indians had was some European virus, for Cartier reports that when the Indians discovered what was wrong with the Frenchmen, they quickly produced an antiscorbutic white pine tea to treat it (Burrage 1906:74-77). Thus we can assume that so long as caloric requirements were met in prehistoric Northeast diets, other nutritional requirements were also met. Given that, we once again have a disjunction between theory and practical results. An elaborate model of nutrition, using all the information currently available on living populations, would tell us little we could not otherwise guess even if archaeological data of sufficient quality and quantity were available. One wonders, given that disjuction, where Wing and Brown's (1979) study of paleonutrition can lead us. Even Earle's attempt to bridge the gap by dealing only with caloric requirements is not a sufficient solution to the dilemma if we use the requirement standards currently accepted for our own society. Most modern Americans and Europeans would find an average intake of 2500 calories per day to be minimal. Women can often get by on fewer than that, but men typically demand more. Yet we can point to other human populations in the world that appear to do well on an average of only 1500 calories per person per day, about what our standards allow for a child in kindergarten. A complex nutritional model for prehistoric populations that does not deal with this fundamental imprecision may have the appearance of accuracy and elegance but actually have neither of those qualities.

Doran and Hodson (1975:315) are generally skeptical regarding potential for mathematical modeling in archaeology. They argue that mathematical models that can use data derived archaeologically are too simple to be useful, and that more complex models require detail not yet available from archaeological data. That generalization seems to apply to the examples just cited. I argue, however, that we have reached a point where we can obtain data that are accurate enough and use them in mathematical models that are complex enough for the results to tell us things that we would not otherwise know. We have, in other words, reached a point where the disjunction is not fatal to all models, and they can be made to provide us with some measure of explanation. However, some ground rules must be kept in mind.

First, models must be testable, which means that they must be simple enough to relate to real archaeological data. Many complex models are not testable because archaeological data are insufficient to refute them. A particular complex model may be valid, but we will never know whether it is or not if it is impossible to test. Such a model is therefore in the last analysis as useless to archaeology as creationism is to biology. The trap, of course, is that such models can appear to be tested by the recitation of case studies, with the consequence that they come to be taken seriously even when they add nothing to our understanding that is not obvious in the case studies taken by themselves.

A second ground rule, which follows logically from the first, is that we must not lose sight of the data base. It should not be necessary to state this simple idea, but it is. If we are to discuss models of process, we cannot do so with models alone, and more than a little attention must be paid to old-fashioned empiricism. A third ground rule is that models must be scaled appropriately to the data we have available. And fourth, a model must tell us, or at least have the potential to tell us, something we could not otherwise either observe directly or discover through simpler means.

THE MODELING OF DISCONTINUITY

We now have somewhat more sophisticated conceptual tools for dealing with discontinuity over time than was once the case. Even if we cannot yet pinpoint the prehistoric disasters that must have occasionally forced rapid readjustments, we can be sure that they occurred. I have argued that we are able to detect such discontinuities archaeologically, and that they occur on a scale comparable to environmental discontinuities that are detectable by independent means. Unknown prehistoric epidemics would have added to the occasional weather-related disasters I discussed earlier. Such epidemics may not have involved human populations directly, as the almost universally fatal chestnut blight of this century demonstrates. We also know that the forests of the Northeast have always been subject to catastrophic changes that interrupted their slow developments to climax states. For example, the forest of northern Minnesota, which is a northern hardwood forest in many ways equivalent to that of most of the Northeast, had a natural fire rotation of 100 years before European settlement began. That is, an area equivalent to the whole was burned every 100 years (Bormann and Likens 1979:662). Any cultural system adapting to such a continuously changing environment would have had to make many adjustments, and the net effect of all those small adjustments would necessarily be a continuously evolving cultural system. Thus, long-term plateaus of adaptation can

have been real only in a general sense. Discontinuity though real at
one scale may seem to be just part of the flow of change at a larger
scale. Moreover, there are many plausible mechanisms to account for
occasional local or regional population declines through the course of
prehistory. Catastrophe theory, a recent branch of mathematics
pioneered by Rene Thom, is particularly well-suited as a model for
such events in prehistory. It is a controversial outgrowth of topology
that focuses upon a set of elementary catastrophes, only the simplest
of which I have included here. It may be that further exploration will
convert catastrophe theory into a powerful new tool for archaeologists (Woodcock and Davis 1978), but for the moment it is mainly
a handy model for illustrating archaeological discontinuity graphi-
cally (Renfrew 1978). Indeed, most mathematicians complain that
you must know the answer before you can use catastrophe models
as expository devices, and that the theory therefore has no predictive
power (Kolata 1977). Just the same, Figure 3.2 illustrates the collapse of a system using a single cusp catastrophe as a model. Here one
might use the Axis A to indicate the degree of focal as opposed to
diffuse adaptation. Axis B can be used to indicate degree of resource
reliability, and Axis C population size. A community tracking from
1-7 on the folded surface will reach a point (5) where the subsistence
system is no longer stable due to extreme focal adaptation and a
decrease in resource reliability. The system will then collapse to a
lower population level (6), after which the community may retreat
from a focal towards a diffuse adaptation before beginning the cycle
again. The process by which a community gets to point 5 is slow due
to the conservatism inherent in adaptation. People rarely invite disaster by leaping to new subsistence strategies, but as Figure 3.2
shows disaster can ultimately occur just the same.

Figure 3.2. A simple cusp catastrophe as a model for archaeological discontinuity. A population tracking on the folded
surface collapses to a lower level
(6) when it reaches a point of
instability.

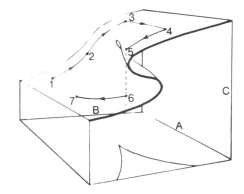

Major discontinuities of this sort probably occurred around 10,000 B.P. in the Northeast, after 1700 B.C. in northern New England, and around the same time in central New York. In at least the latter two cases I suspect that the discontinuities were accompanied by demographic shifts as southern New Englanders expanded northward and, in the case of central New York, the bearers of Frost Island culture did the same. Less dramatic readjustments probably mark the other discontinuities noted by Funk and Rippeteau (1977).

The model is simple, and relates well to archaeological data at an appropriate scale. With the addition of a few more components, it has the capacity to provide us with insights we would otherwise not have, and opens the way toward a special theory of adaptation for the Northeast.

ADAPTATION AND CARRYING CAPACITY

The preceding discussion brings up the issue of carrying capacity and the relevance of this concept in a discussion of cultural adaptation. Cowgill (1975) has summarized the problems that surface when one attempts to use population pressure as an explanation of prehistoric change. Very simply stated, he sees the sort of approach taken by Boserup, in which population pressure is seen as pushing society toward more efficient forms of subsistence (particularly food production), as fallacious. A version of this approach has been stated by Cohen (1975, 1977), who assumes that such pressure exists and goes on to itemize fourteen kinds of archaeological evidence indicative of it. Of course, if the assumption is incorrect as Cowgill concludes it is, then each of the fourteen kinds of archaeological evidence cited by Cohen is indicative of something else. In other words, Cohen's fourteen points are not in themselves evidence of a causitive relationship from population pressure to unidirectional change in the subsistence system, only logical consequences that will follow if the assumption is correct. At the other extreme in this theoretical debate is the view that advances in subsistence efficiency are the cause (not the effect) of population expansion. Clearly there is no advantage to a dogmatic adherence to this extreme point of view either. It is the case that no primate species (humans included) ever lives at the limits of the carrying capacity of its environment. It is also the case that sooner or later any community can come up against a temporary shortage, a serious short-term reduction in carrying capacity. That the shortage is temporary is more than balanced by the fact that it can be lethal for all or part of the group. Thus population and subsistence efficiency are clearly related, but in a complex way that sees the balance tipped first one way then the other by such things as advances in storage techniques, crop failures, the introduction of new cultigens, and long-term climatic deterioration. In adapting to all of these, cultural systems introduce a ratchet effect, diversifying under stress when they can to protect the existing population, and allowing the population to float upwards when such an increase seems not to threaten long-term survival. The consequence is the generally unidirectional character of cultural evolution. Population pressure need be only an occasional problem, and more catastrophic collapse rarer still. It is useful to note Trigger's analysis of the Iroquois case, in which population increase appears to be tied to cultural drives such as sedentism, nucleation, and group productivity, and not directly related to subsistence in any simple way (see Chapter 1). His work confirms that cultural drives intervene and mediate between subsistence and population size.

Grayson has said that on the basis of his analysis of vertebrate fauna from the 750 B.C. Riverhaven No. 2 site and an assessment of the prehistoric availability of these species, "the most popular mammals alone could have supported between 15 and 30 humans per 10 square miles of deciduous forest for an indefinitely long period of time [Grayson 1974:36]." Those numbers translate to about 120 people per 100 km^2, about the density I have calculated for the Hudson-Mohawk drainage and the Middle Connecticut in A.D. 1600 (Table 3.4). It is lower than southeastern New England, where the density was probably closer to 200 per 100 km^2 at that time, but much higher than northern New England, where the aboriginal density was probably under 25 per 100 km^2. If we added other gathered food resources to Grayson's figures, we could easily generate a paper carrying capacity that would far exceed actual population density in the later horticultural Northeast, perhaps by several fold. Clearly we must abandon the concept of carrying capacity at least in its simplistic forms. I have argued that it is not the average carrying capacity that controls population size, but the short-term ability to survive ecological disasters. A village of people facing death by freezing and starvation would find little comfort in Grayson's average figures. Second, any notion of carrying capacity that is to have any utility must include social factors that relate to acceptable nucleation and both inter- and intra-community spacing. The need for *zwischenraum* is no small matter in the long-term survival of any animal community. It fits with the need for birth-spacing in hunter-gatherer societies discussed earlier, because while birth spacing allows necessary female mobility, intra-community spacing guarantees latitude for it. Clearly both temporal and spatial rules of separation are necessary for the long-term survival of these societies (Hickerson 1965).

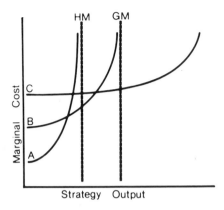

Figure 3.3. Generalized cost curves for hunting (A), gathering (B), and horticulture (C). HM is the maximum yield of hunting and GM is the maximum yield of gathering (after Earle 1980:14).

A third point is that any assessment of carrying capacity must also account for technological variables, particularly in the areas of procurement (or production), storage, and transportation. Figure 3.3 illustrates the point that as separate strategies, hunting, gathering, and horticulture offer different cost/output ratios. Initial cost is high in horticulture, but small additional cost yields much higher output than either hunting or gathering. Moreover, both hunting and gathering strategies quickly come up against output maxima where no amount of additional cost expenditure can significantly increase output. The advantage of horticulture lies not just in its relative productivity and dependability, but also in the increased storage capacity and reduced need for mobility typical of such adaptations. With all of this in mind, I can now turn to a reappraisal of our approaches to adaptation and suggest a format for future research.

A THEORETICAL MODEL OF ADAPTATION

Most of us have adopted a systems perspective for the purposes of examining the complex dynamic qualities of evolving cultures and their environments. Some archaeologists have become temporarily infatuated with general systems theory, and have imagined that we can apply it to archaeological problems. However, the formal application of general systems theory in archaeology is and will probably remain well out of reach, and what we have for the moment is more stance than theory, a systems perspective that is nothing much more than an upgrading of a traditional functionalist perspective. Even this, however, is an improvement over the very modest aspirations of culture history and the clumsy determinism of what Flannery calls "law and order" archaeology, for systems analysis has some explanatory power. Moreover, its limitations are so obvious that it seldom lures us into false explanations of the sort that abound, for example, in the current cannibalism controversy.

Cultural systems are laissez faire systems in which connections and loops are so complex that their evolutions are almost impossible to predict. That is why, like the weatherman, the anthropologist is usually better able to explain why things happened as they did yesterday than predict what will happen tomorrow. There seems always to be something in current trends that we fail to notice until after the fact. Late nineteenth century sages predicted that based on trends then current, New York City would be twenty feet deep in horse manure in a few decades. No one anticipated the automobile. Even more difficult, as the example shows, is the tendency of cultural systems to occasionally change in quantum jumps by incorporating major changes in their structures, by changing the rules in the middle of the game. Such rule changes are, I think, mutations that are genuinely impossible to predict, and will continue to frustrate and embarrass futurologists. Yet once again archaeologists find themselves in the happy position of knowing the outcomes of the systemic processes they are trying to explain. Indeed, the clarity of hindsight is one of the few advantages we have over the forces of darkness in this science. More than that, the excesses of those that would predict the future on the basis of simple extrapolations of current trends should be more than enough to warn us away from the fallacy of false extrapolation into the past. Mark Twain once made great fun of imaginary scientists, basing a reconstruction of a primordial Mississippi River on then-current shortening due to the cutoff of meander loops. By his gratuitous reconstruction the river had once been over a million miles long. The lesson, of course, is that curves that plot change within adapting and thereby evolving systems are by and large sigmoidal. The Gompertz growth curve, of which it is the duty of demographers to periodically remind us, is a perfect example. Thus like several others (Rodin et al. 1978; Rodin 1979), I think that a systems perspective affords us more than just a metaphor. At the very least it helps us avoid simplistic arguments, but more than that it provides us with a vehicle for dealing with adaptation at a practical level while taking into account both the normative and the catastrophic factors discussed earlier.

We can begin a practical assessment of adaptation with a restatement of Crane's law, which holds that there is no such thing as a free lunch. That is,

$$Ep \geq Er$$

where

Ep = energy produced, and

Er = energy required.

Energy produced is greater than or equal to energy required over the long term. Energy required per day can be calculated by the following formula:

$$Er = 3200M + 2000m + 2300F + 1500f$$

where

M = number of males over 15 years,
F = number of females over 10 years,
m = number of males under 15 years, and
f = number of females under 10 years.

Of course the total caloric requirement generated by this formula is based only loosely upon current U.S.D.A. estimates and takes no account of activity levels, air temperature and the like, but it is useful nonetheless. We can calculate energy produced per day using the following formula:

$$Ep = [(M{\cdot}t{\cdot}150) + (F{\cdot}t{\cdot}150)]e \pm s$$

where

t = time in hours,
e = technoenvironmental efficiency, and
s = stored energy.

Note that this formula represents a state adopted by a community for purposes of procurement or production of food. If Ep is too low to equal Er, the state can be altered by increasing t, by adding m and/or f parenthetically within the brackets, or by drawing upon surplus (+s). The value of e is primarily a function of procurement. This state can be expressed as

$$Ep = (M{\cdot}t{\cdot}150)e_1 + (F{\cdot}t{\cdot}150)e_2 \pm s$$

In this case e has two different values depending upon the technoenvironmental efficiency of each of the two separate activities. Further, f and m can be added either as participants on one of these two activities or in separate parentheses to indicate other activities. Indeed, the formula can express any complex state for any population regardless of its size, albeit the formula will be unmanageably long for large complex societies. One need only make sure that all the people accounted for under Er are also accounted for under Ep, even if some of them are allowed to do nothing. As I will show by example, the ±s is an important factor that should be thought of as a reservoir that stands apart from the formula regardless of the mutations the latter might go through. This is a storage reservoir, maximum size of which depends upon storage technology, spoilage rates, productivity, and transportation technology. It turns out that a tendency to increase the size of s is a very important factor in the survival and evolution of adaptative systems.

Limp and Reidhead (1979) have shown experimentally that Ep exceeds Er by a factor of sixty when even very simple techniques are used to harvest fish runs. That releases many people from energy production and makes possible activities not related to subsistence that may nonetheless be regarded as important. Alternatively, the community may decide to maintain a relatively high rate of Ep in order to build up stored energy reserves in the form of smoked fish, or in order to release everyone from the need to produce anything at all for a time. The example shows the importance of experimental archaeology, and its applicability to models of subsistence economies. It also shows us that hunter-gatherers often have considerable latitude in meeting energy requirements. If Ep can be sixty times greater than Er where e is clearly very low, then we are apt to be frustrated in any attempt to generate precise formulas. We can, however, avoid unreasonably complex formulas and the spurious accuracy they imply, by deliberately simplifying them to levels compatible with what we really know empirically.

The formula for Er can even be informative if simplified to:

$$Er = 2000P$$

where

P = number of people in the community

and 2000 is taken as an average daily calorie requirement. The Bull Brook site produced forty-five hot spots that have been assumed by several archaeologists to represent individual nuclear family camps. The semicircular arrangement of the forty-five loci suggests that they were occupied simultaneously. If we assume five people per family band, we get a total congregation of 225 Paleo-Indians, a size that some of us have concluded could not have been maintained for long. However, if we consider that an average caribou weighs 95 kg, and will yield just under 50 kg of edible tissue at about 2300 calories per kg, we see that the assembled Paleo-Indians could have scraped by on only four caribou per day. It would take very little imagination to create a productivity state that would produce an Ep to equal or exceed this level, provided the resource was available. Indeed the most serious constraint on Ep would be the very limited capacity of s so far as we understand the storage capacity of Paleo-Indians. Beyond that, maintenance of the state would depend upon resource availability. Once the resource was no longer at hand, the limited storage would be depleted very rapidly, and the regional band would fragment into several smaller units, each of which could be represented as a separate state. The formula then allows us to see that a family band having five members could subsist for about eleven days on the meat of a single average caribou. This is a useful number, because it seems to be consistent with what we know empirically about the occupation of small kill sites by Paleo-Indians. Specifically, it suggests that small temporary camps could have been occupied for weeks if game was available and meat spoilage was not a serious problem.

The example may seem to belabor the obvious, but I think that it does not. The expression of the adaptive state or series of states of a Paleo-Indian community as a complex and alterable equation makes it possible for us to model different kinds of stress that could have affected the community. There are stress loads that would require radical readaptation, and some that would lead to permanent collapse. One can model the conversion from one state to another as that process was controlled by resources and information about them. Materialists have long had trouble recognizing information as something other than ideology, which they tend to dismiss as a dependent variable. However, information is critical in the maintenance or transformation of adaptive states, and since major discontinuities in the archaeological record may have resulted from breakdowns in adaptive states and the decision-making processes they imply, the role of information in the evolution of cultural systems should not be ignored. To put it another way, information can be factored out when one takes a normative view of adaptation, but remains an important variable if one allows for discontinuities and rapid readjustments.

All of this may seem to contradict the earlier discussion of economic behavior in human ecology and the absence of a requirement of rational thought, but it does not. Information and its use by rational minds to anticipate changes in the environment is a property of human adaptation that gives human populations some advantage over other kinds of adapting populations. However, even rationality is a mixed blessing. Individuals and even whole cultures can commit themselves to the wrong course through a lack or misunderstanding of information, and thereby make ultimate collapse an integral part of an adaptive system. The Paleo-Indian adaptation appears to have been based on a Bayes strategy, to use a term from game theory, and the collapse of that adaptation appears to have paved the way for the expansion of a new adaptation based upon a minimax strategy. As imprecise as they are, the formulas I have presented allow us to model stresses upon the earlier adaptation at a scale consistent with the available data.

There are other rather simple but nonetheless practical advances to be made in the study of adaptation. One of the unexpected benefits of public archaeology has been an increase in the amount of information available regarding site sizes (see Chapter 6). We are accumulating what will soon be a sizeable inventory of sites for which areas have been estimated with relatively high levels of confidence. This unexpectedly makes up in part for our continuing inability to control the time dimension well enough to allow us to determine empirically which subset of known sites for a given period is made up of those sites occupied in a particular year. This problem has plagued most of us at one time or another, because unless you know which sites were used by a particular local system during the course of a yearly round, and at the same time you are sure that you have found all of them, it is nearly impossible to say much about that system on strictly empirical grounds. However, Naroll (1962) has shown that the population of a settlement is approximately

$$P = \frac{m}{10}$$

where P is population and m is floor area in square meters. Once one has identified a central base, it should be possible to estimate its population. Subsequent area determinations for smaller seasonal camps should allow the estimation of average populations for them as well and an indirect means to determine their numbers. The Kings Road site, for example, is such a camp. It covers an elliptical area about 80 x 50 ft (Funk et al. 1969:1), dimensions that convert to about 292 m^2. Naroll's formula yields a population of about twenty-nine people for the site, and Eisenberg's (1978:130) analysis suggests that their activities were restricted to butchering and stone tool manufacture. Le Blanc (1971) has challenged the accuracy of Naroll's simple formula (see also Chapter 5), and Wiessner (1974) has gone on to test it empirically against Bushman data. She concludes that the relationship between population and area is not constant, specifically that the area per person increases as the size of the band increases. Thus while Naroll's formula appears to be fairly accurate for a site the size of Kings Road, her analysis suggests that a site of 59 m^2 would represent a population of about ten people rather than the six predicted by Naroll. Fortunately, these tests seem to be pushing us in the direction of refinement rather than abandonment of this kind of analysis, and we can look forward to second and third order applications of the results. If the figure of 225 Paleo-Indians at Bull Brook and twenty-nine at Kings Road are even approximately correct, the study of Paleo-Indian demography is nearly within our grasp.

Should we eventually be lucky enough to uncover Paleo-Indian skeletal remains in numbers sufficient to allow the generation of a life table, we will have the empirical data necessary to expand the formula for Paleo-Indian populations and refine the caloric demands of their subsets. Even without those empirical data, we could generate a more complex formula using data from Tables 3.2 and 3.3.

Another example is illustrated by Figure 3.4. This figure

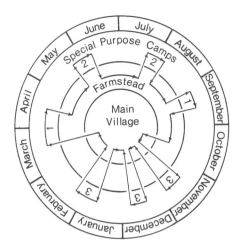

Figure 3.4. Hypothetical seasonal movements of a Massachusett family.

illustrates a hypothetical seasonal round for a Massachusett village as determined by archaeological and ethnohistorical data. The inner core represents the main village, the inner ring farmstead residence, and the outer ring temporary camps. Trips to fishing and fowling camps (1) and to shellfishing and plant gathering camps (2) were made from the farmstead, whereas trips to winter hunting camps (3) were made from the main village. Families spent part of the year in farmsteads away from the main village, and at other times were at possibly even smaller special-purpose camps. A village of 500 inhabitants would not have been unusual, a size that Naroll's formula would require a floor area of 5000 m^2. If one found a few farmstead sites having an average floor area of 80 m^2 each, it would take only the simplest arithmetic to generate an average farmstead population size and an estimate of the total number of farmsteads in use in any particular season, certainly more than we have determined to date by archaeologically traditional empirical techniques. Table 3.4 indicates the approximate total Massachusett population in A.D. 1600. While it is true that most main village sites have been destroyed by modern cities built on the same spots, it should also be clear that we need only sample archaeological and ethnohistorical data to allow an estimation of the total number of main villages. The numbers and distributions of farmsteads and special purpose camps are also predictable based upon accurate estimations of their average floor areas and main village population sizes. Once again the means to study an extinct settlement system and its associated social system appears to be available. That no one has yet taken advantage of it suggests that too many archaeologists are committed to either lofty theorizing or myopic empiricism.

The reports of archaeologists engaged in various nontradiional projects in conservation archaeology have generated a huge new data base. As huge as it is, it is miniscule compared to what we can expect to have in hand by the end of the century. Survey and recording techniques have been improved in recent years to the point that we can now feel more secure about our sampling, and begin to make use of our growing inventory of information on site sizes, locations, ecological contexts, and so on (see Chapter 6). That is not to say that we can abandon caution, of course. The Northeast is a difficult environment in which to conduct archaeological surveys. Even in the Southwest, where it is relatively easy to discover sites, "traditional site surveys have tended to underestimate the number of sites in a survey area by a factor of 5 to 10 and to overestimate the average size of sites by a similar factor [Plog et al. 1977:115]." Nevertheless, newer survey techniques and the very size of the data base we are accumulating are all very promising. Academic archaeologists working on comparatively traditional problems are sure to find avenues opened up by conservation archaeology that they probably did not expect. We are, at this point, about where geologists interested in plate tectonics were just before they began to realize the benefits of data generated by instruments designed and built by the government to monitor the underground testing of nuclear weapons around the world. In short, we are probably about to acquire more than enough data about site areas and locations in the Northeast to begin taking a truly demographic approach to prehistory.

There are further implications of population size as derived from floor area, most of which archaeologists have only rarely considered in the context of adaptation. Naroll (1956:689) suggests a logarithmic relationship between population of the largest settlement and the total number of occupational specialties in the cultural system. The relationship is expressed in the formula

$$P = \left(\frac{S}{2}\right)^3$$

where

P = population of largest settlement, and
S = number of occupational specialties.

The formula indicates that a system having a maximum settlement size of 500 would support about sixteen occupational specializations. These would be different from craft specialties, which involve the manufacture of durable items. The formula

$$P = C^4$$

where

P = population of largest settlement, and

C   = number of craft specialties

indicates that the same system would support about five craft specialties. Finally, Naroll (1956:701) also suggests that we can obtain the number of team types in such a system using the formula

$$P = (\frac{T}{2})^6$$

where

P   = population of largest settlement, and

T   = number of team types.

Our system with a largest settlement of 500 people would according to this formula support about seven team types, whether they be kinship teams, territorial teams, or associational teams.

As approximate as they may be, it is past time that archaeologists consider the numbers generated by Naroll's formulas when assessing adaptation. The results are no less significant than, say, the discovery that a prehistoric community was utilizing anadromous fish resources. Indeed, it seems to me that when considering adaptation we have usually been much too easily satisfied; we have not done ourselves justice. Primary communities of 500 people each may have been typical of sixteenth century Massachusetts, but they were also typical of sixteenth century Maine, where horticulture had not yet been adopted. The population densities of the two areas were quite different, perhaps by a factor of ten, and the distribution and use of smaller seasonal sites quite different as well. Bennett's analysis of the aboriginal food economy of southern New England allows us to see some important points of contrast. Table 3.5 shows the contrast between the aboriginal diet and modern U.S. diet in eleven food groups. One can see the relative importance of horticulture in the aboriginal diet and the effect removal of cultivated plants from that diet would have. Even more important was the storage potential of cultigens as compared to wild or semidomesticated food sources. The Indians of northern New England not only lacked the domesticates that made up well over half the diet of southern New England Indians, but thereby also lacked the foods that would store best for use during lean months. Given this contrast and the contrast between population densities, there are several legitimate questions relating to why both Naroll's formulas and ethnohistorical data from around A.D. 1600 indicate that social, technological, and ideological subsystems of northern and southern New England were nearly equivalent at the time.

Similar questions might be raised regarding the contrasting settlement systems of Maine that existed around A.D. 1000 and A.D. 1600 respectively. The rise of large central villages in northern New England after A.D. 1000 was apparently accompanied by a

Table 3.5. Approximate Food Intake in the United States (1952) and in
Southern New England (1605-1675).

	Food	Percentage Consumption	
		United States 1952	Southern New England 1605-1675
1.	Grain products	22.8	65-
2.	Animal and bird carcasses	21.6	10+
3.	Milk and milk products	15.8	0
4.	Sugars and syrups	15.4	0
5.	Visible vegetable fats	8.5	1-
6.	Vegetables and fruits [a]	6.5	4±
7.	Grain alternatives [a]	2.9	2-
8.	Nuts and leguminous seeds	2.9	8+
9.	Eggs	2.8	1-
10.	Fish and shellfish	0.4	9±
11.	Chocolate	0.4	0
		100.0	100

[a] Potatoes included as grain alternative but excluded from vegetables and
fruits (after Bennet 1955).

decline in the importance of coastal camps. Coastal pit houses, and
presumably winter residence on the coast, may have disappeared
after A.D. 1200 in the St. Croix and St. John drainages. None of
Bourque's (1971:166-216) sites on the Maine coast show evidence
of occupation after A.D. 1100. Indeed, Bourque had trouble finding
any sites postdating A.D. 1100 along the coast, but that may have
been because he was looking in microenvironments that had produced sites dating to the previous period. The more temporary
coastal camps of the Late Prehistoric period may well have been
chosen with other priorities in mind and used so briefly that they can
be easily missed by archaeologists. The Grindle site, which is located
on a shore of a tidal pond rather than on the seacoast, was occupied
both before and after A.D. 1100, suggesting just such a shift. Although this site contains shell fragments, it is not an obvious midden,
and could easily have been overlooked. Thus before A.D. 1000, the
settlement pattern in Maine appears to have been characterized by
dual central places, primary settlement shifting seasonally between
coastal and interior sites. After that date settlement shifted to single

central places at intermediate locations on estuaries. Once we know the sizes of these primary settlements, the sizes and locations of secondary camps, and the resources used at all of them, we should be able to assess the adaptive reasons for the shift in the pattern. Surely it is not sufficient to approach this major adaptive change as merely the presumed consequence of some subtle shift in an external factor such as sea or air temperature.

As a last example of a case of adaptation in the Northeast for which there can and should be a broader and more detailed analysis, I cite the Frost Island phase of central New York. Ritchie (1969: 156-164) long ago noticed that to the degree that we are able to compare them, the Frost Island cultural system shows significant contrasts with the systems that preceded it in central New York. The site distribution and inferred food resources are more strikingly riverine for Frost Island, perhaps an indication of the technological significance of the points of the Susquehanna tradition. The Frost Island system seems neither as diffuse nor as adapted to northern resources as the preceding systems. Further, the Frost Island phase seems to represent a complete cultural system that contrasts in most respects with those of the preceding period in central New York. Its connections, as evidenced by both point types and steatite bowls, are with the lower Susquehanna drainage in southern Pennsylvania. All dated components fit within a relatively narrow time range, and both the technological advantage implied by the broad points as well as available environmental data indicate that there were favorable conditions for migration. Independent invention is out of the question and diffusion seems inadequate to explain such a sharp and pervasive change from the Late to the Terminal Archaic. Finally, to the degree that we are able to examine them, all subsystems of Frost Island appear to contrast with those of earlier systems. The criteria for migration are all met.

However, we are still left with the need to explain why the carriers of the Frost Island system were able to displace the previous inhabitants of central New York. I have argued elsewhere (Snow 1980:251-253) that squash and certain other semidomesticates may have given the Frost Island subsistence subsystem an adaptive advantage. However, we will need more than the recovery of the remains of these plants from Frost Island sites to demonstrate that its system as a whole was a sufficiently dominant one to account for its expansion into New York. We will need more data on site sizes and frequencies per century, which we can then convert into relative population densities. We will need data on the lengths of seasonal occupation of specific site types so that we can assess the relative complexities of the social subsystems. We know from experience that such data can be obtained, and we now have the means to bridge from them to some of the powerful theoretical constructs of contemporary anthropology.

Two different points seem clear from all of this. First, the nature of Frost Island adaptation cannot be assessed by a simple determination of whether or not they were horticulturalists or any other similarly simplistic characterization. We may plumb the sites of later millenia for phytolithic evidence of maize cultivation, but even if we are successful this too will tell us only part of what we should want to know about adaptation. The second point is that the work of both traditional and contemporary archaeologists has long since put these problems in our hands, just as the work of many others has brought their solution within grasp. It is time that Northeastern archaeologists acknowledged this rich legacy and took a leading role in the exploration of prehistoric adaptation.

CONCLUSIONS

I have argued that many theoretical attempts to deal with human adaptation have involved modeling at scales that make the models unavailable to archaeologists. I have argued further that empiricists in archaeology have contributed to disjunction between theory and practice by emphasizing small-scale data that cannot be related to theoretical models. We must emphasize larger scale archaeological data such as site sizes and regional site distributions, data that are for various reasons increasingly accessible to us. At the same time that we are scaling up archaeological data we must scale down theoretical models such that the gap between them can be bridged. Such a compromise is particularly advantageous for the study of adaptation. I have explored the characteristics of adaptation generally and for the Northeast in particular, and have shown how we can relate it to prehistoric demography. The linkage between the data base and theoretical models of adaptation and demography are by way of a set of formulas relating space, population sizes, caloric requirements, and various social dimensions. This set of equations constitutes a theoretical model of adaptation that holds considerable promise for the analysis of prehistoric adaptive systems in the Northeast.

REFERENCES

Baerreis, D.A., and R.A. Bryson
    1965   Climatic episodes and the dating of the Mississippian cultures. *Wisconsin Archaeologist* 46(4):203-220.
Banfield, A.W.F.
    1974   *The mammals of Canada.* University of Toronto Press, Toronto.
Bennett, M.K.
    1955   The food economy of the New England Indians, 1605-75. *The Journal of Political Economy* 63(5):369-397.
Bernabo, J.C., and T.Webb, III
    1977   Changing patterns in the Holocene pollen record of northeastern North America: A mapped summary. *Quaternary Research* 8:64-96.
Bormann, F.H., and G.E. Likens
    1979   Catastrophic disturbance and the steady state in northern hardwood forests. *American Scientist* 67(6):660-669.
Bourque, B.J.
    1971   *Prehistory of the central Maine coast.* Ph.D. dissertation, Department of Anthropology, Harvard University.
Burrage, H.S. (editor)
    1906   *Early English and French voyages, chiefly from Hakluyt, 1534-1608.* Scribner's Sons, New York.
Cleland, C.E.
    1976   The focal-diffuse model: An evolutionary perspective on the prehistoric cultural adaptations of the eastern United States. *Mid-Continental Journal of Archaeology* 1(1):59-76.
Cohen, M.N.
    1975   Archaeological evidence for population pressure in preagricultural societies. *American Antiquity* 40(4):471-475.
    1977   *The food crisis in prehistory: Overpopulation and the origins of agriculture.* Yale University Press, New Haven.
Coombs, G.
    1980   Decision theory and subsistence strategies: Some theoretical considerations. In *Modeling change in prehistoric subsistence economies,* edited by T.K. Earle and A.L. Christenson, pp. 187-208. Academic Press, New York.
Cowgill, G.L.
    1975   Population pressure as a non-explanation. In Population studies in archaeology and biological anthropology: A symposium, edited by Alan C. Swedlund. *Society for American Archaeology Memoir* 30:127-131.
Davis, M.B.
    1965   Phytogeography and palynology of northeastern United States. In *The Quaternary of the United States,* edited by H.E. Wright, Jr. and David G. Frey, pp. 377-401. Princeton University Press, Princeton.

1967 Late-glacial climate in northern United States: A comparison of New England and the Great Lakes region. In *Quaternary paleoecology*, edited by E.J. Cushing and H.E. Wright, Jr., pp. 11-43. Yale University Press, New Haven.

1969 Palynological and environmental history during the Quaternary period. *American Scientist* 57(3):317-332.

Davis, R.B., T.E. Bradstreet, and H.W. Borns, Jr.
1979 Reply to R.J. Mott (1977) regarding an early postglacial boreal forest in New England and adjacent Canadian areas. *Geographie Physique et Quaternaire* 33(1):113-115.

Davis, R.B., T.E. Bradstreet, R. Stuckenrath, Jr., and H.W. Borns, Jr.
1975 Vegetation and associated environments during the past 14,000 years near Moulton Pond, Maine. *Quaternary Research* 5(3):435-466.

Davis, R.B., and T. Webb, III
1975 The contemporary distribution of pollen in eastern North America: A comparison with the vegetation. *Quaternary Research* 5:395-434.

Dice, L.R.
1943 *The biotic provinces of North America*. University of Michigan Press, Ann Arbor.

Doran, J.E., and F.R. Hodson
1975 *Mathematics and computers in archaeology*. Harvard University Press, Cambridge.

Dumond, D.E.
1975 The limitation of human population: A natural history. *Science* 187: 713-721.

Earle, T.K.
1980 A model of subsistence change. In *Modeling change in prehistoric subsistence economies*, edited by T.K. Earle and A.L. Christenson, pp. 1-29. Academic Press, New York.

Eisenberg, L.
1978 Paleo-Indian settlement pattern in the Hudson and Delaware river drainages. *Man in the Northeast, Occasional Publications in Northeastern Anthropology No. 4.*

Fitting, J.E.
1978 Regional cultural development, 300 B.C. to A.D. 1000. In *Handbook of North American Indians*, edited by B.G. Trigger, Vol. 15, pp. 44-57. Smithsonian Institution, Washington, D.C.

Fitzhugh, W.W.
1972 Environmental archaeology and cultural systems in Hamilton Inlet, Labrador: A survey of the central Labrador coast from 3000 B.C. to the present. *Smithsonian Contributions to Anthropology* 16.

Funk, R.E., and B.E. Rippeteau
1977 Adaptation, continuity and change in Upper Susquehanna prehistory. *Man in the Northeast, Occasional Publications in Northeastern Anthropology No. 3.*

Funk, R.E., T.P. Weinman, and P.L. Weinman
    1969   The Kings Road site: A recently discovered Paleo-Indian manifesta-
           tion in Greene County, New York. *New York State Archeological
           Association Bulletin* 45:1-23.
Grant, W.L. (editor)
    1907   *Voyages of Samuel de Champlain.* Scribner's Sons, New York.
Grayson, D.K.
    1974   The Riverhaven No. 2 vertebrate fauna: Comments on methods in
           faunal analysis and on aspects of the subsistence potential of pre-
           historic New York. *Man in the Northeast* 8:23-39.
Griffin, J.B.
    1960   Climate change: A contributory cause of growth and decline of
           northern Hopewell culture. *Wisconsin Archaeologist* 41(2):21-23.
Hassan, F.A.
    1978   Demographic archaeology. In *Advances in archaeological method and
           theory*, Vol. 1, edited by M.B. Schiffer, pp. 49-103. Academic Press,
           New York.
Hickerson, H.
    1965   The Virginia deer and intertribal buffer zones in the upper Mississippi
           valley. In *Man, culture, and animals*, edited by A. Leeds and A.P.
           Vayda, pp. 43-65. American Association for the Advancement of
           Science, Washington, D.C.
Jenness, D.
    1955   The Indians of Canada. *Bulletin of the National Museum of Canada* 65,
           Anthropological Series 15.
Jochim, M.A.
    1976   *Hunter-gatherer subsistence and settlement: A predictive model.*
           Academic Press, New York.
Knight, R.
    1965   A re-examination of hunting, trapping, and territoriality among the
           Northeastern Algonkian Indians. In *Man, culture, and animals*, edited
           by A. Leeds and A.P. Vayda, pp. 27-42. American Association for the
           Advancement of Science, Washington, D.C.
Kolata, G.B.
    1977   Catastrophe theory: The emperor has no clothes. *Science* 196:287,
           350-351.
LeBlanc, S.
    1971   An addition to Naroll's suggested floor area and settlement population
           relationship. *American Antiquity* 36(2):210-211.
Limp, W.F., and V.A. Reidhead
    1979   An economic evaluation of the potential of fish utilization in riverine
           environments. *American Antiquity* 44(1):70-78.
Ludlum, D.M.
    1966   *Early American winters, 1604-1820.* American Meteorological Society,
           Boston.
    1968   *Early American winters II, 1821-1870.* American Meteorological
           Society, Boston.

McArthur, N.
    1970   The demography of primitive populations. *Science* 167:1097-1101.
Naroll, R.
    1956   A preliminary index of social development. *American Anthropologist* 58:687-715.
    1962   Floor area and settlement population. *American Antiquity* 27(4): 587-589.
Peterson, R.L.
    1955   *North American moose.* University of Toronto Press, Toronto.
Plog, F., M. Weide, and M. Stewart
    1977   Research design in the SUNY-Binghamton contract program. In *Conversation archaeology: A guide for cultural resource management studies,* edited by M.B. Schiffer and G.J. Gumerman, pp. 107-120. Academic Press, New York.
Rapport, D.J., and J.E. Turner
    1977   Economic models in ecology. *Science* 195:367-373.
Reidhead, V.A.
    1980   The economics of subsistence change: A test of an optimization model. In *Modeling change in prehistoric subsistence economies,* edited by T.K. Earle and A.L. Christenson, pp. 141-186. Academic Press, New York.
Renfrew, C.
    1978   Trajectory discontinuity and morphogenesis: The implications of catastrophe theory for archaeology. *American Antiquity* 43(2): 203-222.
Rhoades, R.E.
    1978   Archaeological use and abuse of ecological concepts and studies: The ecotone example. *American Antiquity* 43(4):608-614.
Ritchie, W.A.
    1969   *The archaeology of New York State* (2nd ed.). Natural History Press, Garden City, New York.
Rodin, M.B.
    1979   More on systems theory in anthropology. *Current Anthropology* 20(2):413-414.
Rodin, M., K. Michaelson, and G.M. Britan
    1978   Systems theory in anthropology. *Current Anthropology* 19(4): 747-762.
Rouse, I.
    1958   The inference of migrations from anthropological evidence. In Migration in New World culture history, edited by Raymond H. Thompson. *University of Arizona Social Science Bulletin* 27:63-68.
Salmon, M.H.
    1978   What can systems theory do for archaeology? *American Antiquity* 43(2):174-183.
Snow, D.R.
    1977   The Archaic of the Lake George region. In Amerinds and their paleo-environments in northeastern North America. *Annals of the New York Academy of Sciences* 288:431-438.

1980   *The archaeology of New England.* Academic Press, New York.
Spaulding, A.C.
1973   Archeology in the active voice: The new anthropology. In *Research and theory in current archeology*, edited by Charles L. Redman, pp. 337-354. Wiley, New York.
Stommel, H., and E. Stommel
1979   The year without a summer. *Scientific American* 240(6):176-186.
Trigger, B.G.
1979   Review of *Social archeology: Beyond subsistence and dating*, edited by C.L. Redman, et al. *American Scientist* 67(2):246.
Webb, T., III, and J.H. McAndrews
1976   Corresponding patterns of contemporary pollen and vegetation in central North America. *Geological Society of American Memoir* 145: 267-299.
Wendland, W.M., and R.A. Bryson
1974   Dating climatic episodes of the Holocene. *Quaternary Research* 4: 9-24.
Wiessner, P.
1974   A functional estimator of population from floor area. *American Antiquity* 39(2):343-350.
Wing, E.S., and A.B. Brown
1979   *Paleo-nutrition: Method and theory in prehistoric foodways.* Academic Press, New York.
Woodcock, A., and M. Davis
1978   *Catastrophe theory.* Dutton, New York.
Wright, H.E., Jr.
1971   Late Quaternary vegetational history of North America. In *Late Cenozoic glacial ages*, edited by Karl K. Turekian, pp. 425-464. Yale University Press, New Haven.
Wright, J.V.
1978   The implications of probable Early and Middle Archaic projectile points from southern Ontario. *Canadian Journal of Archaeology* 2: 59-78.

4

OLD DATA AND NEW MODELS: BRIDGING THE GAP

WILLIAM A. STARNA
*State University of New York
College at Oneonta*

MODELS IN SCIENTIFIC INQUIRY

In this paper the content of models is discussed on two over-lapping levels, the more general level of epistemology and the more concret level of archaeology. There is no consensus in the philosophy of science on the meaning of the term, "model." This results from the fact that any definition would depend on the function of models, and functions are essentially infinite (Harvey 1969:144). However, although there is a multiplicity of functions models can perform and therefore a multiplicity of possible definitions, several logical, definitional statements about models can be put forward. David L. Clarke (1978:31) asserts that " . . . models are hypotheses or sets of hypotheses which simplify complex observations whilst offering a largely accurate predictive framework structuring these observations—usefully separating 'noise' from information. Which aspect is noise and which counts as information is solely dependent upon the frame of reference of the model." Other definitions range from the exceedingly rigorous, such as "a possible realization in which all valid sentences of a theory T are satisfied is called a model of T [see Suppes 1961:163, citing Tarski 1965]," to the very broad, such as "a model can be a theory, or a law, or a relation, or a hypothesis, or an equation or a rule [Skilling 1964:388A]."

It is probably more appropriate to describe models in terms of function than to attempt to reach an all-inclusive and precise definition. Several such descriptions are available. For example, Clarke (1979:22) contends that "models are usually idealized representations of observations, they are structured, they are selective, they simplify, they specify a field of interest and they offer a partially accurate predictive framework." Providing a categorized description of function, Harvey (1969:141) notes that models may act as cognitive, visualizing devices, as organizational or classificatory devices, as explanatory devices, or as constructional devices in the search for or extension of existing theory. Finally, in a procedural description models are seen to organize data, to make explicit, conscious and definite the nature, direction and content of research, to provide a way of handling complex phenomena, to reveal gaps in our knowledge, to act as generalizing devices, and to make possible an economical summary of actual or anticipated findings (Kaplan 1964:268-272).

There does appear to be a consensus of what models are not, however. Not all models are theories, nor are all theories models. Kaplan (1964:264) puts forward the rather succinct argument that if models are coextensive with theory, then why not just say "theory?" Models are interpretations of a theory or are partial, formalized expressions of a theory. That is, the model contains some, but not all, of the attributes or postulates of a theory, at the same time exhibiting similarity in formal structure. The model must be an ordered set in which the postulates of the theory are satisfied (Harvey 1969:146; Achinstein 1964:329). The theory remains relatively abstract. It neglects certain variables while describing ideal entities in the context of the theory itself (cf. Nagel 1961:95-97, 110-111; Kaplan 1964:263-265; Harvey 1969:144-147). In the interpretation or formal expression of theory a model may serve as a link between the abstract theory and a portion of the reality within the domain of the theory. The model also enables a transfer of the theory into realms which are more familiar, more understandable, more controllable or more easily manipulated (Harvey 1969:146). In essence, "models are pieces of machinery that relate observations to theoretical ideas, they may be used for many different purposes and they vary widely in the form of machinery they employ, the class of observations they focus upon and the manner in which they relate the observations to the theory or hypothesis [Clarke 1979: 21-22]."

Without delving too deeply into the philosophical debate regarding the logical and epistemological relationship between theory and models, it is necessary to point out a possible source of confusion regarding these constructs. It has been stated here that theory is an idealized structure that is abstracted from the domain of reality covered or encompassed by that theory (Harvey 1969:146). Elsewhere it has been noted that models are often idealized representations of observations (Clarke 1979:22). In addition, both theories and models are generalizing structures that are deductively fertile. One could therefore assume that there is no clear or unambiguous distinction between theory and models.

While similarities perceived between the theories, models, and observations outlined above may be necessary for the operation of these constructs they do not detract from the fundamental and necessary differences that are present. Models, theories and observations, occupying different levels of degree, represent isomorphic systems (Kaplan 1964). That is, they exhibit similar formal structures (cf. Harvey 1969:145-146; Nagel 1961; Braithwaite 1960) which allow for the orderly and logical transfer of ordered sets of postulates from one level to another. The critical and fundamental difference between theory and models is stated by Kaplan. "In a strict sense, not all theories are in fact models; in general, we learn something about the subject-matter *from* the theory, but not by investigating properties *of* the theory. The theory *states* that the subject-matter has a certain structure, but the theory does not therefore necessarily *exhibit* that structure in itself [Kaplan 1964: 264-265]." Models can, however, exhibit the structure of the subject matter. As noted earlier, models are the constructs of inquiry that bring the abstractions of the theory to bear on a relatively small segment of reality under the domain of the theory (Harvey 1969: 146). The same axiom holds in the relationship between models and observations. Here too, there is isomorphism between the systems (Clarke 1978:59-60) so that the model acts as the idealized generalizing structure employing observations through induction (Clarke 1978:31). Any perceived difference between the logical and functional relationships of theory and models, on one hand, and models and observations, on the other, are of degree and the foci of investigation and inquiry.

The relationship and interconnectiveness of theories, models and observations are both clear and fundamental to the understanding of their operation and application. As inquiry continues and scientific understanding proceeds, there is the distinct possibility that theories may become models (Achinstein 1965:106; cf. Harvey 1969:148). Then too, the reverse may occur where the models of today will be extended to become the theories, the idealizations, of tomorrow.

For archaeology specifically, there is little doubt as to the validity of this position. For the most part, there is no general theory in our discipline. Instead, we often employ models as temporary devices to represent what we think the structure of a particular set of data or observations or subject matter may, or ought, to be (Harvey 1969:149). Under the conditions where there is no completely specified general theory within the discipline, a model is sometimes used to indicate the theory, actually performing more as an analogue. Nevertheless, these operations and procedures are a means to an end, namely the theorizing of archaeology.

There are many types of models within the philosophy of science and the discipline of archaeology. There is some general agreement regarding what might be termed central kinds of models (cf. Kaplan 1964; Harvey 1969; Clarke 1978). Most appropriate here is the model hierarchy proposed by Clarke (1978:31-33) where there are three broad groups of models arranged in relative levels of sophistication. At the lowest level are iconic models, which are characterized as representing observed attributes as symbols, such as graphs, maps, and histograms. Iconic models fulfill a need for concise documentation and generalizing purposes. At the next highest level are analogue models. These represent sets of observations by substituting analogues which are regarded as congruent with the observations. Clarke (1978:33) correctly contends that analogue models, as they are used presently in archaeology, are the most common and potentially the most dangerous of all models (see Chapter 2). This characterization emerges from the uncritical or uncontrolled application of historical, anthropological, or abstract situations or correspondences to archaeological situations. However, Kaplan (1964: 267) points out that analogues or analogue models are gaining increased attention under headings such as "simulation models," "game theory," and the like (see Chapter 3). Finally, at the top of the hierarchy of model classes are symbolic models. Here observed attributes are represented as symbols integrated and conceptualized into precise, standardized mathematical terms.

For the most part models employed in archaeology are situation analogues or iconic constructs. "These models provide different prehistorians with different conceptual frameworks over which they stretch the same facts but with differing results which can be compared and contrasted for their accuracy or inaccuracy in the light of accumulating evidence [Clarke 1978:33]." There is relatively little application of symbolic models at present. Such models are receiving more attention as the discipline of archaeology advances and grows, for they present the potential of providing the least biased and most powerfully pure deductive systems (Clarke 1978:33).

There are several other broad categories of models that require discussion since they are germaine to the use of models or modeling in archaeology. These are a posteriori and a priori models, and what are termed controlling models (Clarke 1979:25 ff.; cf. Kuhn 1970). This latter category, controlling models, is of great significance in archaeology, generally, and in the Northeast specifically.

The nature of controlling models is complex and either ignored or given short shrift by many archaeologists. "Through exposure to life in general, to educational processes and to the changing contemporary systems of belief we acquire a general philosophy and an archaeological philosophy in particular—a partly conscious and partly subconscious system of beliefs, concepts, values and principles, both realistic and metaphysical [Clarke 1979:25]." This intellectual milieu gives rise to sets of controlling models which emerge or manifest themselves as " . . . the archaeologist's philosophy, the paradigms he chooses to align himself with, the methodologies that he finds most congenial and the aims that this system constrains [Clarke 1979:25]." There is little doubt that controlling models, operating implicitly and without visible structure, are to a great extent those systems that have produced many of the untested and unquestioned assumptions we are burdened with in the Northeast (cf. Ritchie 1965, 1969a; Ritchie and Funk 1973; Byers 1959; Griffin 1967; Funk 1965, 1966).

Beyond this, however, controlling models in the recent history of Northeastern archaeology present another obstacle. The implicit, unstated, and covert operating principles, paradigms, and philosophies of many Northeastern archaeologists have led to the formulation of a conventional wisdom that underlies a great portion of work thus far accomplished (see Chapter 1). This conventional wisdom is most often expressed in data that are left unpublished and therefore inaccessible to many, except those who have had "hands-on" experience or who were otherwise privy to the information. It is sustained by an "old boy" network whose membership is based upon university or institutional affiliation or age grades, and by data that can mean something only if one has logged several decades behind the shovel, and has therefore compiled and filed away in the brain's computer all that has transpired over the years. Unpublished data, here and elsewhere in this paper, refers to data that remain unanalyzed and unsynthesized. They are, in essence, raw data that have been compiled only informally. Their existence is known only to a few, and often its accessibility is restricted. Published data would include brief reports, preliminary reports, or finished reports made available in journals, through dissemination of manuscripts or in written form held in house. Thus, controlling models and their resulting conventional wisdom must be regarded a significant factor in affecting the archaeology that has and will be done in our region.

A posteriori models function to represent something that is already known. In this situation appropriate general theory is required. If no general theory exists the model is in doubt. The application of a posteriori models is by choice, in that the model can exhibit terms and structure which are contained in the theory, or the model can represent an analogue (Harvey 1969:151-152). A posteriori models allow for the facilitation of variable manipulation and testing procedures. However, it must be cautioned that in the absence of sophisticated general theory, little control is obtained over the model-theory relationship. Thus, doubt is cast on whether model conclusions are transferable to the theory, or if a successful test of the model signals a successful test of the theory which the model represents (Harvey 1969:152).

A priori models are more common than a posteriori models and function "to suggest theory, and to allow manipulations and conclusions to be drawn about some set of phenomena even in the absence of full theory [Harvey 1969:153]." This is generally the case with models used in archaeology. For such purposes, the model functions as an analytical construct which is applied to a specified subject. Harvey (1969:153-154) and Braithwaite (1960) discuss a series of logical problems concerning inference and control involved in the use of a priori models. For example, it is not clear whether model concepts are the same as those of the theory under construction. In all cases, there *must* exist congruency between the structure of the model and that of the theory. Importantly, predictions made with the aid of an a priori model, a goal of archaeological modeling theory (Clarke 1978, 1979), must remain open to doubt, "since it is not possible to know in what respects the model represents a theory and therefore the respects in which concepts and structure are similar cannot be assessed [Harvey 1969:153]."

In the scheme of things, including procedural reality, both models reviewed here function in an integrative fashion. "Characteristically, research tends to slip from an *a priori* model of some kind, to the postulating of some theory, to the development of an *a posteriori* model which then has elements added to it so that it then functions as an *a priori* model for the creation of further theory [Harvey 1969:154]."

MODELS IN ARCHAEOLOGY

There is no doubt in the minds of most active archaeologists that modeling is rapidly becoming of paramount concern in the discipline. A number of authors have spoken directly to the current high fashion of model use (cf. Clarke 1979; Redman et al. 1978), while others at least mention the fact that archaeologists use models in their research (Trigger 1978). Models used in archaeology are generally borrowed from sister disciplines and then modified for application to particular research goals. Modification of these pre-existing models is necessary given the change in research and data context. So too, model borrowing and modification and then reuse, can supplement and expand upon the explanatory potential of the original model (Redman et al. 1978:9). There clearly is room, however, for model building to emerge from inside the discipline of archaeology and not necessarily be dependent on allied fields.

The kinds of models used in archaeology are many, their number reflecting the multifaceted aspect of the discipline and the great variety of data contexts encountered by researchers. There are a number of discussions of archaeological model use and compendia of model types (cf. Clarke 1972, 1978, 1979; Redman et al. 1978; Renfrew 1973). A sample of the more commonly employed models, derived primarily from these sources follows.

SYSTEM MODELS

These models are concerned with the relationships of inter-connected parts in a defined system (Harvey 1969:449-480). For archaeologists, the parts of a culture system abstracted from historical or physical situations are investigated. At the simplest level system models postulate isomorphisms among fundamentally different phenomena. They then search for analogy-based principles to provide explanations of the behavior of these "ensembles of interlinked components [Clarke 1979:49]" or "classes" of entities or phenomena (Sutherland 1973:10). Commonly, system models "represent the flow of consequences between ensembles of interlinked variables or the flow of consequences between networks of decisions. . . . Other common system properties may include—constraints, critical thresholds, stochastic oscillation, adaptive regulation and control by positive or negative feedback, convergence upon equilibrium states, replication and related concepts [Clarke 1979:50]." The model assumes that cultural systems are integrated whole systems.

Positive aspects of system models occupy three levels of utility. First, they are useful in reconceptualizing a wide range of relatively broad archaeological problems. Second, by narrowing the scopes of such models, predictive or simulation power increases. Last, with an even more tightly defined system structure containing additional information, it is possible to establish measurable, quantifiable and testable predictions. Nevertheless, the inappropriate selection of system components by the researcher often leads to less than adequate system representation. For example, Clarke (1979:49-50) notes that if component selection is poor, the consequence will be, more often than not, an impressive flow chart with little substance. Developing such a chart does not necessarily explain a process or provide an adequate model. Instead, it usually provides a formulation of the obvious, and no advantage is gained.

System models have enjoyed relatively wide use in archaeology although it is difficult to assess completely their success in explaining human behavior as represented by cultural remains. There is no serious disagreement among archaeologists that system models are "the most promising models for interpreting the evolution of human behavior . . .[Isaac 1972:173]." Also, even though system models and attendant systems theory have offered little in the way of easy answers for archaeology, there is provided " . . . a useful framework that enables the researcher to specify the interrelationship of relevant variables, deduce critical implications for testing the model, and formulate the methodology for conducting investigations [Redman 1978:330]." However, it is well to point out that system models are not beyond criticism in their application to archaeology. Salmon (1978) presents a succinct and devastating critique contending that as long as there remains an absence of general theory concerning systems theory concepts (e.g. negative feedback, positive feedback, etc.) and hence, models, they can have only descriptive and no explanatory force. Nor can general systems theory and therefore system models be looked to for an explicit methodology. "At best they can only direct archaeologists to seek certain types of explanatory principles rather than others, and even here the choices are rather broad. At worst, they amount to the importation of a pseudoscientific jargon which tends to obscure rather than to clarify the issues [Salmon 1978:174]." Nonetheless, the use of system models and systems theory remains popular (cf. Redman 1973; Plog 1975; Clarke 1978).

There are few references to the use of system models in the literature from the Northeast. Those available are illustrative and expository in nature. For example, Snow (1973), in discussing the nature and evolution of Maritime adaptations in aboriginal Maine, employs a series of flow charts to show the primary components of the adaptive system and their relationships. By introducing change in one or several of these components, evidence of which is derived from the archaeological and paleoclimatological record, he is able to explicate shifts in adaptive strategies and their effect on the cultural system as a whole. Cook (1976) applies a form of dimensional analysis to level out a number of systemic variables in dealing with the problem of the so-called Broadpoint complexes along the East Coast of the United States.

LOCATIONAL MODELS

Locational models are derived from a number of subtheories encompassed within the broad designation of spatial theories. For most spatial studies in archaeology, four general theories apply, including anthropological spatial theory, economic spatial theory, social physics theory and statistical mechanics theory (Clarke 1977: 18). Spatial archaeology and its constituent general theories, subtheories and models is directed toward "the retrieval of information from archaeological spatial relationships and the study of the spatial consequences of former hominid activity patterns within and between features and structures and their articulation within sites, site systems and their environments; the study of the flow and integration of activities within and between structures, sites and resource spaces from the micro to the semi-micro and macro scales of aggregation [Clarke 1977:9]."

Anthropological spatial theory rests on the proposition that given the patterned distribution of archaeological remains as a result of the patterned behavior of human populations, the spatial structure is potentially informative about the way the human group organized itself. Economic spatial theory postulates that over time and experience, human groups practicing resource exploitation will move to choices and solutions that will minimize costs and maximize benefits. In general, and to the detriment of the theory, noneconomic factors in regard to choices are ignored and perceptions of cost are often not considered. Social physics theory deals with the notion that although individual human actions are often unpredictable, the actions of the group may form predictable empirical regularities in the interaction between places and populations. Although useful in simulations, this theory is conceptually weak since it is primarily descriptive in nature. Finally, statistical mechanics theory represents an elaboration of the missing statistical and stochastic background that underlies the social physics approach and the analogy between group behavior and elements of that behavior. With this approach a system can be described as a whole without having to understand or be able to describe the detailed behavior of individuals.

The four general theories surveyed briefly above are applied practically through the use of a number of subtheories and their attendant models. Some of these include Von Thünen's model of location theory where the relationships between the spatial distribution of activities and land use around a center, and the law of diminishing returns as distance increases are recognized. Vita-Finzi and Higgs (1970) have modified Von Thünen's model for archaeological application as the "catchment area approach." Webber's locational model considers the location of a site in terms of its being a constituent part of a network with other sites and involved in the movement of resources between and among these sites. Christaller's central place model establishes the relationships between the region served by sites, the functions of the sites and the network of sites, involving the aggregation of site systems as a whole. In addition to these most commonly used location models are within-site location models, sector models, multiple nucleus models, concentric zone models, nearest neighbor statistic models, point pattern models and others.

The relative merits and criticisms of the variety of locational models have been discussed often and at length (cf. Johnson 1977; Clarke 1977; Hodder and Orton 1976; Webber 1971). Here it will suffice to offer the following caveats regarding critical problem areas in the application of locational models. The spatial variation observed in site patterning is to a great extent dependent upon site survival in modern contexts, as filtered by past and present archaeological interests. Consequently, a number of biases are introduced. There is, furthermore, a particular problem that stems from our inability to date prehistoric sites precisely. Also, many locational models demand data of unattainably high quality. Finally, there are constraints and problems associated with the statistical methods and techniques themselves. This includes assumptions of the data base deemed necessary for the statistical methods and techniques to be successful.

To some extent, locational models have supplemented, substituted for, superceded, or replaced traditional settlement pattern and settlement system studies (cf. Smith 1978; Clarke 1977; Winters 1969). This has been accomplished by elaborating on the range of useful elements, assumptions, models, methods, and problems to be tested, in addition to moving away from the static, disaggregated studies common in settlement system and settlement pattern analyses (Clarke 1977:7). Locational models are essentially absent from the literature of the Northeast. Fitting (1972) makes reference to the Von Thünen model in his "The Huron as an ecotype", but offers little else.

ECOLOGICAL MODELS

Ecological models represent a potpourri of approaches to understanding adaptive responses of human populations to environmental constraints. These models do not lend themselves easily to categorization. Instead they occupy analytical perspectives ranging from modeling regional adaptive responses to broad environmental issues, to building models that are concerned with a narrow spectrum of the environment, one or several resources, and the behavioral characteristics of the adapting human group. The latitude of ecological models, their varied application and subject matter, reveals them to be the most innovative in our discipline. In the Northeast, they are the most commonly used.

In many cases, what are often identified as ecological models are in reality descriptions applied to "provide 'scenery' for the cultural and technological 'drama' which is widely considered the province of archaeological investigations [Wilkinson 1972:543]." Other so-called ecological models are far too simplistic and have been applied uncritically by archaeologists. In the Northeast, a prime example is Dice's (1943) biotic province model. This model is descriptive, typological, and static, and upon examination, offers little in terms of archaeological application (see Chapters 2 and 3). For example, it is not possible for a static model to provide explanation for a dynamic system the environment represents. Also, the model is descriptive in form, therefore being restricted to the period for which it was defined. It cannot be used to define, describe, or assist in the understanding of environments several thousands of years older than our own. Several other major problems exist in employing this typological model to environmental dynamics and concomitant human adaptive response (Dincauze 1978:84-85).

It is more appropriate to offer several examples of the application of ecological models than to attempt any form of definition or categorization. In terms of the properties of gross or broad environments and consequent human adaptive responses, Jochim's (1976) predictive model for hunter-gatherer subsistence and settlement is a case in point. The model assumes that human populations are making adaptive strategy decisions in accordance with available resource dynamics within their environments. In another study, Gunn (1975) offers an "envirotechnological" model that is applied to determine how much of the cultural change in a subsistence system can be accounted for by environmental change. A similar model dealing with regional resource availability and climatic change linked to human adaptation is presented by Bettinger (1977). Numerous other examples are in the literature.

Ecological models have also been applied to narrower spectra of the environment. A good example is "Processual cultural ecology of the middle Connecticut River valley" (Paynter 1979), in which several innovative ecological models are presented. They are populationist models that eschew diffusionist explanations. They opt for potential explanations derived from the study of covariation between cultural systems and their natural and social environments. Case studies include a model of hunter-gatherer response to differing paleoenvironments (Curran 1979), modeling expectations for postglacial environmental change to interpret palynology and paleodemography of prehistoric periods (Mulholland 1979), and developing a model relating anadromous fish behavior to watershed characteristics, which in turn are used to generate settlement patterns (Moore and Root 1979). Other examples of ecological modeling are of varying quality and rigor. Fitzhugh (1972) correlates data from regional and local environmental analyses, paleoenvironmental reconstruction, ethnographic models, cultural chronologies, and prehistoric cultural systems, in the modeling of the relationships between cultural systems and the environment. In southern New England, Dincauze and Mulholland (1977) develop several general models of environmental conditions in order to explain the putative low population densities during the Early Archaic. In addition to these examples of ecological modeling is Turnbaugh's (1975) explanation of broadpoint dispersal in eastern North America, Thomas's (1975) "Environmental adaptation on Delaware's coastal plain," Braun's (1974) discussion on the evolution of coastal adaptations in prehistoric eastern New England, and the modeling of subsistence-settlement strategies in the upper Susquehanna Valley by Steponaitis and Mitchell (1978). Although these models are not flawless, they do provide innovative and stimulating alternative perspectives to the discipline (see Chapter 2).

It is probably true that the numbers and kinds of models developed and applied in archaeology are limited only by the creativity of the archaeologist and the range of problems encountered. In fact, in any single archaeological case it is most appropriate to have more than one model so as to cope effectively with different aspects of the situation. "Under this pluralist viewpoint there are many competing models for each archaeological situation, where none may be finally picked out as uniquely and comprehensively 'true' [Clarke 1979:24]." For example, in Clarke's (1972) study of an Iron Age society, he applies a number of different models that are used to identify "target areas" for successive areas or cycles of research. These include post-depositional site models, structural and building models, reconstruction models, social models, economic models, locational models, and others.

SHORTCOMINGS AND MISUNDERSTANDINGS OF MODELS

In completing this survey section on the epistemology of models and their general application in archaeology, it is important to point out real or potential problem areas. The shortcomings to follow should in no way be construed as affecting the validity of models themselves. Instead, they are offered to indicate to archaeologists that care and rigor must be maintained in their use.

In no way should advocacy of the use of models reach the vociferous, finger-pointing polemics that, for example, marked the appearance of the New Archaeology. There is little room in the real world of doing archaeology for attitudes of defensive incorporation and exclusion where models proponents strike the pose that modeling is the only thing worth doing. Neither should traditional archaeologists react defensively to model users. There should be a recognition by both modelers and nonmodelers that a significant portion of the endeavors of archaeologists are the result of their own skills, interests, and nature. Kaplan (1964:277), upon whose writings many of the statements made here are based, wonders " . . . what is wrong, in either art or science, with a man's doing what he does best or enjoys most? The worth of the product must be assessed independently of the motivations which entered into its production. The harm is done when we misconceive the causes of our actions as reasons for them, and so seek to impose the same actions on others [Kaplan 1964:277]." What is to be avoided or objected to is both the condemnation and the indiscriminate advocacy that are evoked by models. Often, model building is made " . . . too much a matter of principle, pro or con, and not enough a matter of the values, esthetic or scientific, achieved in the specific instance [Kaplan 1964:277]."

OVEREMPHASIS OF SYMBOLS

Underlying this shortcoming is an unconscious belief in the magic of symbols. Care must be exercised so that symbolic style or representation is one of thought and not just a mode of expression. In doing so, symbolic representation of the obvious should be avoided, along with pseudo-definitions of symbols. Models that overemphasize symbols are comparable to illustrative experiments. "We learn from them only what we already knew without their help [Kaplan 1964:278]."

OVEREMPHASIS OF FORM

Here an error is committed where what is logically possible in scientific inquiry becomes preeminent to what is actually available in the problematic context. This translates to a situation where a model is always possible, but not necessarily useful in problem solving. Building a model in this case promotes premature closure of the structure being modeled. The result is that a claim is made, or a justification for failure of the mode of inquiry is postulated, that there is an inadequacy in our knowledge of the mathematics or logic of the mode of inquiry, rather than admitting to an inadequacy in our knowledge of the subject matter. Instead, "we tinker with the model when we might be better occupied with the subject matter itself [Kaplan 1964:279]."

OVERSIMPLIFICATION AND OVEREMPHASIS OF RIGOR

Oversimplification is often thought to be at fault when models fail to perform or are of no particular help. Although simplification is a prime tenet of science, the goal of which is to formulate only what is necessary for understanding and not to reproduce a domain of reality completely, it must be done with care. The considerations that lead to a particular simplification are critical. "It is one thing to ignore certain features of a complex reality on the hypothesis that what is being neglected is not essential, at least to a first approximation. It is quite another thing to follow the principle of 'the drunkard's search,' and to simplify in a particular way because then the model would be so much more elegant, or so much easier to work with [Kaplan 1964:280]."

Conversely, there is sometimes an excessive emphasis on exactness and rigor. This occurs when more precision is framed in a model than is allowed by the subject matter. The fact is that models often call for measures that are impossible to attain. To satisfy this demand by stepping outside of the available subject matter is to be avoided.

The imposition of spurious precision is to a certain extent a problem particularly apparent in archaeology. This need not be the case, nor should archaeologists be trapped into opting for such action. There is no reason to expect exact correspondence between models and data in the behavioral sciences in general, and in archaeology in particular. The reasons for this contention are identified by Arrow (1951:83) as (1) the fact that some of the relevant variables in the data base have probably been omitted along with factors that may be individually insignificant, but important in the aggregate, and (2) that the variables that are incorporated into the analysis will not have been measured with great exactness. "Probabilistic considerations thus assume considerable importance; statistical formulations may usefully be built into the model rather than reserved for the treatment of the relations between the model and the data [Kaplan 1964:291]."

Additional problems involve what are termed "map reading," and "pictorial realism." In the former, there is a failure to appreciate the specificity of a model as a structure of representation. Given definitional statements regarding models that, among other things, indicate their idealized structure, it must be recognized that not all of a model's features correspond to some characteristic of its subject matter. The error is seeing something contained in the model that in fact is not part of it. In the latter case, "pictorial realism," the internal structure of the model, its endogenous properties, are misconceived as constituting an image or likeness of what is being modeled. There is a similarity between the model and what it represents. However, the model should not be construed as a literal statement of what is being modeled.

EXPLANATION AND PREDICTION

Archaeologists often equate or assume parity between prediction and explanation in their use of models (e.g. Watson et al. 1971: 5). They see or imply that explanation is a natural or necessary outcome of prediction (e.g. Mulholland 1979), or the reverse (cf. Hempel and Oppenheim 1948:135-175).

There is opposition to this point of view. The questions are whether the ability to predict is a necessary consequence of having a good explanation, or whether predictions must always lead to explanation (Kaplan 1964:346-349). There is no disagreement that prediction is a component of explanation. If prediction is possible it provides the explanation with credibility. But if an explanation does not give rise to predictions is it invalidated or somehow proven unacceptable? According to Watson et al. (1971:5), citing Rudner (1966) and Hempel and Oppenheim (1948), the answer is "yes." There is, they claim, logical equivalence between predictions and explanations in all cases. Kaplan (1964) and Zubrow (1973, citing Rescher 1970) disagree. In the behavioral sciences our knowledge is for the most part limited to what is necessary for an event to occur. However, this same knowledge cannot provide what is sufficient to produce the same event. Therefore, " . . . what we can explain on the basis of that knowledge is not strictly deducible from it, and surely not predictable [Kaplan 1964:347]." Beyond this, even when an explanation exists, there is a limitation to predictability that is a result of the inherent variability and instability of the subject matter, a well-recognized condition in archaeology.

That prediction can proceed without explanation is commonly known. In our discipline, for example, one can predict site locations without having provided an explanation regarding the reasons for the sites being located where they are (cf. Williams et al. 1973). In the long run, if the difference between explanation and prediction is understood, a failure of one to provide the other will not result in one being marked as a nonscientist or to "stand condemned of unscientific speculation [Kaplan 1964:351]."

Whatever the case may be with regard to attaining explanations by the archaeologist, there remains cause for concern in their application and understanding. Explanations do not represent finality, although it is often thought "that when something has been explained it is as though we have conquered a certain amount of territory; a new frontier has been established, and, except for mopping-up operations, nothing remains but to continue our steady advance [Kaplan 1964:351]." Nothing could be further from the truth. For example, in the Northeast there has been a persistent explanation for an apparent absence of Archaic complexes older than about 5000 B.P. Fitting (1968) and Ritchie (1969b:212-213) proposed a period of unfavorable environmental conditions during the earliest millenia of the Archaic, thereby reducing the availability of resources for human populations. They suggested that there was little for human groups to subsist upon, and Early Archaic populations were consequently either absent or sojourned infrequently in the Northeast. Although this explanation was ostensibly framed as an hypothesis, it became indurated in the literature, assuming the status of fact. More than a decade later, this explanation seems faulty. Dincauze and Mulholland (1977:454) have concluded that resource scarcity is not an adequate explanation for apparent low population densities during the period. Instead, the instability of the environment or cultural factors that may suppress population densities may have been operating. In addition, the low site densities may be a distortion resulting from low rates of data recognition and recovery.

Explanations are partial in that only a portion of the factors determining the phenomenon being explained are considered. They are conditional, holding true for only a certain range of phenomena or are applied only when certain conditions are met. Explanations are approximate in that what they describe is more or less inexact from what is observed. They are indeterminate, being true in a general sense, but not in every single case. They are inconclusive, not showing why what is being explained is so, but rather why it is likely that it is so. Explanations are uncertain, confirmation being attained only to a degree. They are intermediate, in that every explanation is subject to being explained by another explanation. Finally, explanations are limited, applying to particular contexts but not to every possible circumstance.

MODELS IN NORTHEASTERN ARCHAEOLOGY:
THE STATE OF THE ART

Without doubt, the preponderance of archaeology carried out within the last three decades in this region exhibits relatively little in the way of modeling. This statement is true in terms of models being explicit structures, statements, or sets of hypotheses that offer relatively accurate predictive frameworks over a simplified body of complex observations. Thus, in Clarke's (1979) terminology there have been few "operational" models formulated, explicated and applied in the Northeast. What have clearly prevailed, instead, are controlling models or paradigms. For the most part Northeastern archaeology has been governed or, in the eyes of some, victimized, by controlling models. To an extent they have affected the selection of the operational models when and where there is a desire to apply them. Certainly in retrospect there is no cause to be overly critical of the apparent lack of application of operational models in archaeology. It is clear to most that work carried on in the 1940s, 1950s, and into the 1960s reflects the growth of the discipline. During this time description, classification, and typology were the goals of archaeology nearly to the exclusion of all else. Such work is exemplified by regional syntheses and culture histories by Ritchie (1944, 1951, 1956, 1958, 1965, 1969a), Byers (1959), Griffin (1952, 1967), the early works of Funk (1965, 1966), and others. Not to be excluded are scores of site reports and preliminary reports too numerous to list here (cf. Moeller 1977). The point is that the state of the art was such as to preclude explicit hypotheses or model building and testing. If research designs, hypothesis building and testing were part of the paradigm of this archaeology, it is not obvious. Rather, the methodological and intellectual machinations of most work is either implicit, unknown, obscure, or uninterpretable. To a great extent this results in the archaeology being " . . . a series of regional schools with cumulatively self-reinforcing archaeological education systems and with regionally esteemed bodies of archaeological theory and preferred forms of description, interpretation and explanation [Clarke 1979:28]." Gaining access to the resulting conventional wisdom is difficult for many since it is to a degree based upon unpublished data known informally only to a few. The axiom must stand in archaeology that if something isn't published, it doesn't exist. This is not to say that reasonable time periods between data collecting and publishing are not acceptable. What is unacceptable is work that remains unpublished. This represents a severe blow to the data base only from which can come model building, model testing, and explanation. Many degreed professionals and graduate students have at one time or another experienced the frustration of critically arguing a point at a meeting or in a seminar only to have their position eroded or destroyed by the presentation of data that had remained unpublished and thus, unavailable.

Since the 1960's, when the New Archaeology and its demand for scientific rigor was introduced, there has been change in the manner in which archaeology is done. Nonetheless, much contemporary Northeastern archaeology remains reminiscent of earlier work. That is, archaeology, in a number of instances, continues to reflect an intense interest in cultural history with the attendant preoccupation with description, classification, typology, and what I term "influence archaeology," that is, diffusional or developmental interpretations and explanations. Examples of these studies can be found in many state and regional journals. In general, they continue to focus on traits and trait complexes and their meanderings. Pottery styles, projectile point types, and other material culture continue to exhibit an uncontrolled and unexplained wanderlust. To the detriment of Northeastern archaeology, and any attempts to deal with processes of human adaptation and change, the state of the art is essentially one of recapitulation of what is already considered known or knowable. There are relatively few new questions being asked.

Although there undoubtedly will be disagreement regarding the above critique, it remains that archaeology in the Northeast has continued to function in a similar manner over the past three or four decades. Certainly the source of this perceived problem is one of controlling models affecting individuals or groups of archaeologists and a concomitant conservatism and resistance to change. Without doubt there is, and continues to be, a conflict between established, inertia-ridden methodologies, paradigms, and perspectives of many archaeologists, and the rather rapidly fluctuating rival paradigms and innovations of developing methodologies (Clarke 1979:26). The Northeast is not unique in this respect.

Criticisms can be leveled at the history of Northeastern

archaeology and its past and ongoing accomplishments. However, these should not be directed at the aspirations, motives, interpretations, and methods of the archaeologists doing what they do or have always done, or doing what they know best. Instead, criticism needs to be directed at many of these same archaeologists for not having taken advantage of some of the changes occurring in the discipline. For the most part, there has been a failure to demonstrate or develop intellectual growth, understanding, and critical perspective with regard to the established and rival paradigms in the discipline. In short, there has been a failure to attempt more in the way of incorporating scientific rigor and new methodology into archaeology, and to assess critically previous accomplishments. Unfortunately, having done something once is not necessarily enough. New questions need to be framed, and there must be attempts to apply whatever tools we have at our disposal.

To be sure, a significant portion of past and ongoing archaeology reflects the traditional paradigms, tenets, and goals of established Northeastern archaeology. These, in turn, yield culture histories, regional and local treatments, synthetic interpretations, and associated classification schemes. At the same time, the data base is expanding. There are a number of excellent works that demonstrate the accomplishment of such goals, including those by Tuck (1971, 1975, 1977), McGee and Tuck (1975), Dragoo (1976), Ritchie (1969a), Ritchie and Funk (1973), Funk (1976), Dincauze (1968, 1976), Sanger (1973), Wright (1966, 1967, 1972, 1974), Snow (1969, 1975), Kent et al. (1971), Stothers (1977), and Keenlyside (1978). I would submit, however, that virtually none of the above studies reflect modeling, model building, or model use as it has been discussed here. They do, however, reflect some of the best of traditional archaeological work. They also constitute legitimate scientific activity (Salmon 1976:376). It is this body of literature that represents what I term the "old data." In using this term I am not in any way implying that these data are bad, inferior, insignificant, or derived incompetently. Neither were they necessarily gathered thirty or forty years ago. What I am suggesting is that many of these data result from research done within the paradigm of controlling models which operate implicitly and without visible or recognized structure. There is little or no evidence of the application of operational models. I am also suggesting that many of these data were accumulated without benefit of explicit research designs or conscious recognition of relevance to problem solving. Some of the old data simply represent desultory information collection, the amassing of subject matter for simple comparative purposes. Done within the proper methodological framework, historically defined, such work fulfills a necessary and critical function within archaeology. Others of the old data were, or are, used to build or refine prehistoric chronologies, or to discover temporal, spatial, or cultural relationships of archaeological complexes (e.g. Snow 1969; Funk 1976; Ritchie and Funk 1973). It is fair to add that some of the old data were accumulated under a number of constraints, including technological, methodological, theoretical, and intellectual. In short, "old data" result from adhering to traditional paradigms.

In contrast, a relatively small number of archaeological research pursuits in the Northeast speak directly, explicitly, and clearly to the application of operational models. These have already been mentioned. There are also a few applications of modeling that appear generally as models of culture change. Included here are Stoltman's (1978) temporal model of the prehistory of eastern North America, and Sanger's (1975) discussion of culture change as an adaptive process in the Maine-Maritimes region. Further examples of model use are those applied to deriving cultural information from stone tools (Bonnichsen 1977). Still, there is a noticeable scarcity of explicit model formulation. There is, however, widespread use of the term "model." For the most part it usually appears in one of the first paragraphs of a monograph or article, or in the conclusion and interpretation chapter. Unfortunately, however, this mention of the term "model" is often no more than lip service. It almost always represents the nearest the authors get to actual modeling. If there are truly models in such works they remain as implicit and obscure as controlling models. They bear little resemblance to operational models.

There is no doubt that controlling models are far and away the guiding force behind both past and ongoing archaeology in the Northeast. Operational models, however, are receiving increased attention. Interest in, and the formulation of, explicit, predictive, and testable models can only enhance archaeological research in our region and promote scientific method and rigor. Model building and application can also provide direction toward gaining new information. Furthermore, by placing modeled information in the structure of scientific inquiry, the goal of explanation will be more fully realized. In attaining this goal it is important to recognize certain difficulties facing both the modelers and the nonmodelers.

First is the problem of dealing with the conventional wisdom that pervades the discipline. Nonrecoverable or nonexistent data, that is, unpublished or otherwise unavailable data, can no longer be a part of the way archaeology is done in the Northeast. Their absence does not allow for the rigorous testing of models or assumptions or other structures of archaeological inquiry, nor do they add to the data base in any meaningful way.

From this emerges the view that " . . . we must develop a heightened awareness of unquestioned assumptions . . . [Dincauze 1978:86]." For nonmodelers and modelers alike this means that what we have believed as knowable or known for the past several decades might very well be questioned. Such examination may support what has been done, or it may call for reformulations. It also means examining critically the fundamental assumptions models and their subject matter are often based upon. For example, modeling social organization among horticulturalists in the Northeast demands more attention (see Chapter 1). It is likely that ceramics and ceramic styles will play an important part in such modeling. However, what assumptions of ceramic styles and their cultural context appearing in the literature have been subjected to rigorous testing? Did women make all the pottery? Did all women make pottery? What mechanisms have been postulated to explain the movement of pottery styles other than postnuptial residence patterns or warfare and the capture of women? What was the role of trade in the Northeast? Did only men trade or does this assumption too require examination? There are many additional time-worn assumptions that must be assessed critically, such as those regarding migration and *in situ* developmental schemes.

In addition to the problem of assumptions emanating from the old data or the old paradigm, there are concerns with regard to the interdisciplinary nature of archaeology as practiced under the new paradigm. For example, if archaeologists are to involve themselves in modeling maintenance strategies and human population responses to the environment and environmental change, there should be a concomitant immersion into the subject matter of ancillary sciences in dealing with this question. For instance, how well do we understand the details of forest succession in terms of human scale (see Chapters 2 and 3)? To what extent do we involve ourselves in understanding in-depth factors affecting the diversity and density of floral and faunal species? How well is resource potential in an area and the actual human exploitation of this potential understood? Have we examined carefully the perceptions we have of a given environment as against the perceptions of the people who lived in it? All of these questions require a deep understanding of a variety of environmental issues, issues that are generally outside the purview of archaeology. It is unfortunate that in many cases our knowledge and application of such information is, at best, naive and superficial.

Another problem area involves many of the modelers. This concerns procedures followed in formulating models and hypotheses and the testing that must follow. In the literature on modeling in the Northeast I have encountered instances of what Fischer (1970: 36-38) identifies as the "fallacy of the potentially verifiable question." The error committed is that somehow there is a perceived division of labor between those who formulate hypotheses and those who test them. The mistake is to attempt to separate two inter-dependent parts of a single process. "Question-framing cannot be undertaken independently of question-answering, for no hypothesis can be demonstrated to be potentially verifiable except in the degree to which it has been partially verified [Fischer 1970:36]." I do not think that archaeology is at a point where it can afford to support both a theoretical and experimental branch. In this light, it is in-cumbent upon modelers to descend from their sometimes ethereal heights and establish the relationships between their models and the subject matter through testing. There needs to be an examination of the models formulated and how they relate to observations. "We can learn to ask questions which are answerable from the data . . . [Dincauze 1978:87]."

Underlying many of the above issues and, by extension, model building, is a series of important and related questions. To what extent is the new paradigm and modeling making use of the old paradigm and its subject matter? What can one paradigm provide the other, if anything? Are the two paradigms interrelated and inter-dependent structures or of separate domains?

There is a large body of data that has been gathered under the old paradigm that begs attention, namely, the results of settle-ment pattern studies (e.g. Ritchie and Funk 1973; Funk 1976). Since settlement pattern studies provide spatial data through indica-tions of site size, site density, site location, site distribution, and site diversification, usually within chronological frameworks, there is an opportunity to interrelate the old data with the new models.

For example, the Mohawk Valley of New York State and its aboriginal inhabitants have received considerable archaeological attention over the past century (Lenig 1965:1-4). Given the time range of research, it is not unexpected that there is a great deal of variation in its quality, direction, and results. Much of the work accomplished in the latter part of the nineteenth century was essen-tially antiquarian in nature, although several individuals demon-strated an expertise that accords them special status. In the late 1940s, William Ritchie, with several avocational archaeologists began the first professional investigations in the valley. This research was directed toward Owasco and protohistoric Mohawk occupations. In 1952, MacNeish published his "Iroquois pottery types," formally presenting the *in situ* hypothesis regarding Iroquois development.

Also in 1952, Ritchie's "Chance horizon" paper appeared, and in 1953, a joint effort with Lenig and Miller on the Owasco in eastern New York was published. The most detailed and comprehensive work on the Mohawk Valley is Lenig's (1965) monograph on the Oak Hill horizon. Since that time, statements on Mohawk Valley archaeology have appeared in the work of Ritchie (1969a), and Ritchie and Funk (1973). A number of site reports concerned with prehistoric and historic occupations are in print. These studies are directly concerned with intrasite settlement patterns.

In general, work carried out over the last several decades is the most thorough and useful. It was accomplished either by professionals or highly competent avocational archaeologists. For the most part, archaeological excavations and research objectives were directed to establish a local cultural chronology, to determine village movements for purposes of understanding culture change, and to explicate intrasite settlement patterns.

Proposed research in the Mohawk Valley (Snow and Starna 1980) focuses on the techno-economic details and cultural dynamics of the acquisition of domesticated plants and the evolution of horticulture. Although dealing with this question will constitute the primary thrust of future archaeological investigations, a series of related research topics should also be considered. There is general agreement that A.D. 1000 marks the first appearance of plant domesticates in the Northeast. Traditionally, corn, beans, and squash are cited. In conventional archaeological terminology, these earliest domesticates distinguish the Late Woodland from the Middle Woodland and are associated with the economy of the Owasco culture or tradition. Combined with the appearance of maize horticulture is village nucleation, reflecting increased sedentism, and perhaps population growth (see Chapter 1).

Settlement pattern data are of considerable importance in considering the shift from hunting and gathering to horticulture. This is due to several factors. First, in the Northeast and elsewhere, hunter-gatherers were fragmented into small mobile populations. They are generally described as practicing a seasonal round of exploitive activities within the framework of scheduling. Their adaptive strategy, or maintenance strategy, was characteristically diffuse (Cleland 1976). Here, the majority of human energy expended in the pursuit of food was directed toward many and varied food resources. Following this, the settlement pattern, identified within a catchment area, reflects the activities of a mobile, techno-economically diversified population. That is, sites are generally small, numerous, and scattered throughout catchment. Most often, sites appear as task specific loci, where the activities carried out during an occupation tended to be mostly of one sort, such as hunting camps, fishing camps, and vegetal preparation camps, although there is nearly always evidence showing several activities taking place at a single site. At the same time, occupations were relatively short, as one would expect given the mobile or even semisedentary nature of such populations.

In contrast, horticultural groups in the Northeast are said to have had focal adaptive strategies (Cleland 1976), where most of the energy of subsistence activities is directed toward one or several food resources. The labor intensive activities of horticulturalists require larger, nucleated, sedentary populations. Populations are regarded as being higher than those of hunter-gatherers due to factors of lengthened female reproductive spans and increased fertility, the ability to intensify crop production as populations increase, and probably lower infant mortality. The last would be a consequence of the removal of practices to limit family size, such as infanticide. For these and other reasons, horticultural practices resulted in, or were concomitant with, increased and nucleated populations, and large permanent or semipermanent settlements. This maintenance strategy is reflected in the archaeological settlement pattern. In general, sites are considerably larger, implying substantially larger numbers of inhabitants, often hundreds, than sites of hunter-gatherers. The sites evidence the presence of dwellings, storage areas, and often, fortifications. Task-specific sites such as hunting camps and fishing camps persist, although they are nearly always associated with the large villages. Many times, villages are positioned near major waterways or along tributaries to the main waterways. There is also a relationship between the village location and surrounding arable lands. In summary, there is a relatively clear distinction between the settlement patterns of hunter-gatherers and horticulturalists.

From about A.D. 1000 until A.D. 1300, the full time range of the Owasco culture or tradition, the majority of known components in the Mohawk Valley were situated along the floodplain of the Mohawk River or on the immediately adjacent kame terraces. By the beginning of the fourteenth century Lenig (1965, 1977) sees a trend of village movement away from the river. This movement continues throughout the fifteenth century and by the early sixteenth century villages are located at a maximum distance from the Mohawk River, nearly 11 km north. With the beginning of the seventeenth century, this trend was reversed and by the early decades of that century the majority of villages were located once again on the floodplains and adjacent terraces. Of the sixteen components attributed to the period of A.D. 1500-1620, thirteen are located north and three south of the river.

A few possible explanations are given for village movements as just described. The generalized trend away from the river beginning in the fourteenth century has been often explained as a defensive maneuver by the Mohawk. However, Lenig (1977) contends that the remoteness of villages from the river does little to enhance their defense. He points out that it is exceedingly difficult to hide a village of several hundred people, spewing smoke from scores of fires, with the added cacophony of yelling children and barking dogs. Further, given the expertise of the enemies of the Mohawk, it is equally hard to imagine that they would be hindered in their approach to attack a village deep in the woods. He concludes that reasons for the apparent trend of movements away from the river are unknown at present.

While Lenig can offer no satisfactory explanation for village movement away from the river, he feels that there is an obvious reason for the return of villages to the river. The rapid development of the fur trade with the Dutch in the Hudson Valley and the desire of the Mohawk to act as middlemen in this trade made it imperative for them to control the river, a primary trade route into the interior. Therefore, they moved their villages to strong points adjacent to it.

At face value, Lenig's hypothesis regarding village movements is appealing. In fact, it may eventually prove to be perfectly valid. However, there are a number of questions and problems associated with his position that require attention. First, there has never been any systematic areal site survey work done in the Mohawk Valley. It is interesting to note that few new sites have been located beyond those known from the late nineteenth century and into the early decades of the twentieth century. As a consequence, the trends of village movements noted by Lenig and others must be examined more closely. In the absence of careful surveys, the observation that Owasco sites are located only along the floodplain of the Mohawk River cannot be verified. A second problem exists regarding sites from the fourteenth, fifteenth, and sixteenth centuries. It is possible that there are other sites, either at the known maximum distance from the river of nearly 11 km, north or south, or at intervening distances. Major tributaries south of the Mohawk River have never been adequately examined, and the same can be said of tributaries to the north.

There could also be problems with the chronology as it has been developed for the valley, and this could have far-reaching implications regarding village periods and village movements. The chronology is a relative one based upon ceramic seriation. Lenig (1977) contends that it is accurate, resting upon a firm foundation provided by radiocarbon dates for the time period prior to the sixteenth century and by datable European goods for the seventeenth century. Again, however, a question must be raised. For the entire Middle and Late Woodland, there are only four radiocarbon dates from the Mohawk Valley. They consist of four dates from four different sites. Separate from this issue, although ultimately dependent upon a radiocarbon baseline, is the question of the development of the ceramic seriation. No sampling techniques, procedures, or designs were applied in making ceramic collections from sites of the Late Woodland. There is also doubt regarding the numerical adequacy of the samples. It may very well be that the present chronology may stand up to testing and therefore be verified as accurate, but it must be tested. Accordingly, a model has been developed with a number of test implications for the acquisition of horticulture by human groups in the Mohawk Valley.

Domesticated plants appeared in the Northeast generally during the centuries of the Middle Woodland. The mechanism for their appearance is considered to have been diffusion, and the direction of the diffusion was from the south. At the initial arrival of domesticates in the Northeast, in-place populations were hunter-gatherers practicing a diffuse maintenance strategy, the ramifications of which were discussed previously. Small, dispersed, mobile populations of hunter-gatherers found themselves adding domesticated plants to their subsistence inventory. It is hypothesized that their conversion to horticulture was relatively slow, and carried out in increments, to the extent that only by degrees did domesticated plants gain a foothold, eventually becoming the most significant food in terms of bulk and nutritional value (Heidenreich 1971). Given this incremental adjustment to horticulture, the following scenario is offered. Initially, within the constraints of a hunter-gatherer settlement pattern, domesticated plants were acquired and intensified. The sites associated with this period are proto-Owasco and possibly earlier. These sites should generally reflect a settlement pattern of camps and hamlets dispersed throughout the valley, and not relegated to the river's immediately adjacent floodplains and terraces. As domesticated crop use intensified, along with a concomitant increase in populations, stresses were placed on both the human populations and the surrounding arable lands. A number of factors probably came into play. Due to requirements of practicing horticulture, such as sedentism and the maintenance of arable lands, populations nucleated and apparently fortified themselves. Horticulture is a labor-intensive activity requiring relatively substantial and well-organized populations, and sufficient arable land. It is hypothesized that the larger thirteenth, fourteenth, and fifteenth century villages reflect this nucleation. Although they have presently been found only far back from the river, it is suspected that un-known others may be closer, but not necessarily on, the river. Soils back from the river and at higher elevations on the hills bordering the valley are thin, less fertile, and not as capable of being as quickly replenished with nutrients as those of the floodplain. With the increases in, and nucleation of, populations, and the associated need to intensify horticultural production, these thin soils failed or began to fail. This forced the populations to seek large tracts of arable land that could withstand heavy crop utilization for extended periods of time, and continue to produce sufficiently. It is further hypothesized that the gravitation of villages to the river in the late sixteenth and early seventeenth centuries reflects such a decision. The floodplains of the Mohawk River are vast, fertile, easily-worked areas. Flooding every spring replenished depleted soils and at the same time prevented heavy vegetation from growing. The efforts of labor intensive slash-and-burn horticulture, as practiced in the hills and forests back from the river, could be reduced considerably.

In order to gather data to test the model outlined here, surveying, testing, and field checking the scores of sites already known and expected to be discovered in the study area will have to be carried out. Eventually, sites will be isolated with which to test the model and its implications for understanding and explaining the details and cultural dynamics of the acquisition of horticulture.

From a methodological and theoretical point of view the case can be made that the old data provide a perfectly proper infor-mation base from which innumerable hypotheses and models can be generated and tested. This position is in direct opposition to those archaeologists who have suggested that previously collected data are somehow inferior and should therefore be abandoned or ignored (cf. Funk and Rippeteau 1977:4-5). Following this is a similar con-tention that the data used to suggest an hypothesis or hypotheses may not be legitimately used to test the same hypothesis or hypoth-eses (LeBlanc 1973; Salmon 1975). Both of these claims are in-correct. LeBlanc discusses a number of propositions to support this latter statement. First, data themselves have no memory. Using data for whatever purposes does not change their reality. Also, data used to formulate a hypothesis are not so contaminated that they cannot be legitimately used to test the hypothesis. Unfortunately the charge of circular reasoning is often made in an attempt to impugn such a procedure. "While circularity does exist when data used to derive an H (hypothesis) are also used to test it, these data form a necessary part of the test. Such data is seldom (and seldom taken to be) sufficient to confirm the H and, finally, it certainly cannot be ex-cluded from test data [LeBlanc 1973:204]." In scientific inquiry it is well to keep in mind that testing is not always a matter of using new data, for it can also involve looking at the old data from a fresh perspective or a different point of view. Second, the logic underlying hypothesis testing is atemporal. "Therefore, the order of data collecting, deduction of test implications for hypotheses, and testing is irrelevant to the validity of the reasoning involved [LeBlanc 1973: 200]."

Finally, hypotheses are in no way logically dependent on actual data, whether collected or potentially collectable. This is not to say that hypotheses cannot be suggested from or tested against actual data, but that hypotheses can also be fabricated or even hallucinated (Salmon 1975:461-462). The source from which hypotheses are suggested makes no difference in determining their logical implications or whether or not they are confirmed. Only the empirical truth of the hypotheses' implications are dependent on the data. Therefore, testing hypotheses is a matter of assessing their implications.

I do not think that there is any longer disagreement among archaeologists that archaeology can, or should, be a science, even though there is disagreement regarding its conceptual structure (Read and LeBlanc 1978). Science is a cumulative process consisting of a succession of explicit interrelated structures of inquiry and interpretation. These structures are part of a continuum that has direction. In a real sense the old paradigm, which has provided the old data, represents structures of archaeological inquiry and interpretation that for the most part have been directionless, saltatory, noncumulative, and implicit. What should be cumulative progress towards exact knowledge appears instead as a succession of contemporary mythologies whose validities are judged by authority (Clarke 1979:63; Read and LeBlanc 1978:307).

However, archaeological science in the Northeast can be maintained and developed to become a cumulative process. This requires a wedding of the old paradigm and its old data, and the new paradigm and its scientific methodology. The old data can provide significant and crucial input for the explicit building and testing of archaeological models, which in turn " . . . can provide the progressive cycle by means of which fresh information is gained, theory is accumulated and the cumulative knowledge within the discipline is expanded [Clarke 1979:63]."

ACKNOWLEDGEMENTS

    I would like to express thanks and appreciation to the following indi-
viduals who either commented on earlier drafts of this paper, offered sound
advice during its writing, or simply listened: Donald R. Hill, Douglas W. Shrader,
Dean R. Snow, and George H. Young. As is customary, I assume full responsibility for any and all shortcomings.

REFERENCES

Achinstein, P.
    1964   Models, analogies, and theories. *Philosophy of Science* 31:328-350.
    1965   Theoretical models. *British Journal of the Philosophy of Science* 16:
           102-120.
Arrow, K.J.
    1951   *Social choice and individual values.* Wiley, New York.
Bettinger, R.L.
    1977   Aboriginal human ecology in Owens Valley: Prehistoric change in the
           Great Basin. *American Antiquity* 42(1):3-17.
Bonnichsen, R.
    1977   Models for deriving cultural information from stone tools. *National
           Museum of Man, Archaeological Survey of Canada Mercury Series
           No. 60.*
Braithwaite, R.B.
    1960   *Scientific explanation.* Harper Torchbooks, New York.
Braun, D.P.
    1974   Explanatory models for the evolution of coastal adaptation in pre-
           historic eastern New England. *American Antiquity* 39(4):582-596.
Byers, D.S.
    1959   The Eastern Archaic: Some problems and hypotheses. *American
           Antiquity* 24(3):233-256.
Clarke, D.L.
    1978   *Analytical archaeology* (2nd ed.). Columbia University Press, New
           York.
    1979   *Analytical archaeologist: Collected papers of David L. Clarke,* edited
           by his colleagues. Academic Press, New York.
Clarke, D.L. (editor)
    1972   *Models in archaeology.* Methuen, London.
    1977   *Spatial archaeology.* Academic Press, New York.
Cleland, C.E.
    1976   The focal-diffuse model: An evolutionary perspective on the pre-
           historic cultural adaptations of the eastern United States. *Mid-
           Continental Journal of Archaeology* 1(1):59-76.
Cook, T.G.
    1976   Broadpoint: Culture, phase, horizon, tradition, or knife. *Journal of
           Anthropological Research* 32(4):337-357.

Curran, M.L.
 1979 Studying human adaptation at a Paleo-Indian site: A preliminary report. In Ecological anthropology of the middle Connecticut River valley, edited by Robert Paynter. *Research Reports* 18. Department of Anthropology, University of Massachusetts, Amherst.
Dice, L.R.
 1943 *The biotic provinces of North America.* University of Michigan Press, Ann Arbor.
Dincauze, D.F.
 1968 Cremation cemeteries in eastern Massachusetts. *Papers of the Peabody Museum of Archaeology and Ethnology* 59(1).
 1976 The Neville site: 8000 years at Amoskeag. *Peabody Museum Monographs* 4. Peabody Museum, Harvard University.
 1978 "Common sense" and scientific insight. *Archaeology of Eastern North America* 6:83-87.
Dincauze, D.F., and M.T. Mulholland
 1977 Early and Middle Archaic site distributions and habitats in southern New England. In Amerinds and their paleoenvironments in northeastern North America. *Annals of the New York Academy of Sciences* 288:439-456.
Dragoo, D.W.
 1976 Some aspects of eastern North American prehistory: A review 1975. *American Antiquity* 41(1):3-27.
Fischer, D.H.
 1970 *Historians' fallacies.* Harper and Row, New York.
Fitting, J.E.
 1968 Environmental potential and the postglacial readaptation in eastern North America. *American Antiquity* 33(4):441-445.
 1972 The Huron as an ecotype: The limits of maximization in a western Great Lakes society. *Anthropologica* (new series) 14(1):3-18.
Fitzhugh, W.W.
 1972 Environmental archeology and cultural systems in Hamilton Inlet, Labrador. *Smithsonian Contributions to Anthropology* 16.
Funk, R.E.
 1965 The Archaic of the Hudson Valley—New evidence and new interpretations. *Pennsylvania Archaeologist* 35(3-4):139-160.
 1966 *An Archaic framework for the Hudson Valley.* Ph.D. dissertation, Columbia University.
 1976 Recent contributions to Hudson Valley prehistory. *New York State Museum and Science Service Memoir* 22.
Funk, F.E., and B.E. Rippeteau
 1977 Adaptation, continuity and change in Upper Susquehanna prehistory. *Man in the Northeast, Occasional Publications in Northeastern Anthropology No. 3.*
Griffin, J.B.
 1967 Eastern North American archaeology: A summary. *Science* 156: 175-191.

Griffin, J.B. (editor)
  1952 *Archeology of the eastern United States.* University of Chicago Press, Chicago.
Gunn, J.
  1975 An envirotechnological system for Hugup Cave. *American Antiquity* 40(1):3-21.
Harvey, D.
  1969 *Explanation in geography.* Edward Arnold, London.
Heidenreich, C.E.
  1971 *Huronia: A history and geography of the Huron Indians, 1600-1650.* McClelland and Stewart, Toronto.
Hempel, C.G., and P. Oppenheim
  1948 Studies in the logic of explanation. *Philosophy of Science* 15:135-175.
Hodder, I., and C. Orton
  1976 *Spatial analysis in archaeology.* Cambridge University Press, London.
Isaac, G.L.
  1972 Early phases of human behavior: Models in Lower Paleolithic archaeology. In *Models in archaeology*, edited by D.L. Clarke, pp. 167-199. Methuen, London.
Jochim, M.A.
  1976 *Hunter-gatherer subsistence and settlement: A predictive model.* Academic Press, New York.
Johnson, G.A.
  1977 Aspects of regional analysis in archaeology. *Annual review of anthropology* 4:479-508.
Kaplan, A.
  1964 *The conduct of inquiry.* Chandler, New York.
Keenlyside, D.L.
  1978 Late prehistory of Point Pelee, Ontario and environs. *National Museum of Man, Archaeological Survey of Canada Mercury Series No. 80.*
Kent, B.C., I.F. Smith, III, and C. McCann (editors)
  1971 Foundations of Pennsylvania prehistory. *Anthropological series of the Pennsylvania Historical and Museum Commission* 1.
Kuhn, T.
  1970 *The structure of scientific revolutions* (2nd ed.). University of Chicago Press, Chicago.
LeBlanc, S.A.
  1973 Two points of logic concerning data, hypotheses, general laws, and systems. In *Research and theory in current archeology*, edited by C.L. Redman, pp. 199-214. Wiley, New York.
Lenig, D.
  1965 The Oak Hill horizon and its relation to the development of Five Nations Iroquois culture. *New York State Archeological Association Researches and Transactions* 15(1).
  1977 Of Dutchmen, beaver hats and Iroquois. In Current perspectives in northeastern archeology. *New York State Archeological Association Researches and Transactions* 17(1):71-84.

MacNeish, R.S.
1952   Iroquois pottery types: A technique for the study of Iroquois prehistory. *National Museum of Canada Bulletin* 24.

McGhee, R., and J.A. Tuck
1975   An Archaic sequence from the Strait of Belle Isle, Labrador. *National Museum of Man, Archaeological Survey of Canada Mercury Series No. 34.*

Moeller, R.W.
1977   *Archaeological bibliography for eastern North America.* Eastern States Archaeological Federation and American Indian Archaeological Institute.

Moore, J.A., and D. Root
1979   Anadromous fish, stream ranking and settlement. In Ecological anthropology of the middle Connecticut River valley, edited by Robert Paynter. *Research Reports* 18:27-44. Department of Anthropology, University of Massachusetts, Amherst.

Mulholland, M.T.
1979   Forest succession and human population change in a temperate forest environment. In Ecological anthropology of the middle Connecticut River valley, edited by Robert Paynter. *Research Reports* 18:45-56. Department of Anthropology, University of Massachusetts, Amherst.

Nagel, E.
1961   *The structure of science.* Harcourt, Brace and World, New York.

Paynter, R. (editor)
1979   Ecological anthropology of the middle Connecticut River valley. *Research Reports* 18. Department of Anthropology, University of Massachusetts, Amherst.

Plog, F.T.
1975   Systems theory in archaeological research. *Annual Review of Anthropology* 4:207-224.

Read, D.W., and S.A. LeBlanc
1978   Descriptive statements, covering laws, and theories in archaeology. *Current Anthropology* 19(2):307-335.

Redman, C.L.
1973   Research and theory in current archeology: An introduction. In *Research and theory in current archeology,* edited by C.L. Redman, pp. 5-20. Wiley, New York.
1978   Mesopotamian urban ecology: The systemic context of the emergence of urbanism. In *Social archeology,* edited by C.L. Redman, pp. 329-347. Academic Press, New York.

Redman, C.L. (editor)
1978   *Social archeology.* Academic Press, New York.

Renfrew, C. (editor)
1973   *The explanation of culture change: Models in prehistory.* Duckworth, London.

Rescher, N.
1970   *Scientific explanation.* Free Press, New York.

Ritchie, W.A.
    1944   The pre-Iroquoian occupations of New York State. *Rochester Museum of Arts and Sciences Memoir* 1.
    1951   A current synthesis of New York prehistory. *American Antiquity* 17(2):130-136.
    1952   The Chance horizon, an early state of Mohawk Iroquois cultural development. *New York State Museum Circular* 29.
    1956   Prehistoric settlement patterns in northeastern North America. In *Prehistoric settlement patterns in the New World*, edited by Gordon R. Willey, pp. 72-80. Viking Fund Publications in Anthropology 23, New York.
    1958   An introduction to Hudson Valley prehistory. *New York State Museum and Science Service Bulletin* 367.
    1965   *The archaeology of New York State.* Natural History Press, Garden City, New York.
    1969a   *The archaeology of New York State* (2nd ed.). Natural History Press, Garden City, New York.
    1969b   *The archaeology of Martha's Vineyard.* Natural History Press, Garden City, New York.
Ritchie, W.A., and R.E. Funk
    1973   Aboriginal settlement patterns in the Northeast. *New York State Museum and Science Service Memoir* 20.
Ritchie, W.A., D. Lenig, and P.S. Miller
    1953   An early Owasco sequence in eastern New York. *New York State Museum Circular* 32.
Rudner, R.S.
    1966   *Philosophy of social science.* Prentice-Hall, Englewood Cliffs, New Jersey.
Salmon, M.H.
    1975   Confirmation and explanation in archaeology. *American Antiquity* 40(4):459-464.
    1976   "Deductive" versus "inductive" archaeology. *American Antiquity* 41(3):376-381.
    1978   What can systems theory do for archaeology? *American Antiquity* 43(2):174-183.
Sanger, D.
    1973   Cow Point: An Archaic cemetery in New Brunswick. *National Museum of Man, Archaeological Survey of Canada Mercury Series No. 12.*
    1975   Culture change as an adaptive process in the Maine-Maritimes region. *Arctic Anthropology* 12(2):60-75.
Skilling, H.
    1964   An operational view. *American Scientist* 52:388A-396A.
Smith, B.D. (editor)
    1978   *Mississippian settlement patterns.* Academic Press, New York.

Snow, D.R.
  1969   *A summary of excavations at the Hathaway site in Passadumkeag, Maine, 1912, 1947, and 1968.* Department of Anthropology, University of Maine, Orono.
  1973   *The evolution of maritime adaptation in aboriginal Maine.* Paper presented at the 72nd annual meeting of the American Anthropological Association, New Orleans.
  1975   The Passadumkeag sequence. *Arctic Anthropology* 12(2):46-59.
Snow, D.R., and W.A. Starna
  1980   *A preliminary research design for the Mohawk Valley project.* Paper read at the Conference on Iroquois Research, Rensselaerville, New York.
Steponaitis, L.C., and W.W. Mitchell
  1978   Subsistence settlement strategies: A predictive model for the upper Susquehanna River valley. In *The I-88 archaeological report.* Public Archaeology Facility, State University of New York, Binghamton.
Stoltman, J.B.
  1978   Temporal models in prehistory: An example from eastern North America. *Current Anthropology* 19(4):703-746.
Strothers, D.M.
  1977   The Princess Point complex. *National Museum of Man, Archaeological Survey of Canada Mercury Series No. 58.*
Suppes, P.
  1961   A comparison of the meaning and uses of models in mathematics and the empirical sciences. In *The concept and role of the model in mathematics and nature and social sciences.* Synthese Library, Dordrecht.
Sutherland, J.W.
  1973   *A general systems philosophy for the social and behavioral sciences.* George Braziller, New York.
Tarski, A.
  1965   *Introduction to logic.* Oxford Univeristy Press, New York.
Thomas, R.A., D.R. Griffith, C.L. Wise, and R.E. Artusy, Jr.
  1975   Environmental adaptation on Delaware's coastal plain. *Archaeology of Eastern North America* 3:35-90.
Trigger, B.G.
  1978   *Time and traditions.* Columbia University Press, New York.
Tuck, J.A.
  1971   *Onondaga Iroquois prehistory: A study in settlement archaeology.* Syracuse University Press, Syracuse.
  1975   Prehistory of Saglek Bay, Labrador: Archaic and Palaeo-Eskimo occupations. *National Museum of Man, Archaeological Survey of Canada Mercury Series No. 32.*
  1977   A look at Laurentian. In Current perspectives in northeastern archeology. *New York State Archeological Association Researches and Transactions* 17(1):31-40.

Turnbaugh, W.A.
1975   Toward an explanation of the broadpoint dispersal in eastern North American prehistory. *Journal of Anthropological Research* 31(1): 51-68.

Vita-Finzi, C., and E. Higgs
1970   Prehistoric economy in the Mount Carmel area of Palestine: Site catchment analysis. *Proceedings of the Prehistoric Society* 36:1-37.

Watson, P.J., S.A. LeBlanc, and C.L. Redman
1971   *Explanation in archaeology.* Columbia University Press, New York.

Webber, M.J.
1971   Empirical verifiability of classical central place theory. *Geographical Analysis* 3:15-28.

Wilkinson, P.F.
1972   Ecosystem models and demographic hypotheses: Predation and prehistory in North America. In *Models in archaeology*, edited by D.L. Clarke, pp. 543-576. Methuen, London.

Williams, L., D.H. Thomas, and R. Bettinger
1973   Notions to numbers: Great Basin settlements as polythetic sets. In *Research and theory in current archeology*, edited by C.L. Redman, pp. 215-238. Wiley, New York.

Winters, H.D.
1969   The Riverton culture. *Illinois State Museum Reports of Investigations* 13.

Wright, J.V.
1966   The Ontario Iroquois tradition. *National Museum of Canada Bulletin* 210.
1967   The Laurel tradition and the Middle Woodland period. *National Museum of Canada Bulletin* 217.
1972   The Shield Archaic. *National Museum of Man Publications in Archaeology* 3.
1974   The Nodwell site. *National Museum of Man, Archaeological Survey of Canada Mercury Series No.* 22.

Zubrow, E.
1973   Adequacy criteria and prediction in archaeological models. In *Research and theory in current archeology*, edited by C.L. Redman, pp. 239-260. Wiley, New York.

5

APPROACHES TO DEMOGRAPHIC PROBLEMS IN THE NORTHEAST

DOUGLAS H. UBELAKER
Smithsonian Institution

Although the field of prehistoric demography currently attracts considerable attention in anthropological scholarship (Hassan 1978), it is hardly a new subject. Interest in the number and composition of the New World aborigines extends back almost to the discovery of the New World when theories were plentiful regarding their composition, size, and origins. Most of these theories were rooted in erroneous conceptions of the geography of the New World and a biblical historical perspective, which resulted in widely diverging concepts of American Indian demography. Many authors felt there were so few Indians present that someone else must have produced the great temple mounds (Tooker 1978). Others, such as Las Casas estimated greater numbers than would presently be accepted.

Today our methodology and sense of geography are much improved, but our impressions of prehistoric demography are still divergent (Ubelaker 1976a), reflecting the variability in research methodology and the inherent weakness in the baseline data. This essay explores areas of demographic interest in the Northeast in terms of the variety of methods available, the nature of the data, and the assumptions and limitations which must be considered in evaluating research results.

Paleodemography is more than just estimating numbers of Indians. Recent research focusing on aboriginal Northeastern prehistoric populations has investigated not only population size but such factors as village size, number of occupants per house, family size, population composition (ratios of males to females or of adults to subadults), rates of mortality or fertility, and population growth. Much of this research overlaps strongly into areas of prehistoric nutrition, subsistence, epidimiology, and population dynamics. Scholarly publications on these subjects date back into the nineteenth century with Morse's 1822 compilation of American Indian statistical data, Schoolcraft's 1851-1857 somewhat disorganized but valuable encyclopedic volumes, and various works on Indian history, such as DeForest (1853) and Ruttenber (1872). Research in these areas intensified with the founding of the Bureau of American Ethnology, the publication of the first *Handbook of North American Indians* (Hodge 1907-1910), Mooney's 1928 essay on "The aboriginal population of America north of Mexico," and Kroeber's 1939 "Cultural and natural areas of native North America." The trend has continued with numerous subsequent studies based on both ethnological and archaeological data.

Since 1970 numerous publications have appeared offering new direction to paleodemographic studies in the Northeast. Notable among these are works by Asch (1976), Buikstra (1976), Cook (1976), Feest (1973), Lovejoy et al. (1977), Mensforth et al. (1978), Moore et al. (1975), Snow (1980), Ubelaker (1974), and a variety of contributors to Volume 16 of the new *Handbook of North American Indians* (Trigger 1978). These publications and others in other areas illustrate a variety of approaches to paleodemographic problems, which can be grouped under two general headings, ethnohistorical approaches and archaeological approaches.

The ethnohistorical approach to population reconstruction was used almost exclusively in the early literature and continues to be useful today. This method turns to diaries, journals, and letters of contemporary observers and usually yields data on population size, dates, and severity of epidemics, but rarely data on family size, house size, etc. Data from such sources dominate early attempts at population reconstruction by Ruttenber, Schoolcraft, DeForest, and others. Cook (1976) relied almost exclusively on this approach in his recent treatise "The Indian population of New England," and it is used extensively in Feest's (1973) work on Virginia Algonquians and by numerous authors in the new *Handbook of North American Indians* volume on the Northeast (Trigger 1978). My own analysis of archival documents revealed that Mooney utilized this approach in his essay on "The aboriginal population of America north of Mexico," edited by Swanton and published posthumously in 1928. This work is of special historical importance since it was the basis of Kroeber's 1939 treatise on "Cultural and natural areas of native North America" and comprised the definitive statement on American Indian population size for decades. Mooney's sources for the

Northeast included the Jesuit Relations (see JR), the journals of John Smith (Arber 1884), Lawson (1860), and Strachey (1849), letters by Thomas Mayhew (1806) and other missionaries, and later interpretive works by Gookin (1806), DeForest (1853), and Schoolcraft (1851-1857).

The usefulness of this inductive approach completely depends upon the availability and accuracy of relevant documents. The approach assumes that early statements are accurate themselves or that they can be accurately interpreted. The limitations of this approach are numerous. By definition, an observation by a contemporary European observer does not extend into the prehistoric period or even to the time of initial European contact (see Chapter 1). Usually at least several decades had passed before the first serious observations were recorded. In nearly all cases, this was time for disease and cultural conflicts to have extensive effects on aboriginal demographic structure. Some early observers vaguely reference the previous condition (e.g. "they were much more numerous before the epidemics"), but such statements are usually general and inconclusive if present at all. This situation has led to considerable confusion in the literature. For example the Mooney-Kroeber estimates of aboriginal population size at the time of contact recently have been criticized extensively as being much too conservative. My analysis of the Mooney notes revealed however, that for many groups Mooney was trying mainly to establish the earliest reliable estimate of population size. For example, the published Mooney-Kroeber estimate for the Massachusett is 3000. Mooney's notes attribute this estimate to John Smith who said in June, 1616, "The Sea Coast as you passe, shewes you all along large corne fields, and great troupes of well proportioned people . . . if there be neer three thousand people upon these Iles [Arber 1884:205]." Mooney's notes acknowledge that Smith's estimates apply only to those people along the coast and they may have been more numerous prior to the time of Smith's observations. Similarly Mooney's published estimate for the Wampanoag is 2400 but his unpublished notes comment "we may assume that the Wampanoag, before their losses by epidemics, may have numbered at least 3,500 souls and perhaps more [Ubelaker 1976b:251]."

The second major limitation to the direct ethnohistorical approach consists of errors in the estimates themselves. Sources for error are numerous with early estimates but consist primarily of (1) reliance upon general impressions or estimates of others rather than actual head or house counts, (2) poor knowledge of the extent of the group described (e.g. the estimate may be for one or two villages when the group actually had many villages), (3) estimates made when the group was not completely assembled due to seasonal activities or chance events which temporarily reduced the populations, and (4) intentional falsification or exaggeration of the data for political purposes. Interpretation of these early sources basically boils down to a determination of the extent of the observers' familiarity with the group concerned and the reasons why the estimate is being made. Observations made by someone who lived among the group for an extended time are naturally more valuable than those of a passer-by. Estimates made by an early colonist who needed accurate estimates of the numbers of his Indian neighbors may be more reliable than those of the missionary who may have been trying to impress his religious superiors back home in Europe. It is largely differences in interpretation of such sources that lead to the widely diverging estimates of population size found in the literature. For example, Mooney flatly rejected estimates by Daniel Gookin as incorporating "his usual exaggeration [Ubelaker 1976b:249]." Cook regards Gookin's estimate of 3000 men for Massachusetts as "an apparent absurdity" that should be used "only with serious reservation [Cook 1976:30]." In contrast, in the recent *Handbook* volume, Salwen (1978) relies heavily on Gookin's figures.

Variance in the estimates of the general Northeastern population also reflects the factors discussed above. The new volume of the *Handbook of North American Indians* (Trigger 1978) estimates the number for the Northeast at about 250,000. The 1928 Mooney estimate for the equivalent area was about 208,100. Cook's (1976) estimate for New England was 71,900. Mooney's estimate for the same area was about 34,100 (see Chapter 3).

The indirect ethnohistorical approach consists of gathering ethnohistorical data for one group (direct approach) and then extending that data to populations in neighboring areas or in areas which are environmentally, culturally, or historically similar. Basically it involves applying data from one group to another and has been employed with such diverse data as population size, population density, male-female ratios, house size, family size and composition, and all aspects of mortality. In many instances where direct data are lacking it represents the only method available for supplying this information. Perhaps the best known example is Dobyns's (1966) classic study of depopulation rates and population size in American Indians. In this study, Dobyns established for several groups in the western hemisphere the ratio of population numbers at the time of European contact to the numbers at the point of nadir (maximum point of population decline). The result was a postulated "standard" hemispheric depopulation ratio of 20 to 1 which could be applied across the hemisphere. When Dobyns applied it, he produced a New

World aboriginal population size of just under 100 million and an average density of 2.1 persons per km^2. The merits of this approach are obvious. It enables one to extend data to groups and into areas where such data are not otherwise available. Unfortunately, the limitations are obvious as well. All of the problems mentioned earlier with the direct approach apply to the first step here in establishing the "standards" in the well-documented areas. An additional problem of sampling then enters when the data are projected. The projection assumes that the standard represents the true average figures for the hemisphere and incorporates all variability that existed in the total sample. This of course is difficult to accept without reservation.

In 1962 Naroll advanced a method for calculating population size from floor area within houses which has attracted considerable attention from archaeologists (see Chapters 1 and 3). Naroll studied the relation between floor size and number of house occupants in eighteen groups distributed worldwide and suggested that population size can be estimated by dividing the square meter floor area of all dwellings by a factor of ten. Of course the archaeologist must first determine what proportion of the dwellings present have been located and excavated, which structures were actually used as dwellings and not for storage, ceremonies, etc., and how many dwellings were occupied contemporaneously. Then the sampling problem enters when Naroll's data are extended beyond their sources. The ratio of floor size to population size apparently varies considerably with climate, available building materials, intended permanency of the dwelling, and such unpredictable cultural factors as whether the dwelling is also planned for grain storage and/or to house animals. Wedel (1979) has recently shown that the application of Naroll's formula to data from the Great Plains may be quite questionable.

The use of model life tables represents another indirect approach to prehistoric demographic reconstruction. Bocquet and Masset (1977), Petersen (1975), and others have argued effectively that model tables developed from modern, well-documented data offer important leads to the prehistoric situation. Use of these tables usually involves establishing one secure variable, such as mortality of adults from skeletal data, and then projecting values of child mortality, life expectancy, fertility, and family size by comparison with the tables. Weiss (1973) has recently developed model tables from archaeological sources and "primitive" contemporary populations which also have been used in this manner. Once again, assuming the model tables correctly represent their source populations, can they be extended to populations in different environments and from different time periods? The answer may prove to be generally "yes" but until more data are in we should continue to use this approach cautiously.

Archaeological approaches to prehistoric demographic problems are used most frequently. Numerous studies, including some excellent ones in the Northeast, have examined settlement patterns and the distribution of communities relative to their environments. Such studies yield data on where people lived and why and how changing environmental conditions affected this pattern. Archaeological data have been used to estimate population size from the number of settlements (Cook and Heizer 1965), number of houses in the settlements (Cook and Heizer 1968), size of individual houses (Naroll 1962; Wiessner 1974), number and size of refuse mounds (Ascher 1959; Cook and Treganza 1950; Glassow 1967), and detailed analysis of faunal remains (Grayson 1974). Problems with these approaches are well known and summarized with the following questions. How does one establish the temporal relationships of several adjacent settlements when dating methods have standard errors of many years? How many houses within a given community were occupied contemporaneously and how many persons lived in each? Do four adjacent settlements reflect four contemporary populations or one mobile group that moved four times? What proportion of the diet is reflected in nonperishable bone and shell and does that pile of bone and/or shell represent continued long term use or one great feast? In most of the archaeological approaches there are more questions than answers, but with increasingly sophisticated excavation and analysis and more creative use of existing ethnographic data, this ratio may shift favorably.

To many investigators (Howells 1960; Brothwell 1971, 1972), the most direct source of demographic information is the skeleton itself. Careful analysis of good samples of human skeletal material can provide data on life expectancy, death rates, age-specific mortality, male/female ratios, the demographic impact of disease, nutrition, and subsistence, and even population size when certain variables can be controlled. Numerous innovative studies have been produced not only in the Northeast, but throughout the New World. The quality of such investigations largely depends on the control of error introduced from two major sources, sampling and methodology.

Sampling probably produces the greatest error in such studies, although it is at times difficult, if not impossible to detect. Most skeletal samples are produced by excavation of cemetery areas discovered because of their proximities to known habitation sites, or due to chance soil disturbances caused by erosion, construction activities, rodent burrows, etc. The completeness of the resulting sample in a museum or university collection depends on the following factors:

1. Was the cemetery complete when excavated, or was part of it destroyed prior to discovery? This is especially important in salvage excavations around construction sites, reservoir projects, etc.
2. Are the total limits of the cemetery known and if so what percentage has been excavated?
3. Does the cemetery contain spatial variability and is this variability properly sampled by the excavation?
4. Did the population inter all of the deceased in the cemetery or were certain individuals or classes of individuals treated differently?
5. Was the entire excavated sample preserved or were some infant skeletons or skeletons in areas with certain soil conditions not preserved?
6. Were any skeletons lost or destroyed during the processes of excavation, removal, shipment, and cleaning?
7. Did collection policy eliminate any skeletons from the sample?

Any one of these factors, if not properly detected and evaluated, can render analysis meaningless. Excavation should aim to recover as large a sample as possible and/or to utilize sampling procedures which establish the representativeness of the material recovered. Excavation should proceed carefully to minimize bone destruction and to detect skeletons that are poorly preserved. Field notes should be copious, especially in recording those data that may be destroyed during excavation and removal. Museum collections should be carefully researched to reveal past collection policies or storage problems which may have affected the sample. Analysis should be problem oriented and allow for unanticipated problems. For example, the statistic life expectancy at birth should not be presented for a sample in which infant skeletons were not preserved. For the same sample, age-specific mortality figures or adult life expectancy would provide valuable comparative figures which were not affected by the missing infants.

Methods utilized in analysis can also introduce considerable error. For example, to estimate the age of the individual at death, physical anthropologists apply methods developed from modern samples. The approach is an extension of the principle of uniformitarianism. It assumes that the biological process of aging is the same today as in the past and thus modern data and observations can be applied to prehistoric skeletons. To estimate age at death for a child skeleton, physical anthropologists frequently turn to modern studies of the timing of dental development and long bone growth (Ubelaker

1978). For adults, we look at cranial suture closure, the extent of dental attrition, the extent of epiphyseal union, arthritic changes on long bone joint surfaces, vertebrae, and other areas of the skeleton, pubic symphyseal metamorphosis, ossification of cartilage, and histological changes in bones and teeth. Nearly all of the original studies of these age changes were conducted on modern material, since only modern samples are available with documented ages at death. Actually we know that considerable variability exists among different populations in the rate of age change in at least some aspects of skeletal and dental development. The rate of long bone growth in children varies considerably among different populations, as evidenced by the great variance in adult stature at the culmination of the longitudinal growth process. We know that non-White dentitions usually develop and erupt earlier than in modern Whites. Rates of dental attrition and arthritic involvement of the skeleton probably also vary considerably between modern and prehistoric populations. The methods are nonetheless used because they are convenient, or simply because they are the only ones available. Because it is impossible to obtain prehistoric samples of documented age at death, this practice must continue. We can look critically at and improve existing methods by (1) examining the nature of the samples they are based upon, (2) documenting the variability within the base sample and the accuracy of the method applied to its base sample, (3) establishing the accuracy of the method applied to a sample which differs from the base sample, and (4) guessing at the accuracy or directional error when the method is applied to a prehistoric Indian sample. For example, the McKern and Stewart (1957) method of estimating adult age at death from the morphology of the pubic symphysis is based on their study of casts taken from 349 male Korean War dead whose ages at death ranged from seventeen to fifty years. Obviously this method has limited value for females and for individuals above or below these age limits. To use it even for adult males one has to assume that the rate of age change was the same for prehistoric Indians as for young American males who died in the Korean War. We know the error involved when the method is applied to the original sample, but we do not know the error involved when the method is applied to other samples.

New methods of estimating age at death from dental and skeletal microstructure are now available and appear especially promising. The dental technique (Gustafson 1950; Maples 1978) involves preparing sections of teeth and microscopically examining seven structural variables. The methods yield estimates with standard errors as low as 3.6 years but have not been utilized extensively because many anthropologists are reluctant to sacrifice teeth, and because attrition rates are usually much greater in prehistoric samples.

Methodology based on microstructure of cortical bone has been used in prehistoric studies (Ubelaker 1974) and has received considerable attention in the recent methodological literature (Bouvier and Ubelaker 1977; Thompson 1978; Kerley and Ubelaker 1978). The original regression formulae (Kerley 1965) offer standard errors as low as 3.66 years and utilize counts of primary osteons, secondary osteons, osteon fragments, and circumferential lamellar bone in four circular microscopic fields located along the periosteal margin of the long bone cortex. For details of the methods, consult Kerley (1965) and the recent revision by Kerley and Ubelaker (1978). Additional methods are now available by Ahlqvist and Damsten (1969), Singh and Gunberg (1970), and Thompson (1978), which offer different approaches using different structures, fields, and regression equations.

The problem with all of the microscopic methods is that they are destructive and they are based on modern samples. The published standard errors adequately reflect the variability within the original samples, but the error involved in the application to a prehistoric sample remains unknown. Since prehistoric samples of known age at death are not available, it is difficult to estimate the magnitude of the problem.

One approach to this problem is to examine the error involved when the methods are applied to samples which differ markedly from the original samples the methods were derived from. The Kerley method is based upon his analysis of cross sections taken from the femora, tibiae, and fibulae of 126 predominately White and healthy U.S. military personnel of known age and sex. Recently I applied the Kerley method to a sample of skeletons of economically depressed urban Blacks from the Dominican Republic. The sample was collected in 1974 by the scientific staff at the *Museo del Hombre Dominicano* in Santo Domingo, Dominican Republic in collaboration with me. The sample is comprised of 158 skeletons of known age at death and sex which were removed from local cemeteries as a solution to space problems. Most individuals represented laborers who died in Santo Domingo. Most were born in Santo Domingo, although some had migrated to the city from the neighboring countryside or from Haiti. All were socially classified as Black or mulatto. Age at death and sex were recorded from cemetery records and were derived from national social security information.

In 1975, I removed complete cross sections from the midshafts of the tibia, fibula, femur, radius, ulna, humerus, and clavicle of each individual and later they were converted to undecalcified ground thin sections. Sections were eliminated from the sample which (1) displayed loss of bone from the periosteal surface due to erosion in the soil or fragmentation during the preparation process, (2) displayed excessive infiltration of soil or organic debris within the periosteal margin of the cortex, (3) were from cross sections which displayed evidence of pathological disturbance, and (4) were from skeletons of questionable age at death. The resulting sample was composed of sections from 114 femora, 108 tibiae, and 102 fibulae of 55 males and 59 females whose confirmed ages at death ranged from 15 to greater than 90 years. Ages were estimated using Kerley's (1965) profile chart and the field size recommended by Kerley and Ubelaker (1978). Estimated ages were then compared to actual ages to assess the accuracy of the Kerley method when applied to this sample.

Error of the estimates ranged from 0 to 47 years with an average error of 10.43 years. Forty-two percent of the estimated ages were within 5 years of actual age, 62 percent within 10 years, and 95 percent within 28 years. Estimates for females were more accurate than those for males. Average error for the 59 female estimates was only 8 years while the 55 male estimates were off an average of 13 years. Average error for individuals with actual ages less than 50 years was only 5.5 years, considerably less than the average error (12.6 years) for those over 50 years.

Based on this evidence, there is no question that the error increases when the method is applied to different samples. The impact of this error on demographic reconstruction is not severe however, because estimates above and below actual age tend to cancel each other in a large sample. The average actual age of the sample is 58.8 years, while the average of the estimated ages is 54.6. This comparison is especially encouraging in the female sample where actual average age is 59.5 years and estimated average age is 59.2 years.

Figure 5.1 compares the actual age distribution of the sample with the distribution of estimated ages, arranged in the form of a partial mortality curve. The difference between the two curves represents the error involved in our attempt to estimate demographic reality and hints at the possible error involved in our prehistoric estimate. Since the Santo Domingo and Kerley samples represent extreme contrasts, it is doubtful that the error involved in a prehistoric sample would be greater than that shown in Figure 5.1, and probably would be considerably less. With more studies of this type, perhaps involving samples from the Northeast, it may eventually be possible to devise special regression equations for prehistoric populations or to simply adjust the estimates by an established factor.

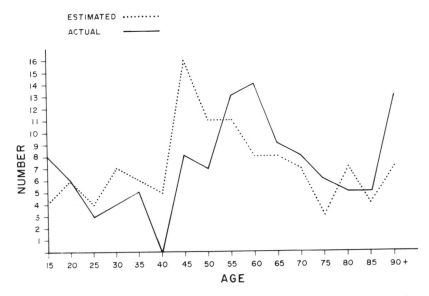

Figure 5.1. Comparison of the actual age distribution of the Santo Domingo sample with the age distribution estimated from the microscopic examination of femoral sections.

APPLICATION IN THE NORTHEAST

Although numerous reports of human skeletal remains appear in the Northeast literature, few contribute meaningfully to demographic understanding due to the limitations discussed earlier. Most reports deal with small samples that provide useful biological data on disease, morphology, or stature. They are not suitable for demographic reconstruction since it is not known how much of the entire cemetery sample they represent, or the size and composition of the living sample they represent. Doyle and Faingnaert (1976) and Faingnaert and Doyle (1977) offer detailed descriptions of such samples from Pennsylvania.

Simmons (1970) described a cemetery from Rhode Island in such great detail that it may be useful for demographic reconstruction. Here again, the investigation must assess the sampling of the cemetery and interpret how representative are the cemetery and resulting sample. Problems of poor preservation must be dealt with as well.

Probably the greatest potential for demographic reconstruction in the Northeast rests with the analysis of ossuaries. Ethnographic sources indicate that in some groups, bodies of the dead were assembled periodically for communal burial. The resulting "ossuaries" are especially valuable for demographic reconstruction since they are not subject to the sampling limitations of most cemetery samples. They essentially contain all of the dead from the contributing population, rather than the usual unknown sample from it. Unfortunately, while many ossuaries have been located in the Northeast, relatively few have been professionally excavated, and very few have been used in demographic studies.

An excellent opportunity for demographic reconstruction comes from Kenneth Kidd's (1953) excavation of a probably Huron ossuary in Simcoe County, Ontario. Archaeological details of the excavated ossuary matched so closely with Jean de Brebeuf's historical description that Kidd cautiously suggested they were one and the same. If so, the resulting sample offers an excellent opportunity to not only verify information in the historical account, but to add important data on sex ratios, life expectancy, and age-specific mortality.

Anderson's (1964) analysis of an Iroquois ossuary near Toronto presents valuable data on the number of individuals represented, the relative representation of different types of bones, and the age distribution. The ossuary cannot be traced directly to the historic record, but it clearly offers an excellent sample for demographic analysis.

Churcher and Kenyon's (1960) report on the Tabor Hill ossuaries, also near Toronto, demonstrated the importance of ossuary samples for demographic reconstruction. They estimated the number of individuals present in the ossuary, the age and sex distribution, as well as the size of the living population. Unfortunately, part of their sample had been removed by construction equipment prior to their salvage excavation and analysis.

A final example of the relevance of careful skeletal analysis to problems of prehistoric demography in the Northeast can be seen from my own study of prehistoric ossuaries in Maryland. In 1953 and 1971, two prehistoric Late Woodland period ossuaries were located and subsequently excavated on the Juhle farm near Nanjemoy Creek in Charles County, Maryland (Ubelaker 1974). The two ossuaries contained at least 131 and 188 skeletons respectively, mostly represented by disarticulated remains. Ethnohistorical and archaeological evidence suggests that each ossuary represents nearly all individuals who died during a culturally prescribed time period. After death, bodies were probably stored above ground and then later communally buried in the ossuaries. Like the ossuary examples discussed above, this sample is of special value for demographic reconstruction since it is not subject to the sampling limitations of most cemetery samples. We know that all of the sample was excavated, that most of those who died during that period of time are included in the sample and that few bones were lost due to soil preservation, excavation technique, museum accession policy, or other factors.

After a careful inventory of the bone elements present and a determination of the minimum number of individuals, I assessed age at death using several different methods. For subadults, age at death was determined independently from the degree of dental calcification of the teeth (Moorrees et al. 1963a, 1963b), dental eruption (Schour and Massler 1944), and femoral length (Stewart 1968). Figure 5.2 compares the partial mortality curves for one ossuary resulting from the three methods. Differences among the curves reflect the varying accuracy of· the methods, as well as differences in the sample sizes of the bones used in each method.

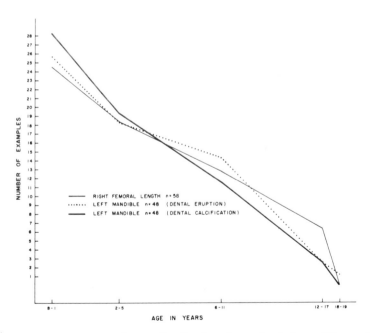

Figure 5.2. Comparison of age distribution determined from (1) maximum length and epihyseal union of right femora, (2) dental eruption in left mandibles, and (3) dental calcification in left mandibles from Ossuary I. All normalized to n=62 (Ubelaker 1974:50).

Adult ages at death were estimated using two methods, pubic symphysis morphology (McKern and Stewart 1957; Gilbert and McKern 1973) and a modification of Kerley's microscopic method (Ahlqvist and Damsten 1969). Adult mortality curves produced by the two methods for both ossuaries are shown in Figure 5.3. As with the subadult curves, two factors contribute to the differences shown, (1) the relative accuracy of the methods and (2) differences in sample size of the bones used in each method. I chose estimates determined by femoral length (subadults) and by microscopic structure (adults) for the final mortality curves primarily because they were derived from the largest samples, but Figures 5.2 and 5.3 clearly show the problems involved.

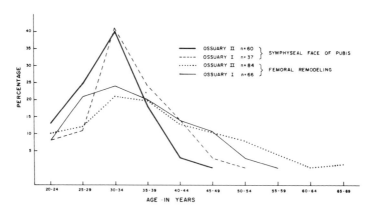

Figure 5.3. Comparison of adult mortality curves from Ossuaries I and II as determined from the appearance of the symphyseal faces of the pubes and the degree of microscopic cortical remodeling in the femora (Ubelaker 1974:58).

The resulting composite mortality data not only provide important information about age-specific mortality, life expectancy, and probability of death at different age intervals, but also an opportunity to reconstruct population size. Population size can be calculated by the formula

$$P = \frac{D \, e_0^0}{T}$$

where

P = population size
D = the total number of dead
e_0^0 = life expectancy at birth, and
T = the time interval in years.

For the ossuaries all of these variables have been determined except T, the actual number of years. Ethnographic documentation of similar practices in the Great Lakes area established the time interval there at about 10 to 12 years. In the mid-Atlantic area, the figure was unknown. An approach to deriving this figure for the Maryland ossuaries involves observation of bone articulations during excavation. Since the ossuary represents all individuals who died during a fixed number of years, the sample to be buried would have included individuals in various stages of disarticulation. Those who died just before the burial ceremony would be whole cadavers and would be represented archaeologically by whole, articulated skeletons. Some individuals would have been partially decomposed at time of burial. Their bodies would have "come apart" during the transfer to the burial pit and be represented by articulated but isolated skeletal groups (hands, feet, vertebral sections, etc.). Logically as the time interval between ossuary deposits increases, so should the ratio between disarticulated and articulated bones. Data from one ossuary suggested a time interval of about three years, which together with the other data suggests a living population size of 914 from one ossuary and 1441 from the other. These estimates suggest that several villages were burying their dead communally in the ossuaries and that the area occupied historically by the Conoy may have supported more than 7000 persons. These data are consistent with John Smith's village warrior counts in the early seventeenth century (Arber 1884), but substantially greater than the well-known Mooney (1928) and Kroeber (1939) estimates for the Conoy. The ossuary data do not necessarily represent the last word on population size, but they do indicate the value of skeletal analysis when certain variables can be controlled.

In summary, a variety of approaches to prehistoric demographic reconstruction and samples are now available. All of them have certain limitations, but show promise for the future with more detailed excavation, better control of the variables involved, and a more critical look at some of the past assumptions. Clearly future research must become even more interdisciplinary or at least more cognizant of data in related disciplines.

REFERENCES

Ahlqvist, J., and O. Damsten
1969   A modification of Kerley's method for the microscopic determination
       of age in human bones. *Journal of Forensic Sciences* 14:205-212.
Anderson, J.E.
1964   The people of Fairty: An osteological analysis of an Iroquois ossuary.
       National Museum of Canada Bulletin 193.
Arber, E. (editor)
1884   *Captain John Smith, Works 1608-1631.* The English scholar's library
       No. 16, Birmingham.
Asch, D.
1976   The Middle Woodland population of the lower Illinois Valley. *North-
       western Archeological Program Scientific Papers* 1.
Ascher, R.
1959   A prehistoric population estimate using midden analysis and two pop-
       ulation models. *Southwestern Journal of Anthropology* 15:168-178.
Bocquet, J.P., and C. Masset
1977   Estimateurs in paléodémographie. *L'Homme* 17(4):65-90.
Bouvier, M., and D.H. Ubelaker
1977   A comparison of two methods for the microscopic determination of
       age at death. *American Journal of Physical Anthropology* 46(3):
       319-394.
Brothwell, D.R.
1971   Paleodemography. In *Biological aspects of demography*, edited by
       W. Brass, pp. 111-130. Taylor and Francis, London.
1972   Paleodemography and earlier British populations. *World Archaeology*
       4:75-87.
Buikstra, J.
1976   Hopewell in the lower Illinois Valley. *Northwestern Archeological
       Program Scientific Papers* 2.
Churcher, C.S., and W.A. Kenyon
1960   The Tabor Hill ossuaries: A study in Iroquois demography. *Human
       Biology* 32:249-273.
Cook, S.F.
1976   The Indian population of New England in the seventeenth century.
       University of California (Berkeley) Publications in Anthropology 12.
Cook, S.F., and R.F. Heizer
1965   The quantitative approach to the relation between population and
       settlement size. *Contributions of the University of California Archae-
       ological Research Facility* 64.
1968   Relationships among houses, settlement areas and population in
       aboriginal California. In *Settlement archaeology*, edited by K.C.
       Chang, pp. 79-116. National Press, Palo Alto, California.
Cook, S.F., and A.E. Treganza
1950   The quantitative investigations of Indian mounds. *University of
       California Publications in American Archaeology and Ethnology* 40:
       223-262.

DeForest, J.W.
  1853   *History of the Indians of Connecticut.* Hamersley, Hartford.
Dobyns, H.F.
  1966   Estimating aboriginal American population, 1: An appraisal of techniques with a new hemispheric estimate. *Current Anthropology* 7(4): 395-416.
Doyle, W., and D. Faingnaert
  1976   A report on the skeletal remains of the McKees Rocks site, a late prehistoric village. *Pennsylvania Archaeologist* 46(4):11-27.
Faingnaert, D., and W. Doyle
  1977   A report on the skeletal remains of the Ohioview site, a late prehistoric village. *Pennsylvania Archaeologist* 47(4):8-26.
Feest, C.F.
  1973   Seventeenth century Virginia Algonquian population estimates. *Quarterly Bulletin of the Archaeological Society of Virginia* 28(2): 66-79.
Gilbert, B.M., and T.W. McKern
  1973   A method for aging the female os pubis. *American Journal of Physical Anthropology* 38(1):31-38.
Glassow, M.A.
  1967   Considerations in estimating prehistoric California coastal populations. *American Antiquity* 32:354-359.
Gookin, D.
  1806   Historical collections of the Indians of New England. In *Collections of the Massachusetts Historical Society for the year 1792, First Series* 1: 141-229.
Grayson, D.K.
  1974   The Riverhaven No. 2 vertebrate fauna: Comments on methods in faunal analysis and on aspects of the subsistence potential of prehistoric New York. *Man in the Northeast* 8:23-39.
Gustafson, G.
  1950   Age determinations on teeth. *Journal of the American Dental Association* 41:45-54.
Hassan, F.A.
  1978   Demographic archaeology. In *Advances in archaeological method and theory*, Vol. 1, edited by M.B. Schiffer, pp. 49-103. Academic Press, New York.
Hodge, F.W. (editor)
  1907-1910   Handbook of American Indians north of Mexico (2 Vols.). *Bureau of American Ethnology Bulletin* 30.
Howells, W.W.
  1960   Estimating population numbers through archaeological and skeletal remains. In *The application of quantitative methods in archaeology*, edited by Robert Heizer and Sherburne Cook, pp. 158-176. Quadrangle Books, Chicago.

JR = Thwaites, R.G. (editor)
   1896-1901   *The Jesuit relations and allied documents: Travel and explorations of the Jesuit missionaries in New France, 1610-1791* (73 Vols.). Burrows, Cleveland (reprinted by Pageant, New York, 1959).
Kerley, E.R.
   1965   The microscopic determination of age in human bone. *American Journal of Physical Anthropology* 23:149-163.
Kerley, E.R., and D.H. Ubelaker
   1978   Revisions in the microscopic method of estimating age at death in human cortical bone. *American Journal of Physical Anthropology* 49:545-546.
Kidd, K.E.
   1953   The excavation and historical identification of a Huron ossuary. *American Antiquity* 18(4):359-379.
Kroeber, A.L.
   1939   Cultural and natural areas of native North America. *University of California Publications in American Archaeology and Ethnology* 38.
Lawson, J.
   1860   *The history of Carolina, containing the exact description and natural history of that country.* Strother and Marcom, Raleigh.
Lovejoy, C.O., R.S. Meindl, T.R. Pryzbeck, T.S. Barton, K.G. Heiple, and D. Kotting
   1977   Paleodemography of the Libben site, Ottawa county, Ohio. *Science* 198:291-293.
Maples, W.R.
   1978   An improved technique using dental histology for estimation of adult age. *Journal of Forensic Sciences* 23(4):764-770.
Mayhew, T.
   1806   Of the progress of the gospel among the Indians at Martha's Vineyard and Nantucket. In *Collections of the Massachusetts Historical Society for the Year 1792* (1st series) 1:201-205.
McKern, T.W., and T.D. Stewart
   1957   Skeletal age changes in young American males. *Technical Report* EP-45. U.S. Army Environmental Protection Research Division, Quartermaster Research and Development Center, Natick, Massachusetts.
Mensforth, R.P., C.O. Lovejoy, J.W. Lallow, and G.J. Armelagos
   1978   The role of constitutional factors, diet, and infectious disease in the etiology of porotic hyperostosis and periosteal reactions in prehistoric infants and children. *Medical Anthropology* 2(1):1-59.
Mooney, J.
   1928   The aboriginal population of America north of Mexico. *Smithsonian Miscellaneous Collections* 80(7):1-40.
Moore, J.A., A.C. Swedlund, and G.J. Armelagos
   1975   The use of life tables in paleodemography. *Society for American Archaeology Memoir* 30:57-70.

Moorrees, C.F.A., E.A. Fanning, and E.E. Hunt, Jr.
1963a Formation and resorption of three deciduous teeth in children. *American Journal of Physical Anthropology* 21:205-213.
1963b Age variation of formation stages for ten permanent teeth. *Journal of Dental Research* 42(6):1490-1502.

Morse, J.
1822 *A report to the Secretary of War of the United States on Indian affairs.* A. Converse, New Haven.

Naroll, R.
1962 Floor area and settlement population. *American Antiquity* 27(4): 587-589.

Petersen, W.
1975 A demographer's view of prehistoric demogarphy. *Current Anthropology* 16(2):227-245.

Ruttenber, E.M.
1872 *History of the Indian tribes of Hudson's River.* Munsell, Albany.

Salwen, Bert
1978 Indians of southern New England and Long Island: Early period. In *Handbook of North American Indians*, edited by Bruce G. Trigger, Vol. 15, pp. 160-176. Smithsonian Institution, Washington, D.C.

Schoolcraft, H.R.
1851-1857 *Historical and statistical information respecting the history, condition and prospects of the Indian tribes of the United States* (6 Vols.). Lippincott, Grambo, Philadelphia.

Schour, I., and M. Massler
1944 *Development of the human dentition* (2nd ed.). American Dental Association, Chicago.

Simmons, W.S.
1970 *Cautantowwit's house.* Brown University Press, Providence.

Singh, I.J., and D.L. Gunberg
1970 Estimation of age at death in human males from quantitative histology of bone fragments. *American Journal of Physical Anthropology* 33:373-382.

Snow, D.R.
1980 *The archaeology of New England.* Academic Press, New York.

Stewart, T.D.
1968 Identification by the skeletal structures. In *Gradwohl's legal medicine* (2nd ed.), edited by Francis E. Camps, pp. 123-154. John Wright and Sons, Bristol.

Strachey, W.
1849 *The historie of travaile into Virginia Britannia.* Hakluyt Society, London.

Thompson, D.D.
1978 *Age related changes in osteon remodeling and bone mineralization.* Ph.D. dissertation, University of Connecticut, Storrs.

Tooker, E.
    1978   History of research. In *Handbook of North American Indians*, edited by Bruce G. Trigger, Vol. 15, pp. 4-13. Smithsonian Institution, Washington, D.C.

Trigger, B.G.
    1978   *Handbook of North American Indians*, Vol. 15. Smithsonian Institution, Washington, D.C.

Ubelaker, D.H.
    1974   Reconstruction of demographic profiles from ossuary skeletal samples: A case study from the tidewater Potomac. *Smithsonian Contributions to Anthropology No. 18.*
    1976a   Prehistoric New World population size: Historical review and current appraisal of North American estimates. *American Journal of Physical Anthropology* 45:661-665.
    1976b   The sources and methodology for Mooney's estimates of North American Indian populations. In *The native population of the Americas in 1492*, edited by W.M. Denevan, pp. 243-288. University of Wisconsin Press, Madison.
    1978   *Human skeletal remains, excavation, analysis, interpretation.* Taraxacum, Washington, D.C.

Wedel, W.R.
    1979   House floors and native settlement population in the central Plains. *Plains Anthropologist* 24(84, pt. 1):85-98.

Weiss, K.M.
    1973   Demographic models for anthropology. *Society for American Archaeology Memoir* 27.

Wiessner, P.
    1974   A functional estimator of population from floor area. *American Antiquity* 39(2):343-350.

6

PROBABILITY SAMPLING AND ARCHAEOLOGICAL
SURVEY IN THE NORTHEAST:
AN ESTIMATION APPROACH

FRANCIS P. McMANAMON
National Park Service, Boston

In 1976 William Lovis published the results of his attempt to use probability sampling in the densely vegetated forests of Michigan (Lovis 1976). Despite several methodological and technical weaknesses of his article (Nance 1979), Lovis's effort was commendable because he attempted to insert some quantitative support for his conclusions about the population of archaeological resources within his study area. Northeastern archaeologists can learn from Lovis's mistakes and improve their survey methods and techniques. One might reasonably have expected a number of articles discussing this topic to appear in the wake of Lovis's article. The results, however, have been slim (McManamon 1978, 1980, 1981a; Casjens et al. 1980; Thorbahn 1980).

This fortunately has not been the case generally for discussions of probability sampling among archaeologists. Notwithstanding a recent diatribe to the contrary (Hole 1980), several articles and commentaries have appeared since the mid-1970s reflecting increased sophistication within the discipline regarding the appropriateness and applications of probability sampling (e.g. Redman 1974). Cowgill (1975:262), Plog (1978:284-5), and Mueller (1978:109) have pointed out that the principal advantage of probability sampling is that it permits a quantified measurement of the reliability, or precision, of estimates based upon the sample. A refreshingly candid and clear discussion by Cowgill (1975) of the inappropriateness of probability sampling, or certain types of it, for some investigations has also done archaeologists a great service. Recognition of the weaknesses of probability sampling is as important as understanding its strengths. Probability sampling is in many cases unlikely to be an effective means of discovering sites. In addition, for study areas where sites are rare or spatially clustered, a probability sample lacking appropriate stratification will be both inefficient and ineffective for estimation (Redman 1974:22; Schiffer et al. 1978:2).

A second important point made clear by recent discourses (e.g. Read 1975; Thomas 1975; Nance 1979) is the crucial distinction between the sample unit and the unit of analysis. The sample unit is the unit selected during the sampling procedure. If a population consists of known sites in a study area and a sample of sites is selected for analysis, the site is both the sample unit and the unit of analysis. On the other hand, if a study area is divided into a sample frame of 1000 one-hectare quadrats and sites discovered within the sampled quadrats are analyzed, the quadrats are the sample units and the sites are the units of analysis. It is possible, as will be demonstrated, for quadrats to serve as units of analysis as well as sample units (Thomas 1975; Nance 1980). Distinction and clarity regarding these two kinds of units is essential. When sample units are not also the units of analysis, one is engaged in cluster sampling. Since estimates of population parameters are made using different formulas depending upon whether the sample is simple random, stratified random, or cluster, clear thinking about what the sample units are and what the units of analysis are is crucially important (Read 1975; Nance 1979).

The third point recently made clear regarding probability sampling in archaeology involves subsampling (Nance 1979, 1980). If inspection of a sample unit, such as a quadrat, is insufficient to discover all of the items of interest within it (e.g. sites of a particular size), the items have been subsampled. Subsampling can lead to biased estimates of site frequency if the site discovery technique employed favored the discovery of some kinds of sites over others (e.g. large vs. small), unless the bias is accounted for when the estimates are made. As a discovery procedure, subsampling also can be inefficient (Nance 1979:174). The likely success of a subsampling scheme depends upon (1) the number of subunits tested, (2) the area of the collective subunits relative to the area of the sample unit, (3) the area of the sites of interest, and (4) the frequency of sites within the sample unit. For areas like the Northeast where sites within sample units are not easily discoverable, the search procedures and discovery techniques used within sample units must be designed to detect at least the kinds of sites of interest for the planned analysis.

The investigation described and assessed in this article is an attempt to use probability sampling in the Northeast. One goal of this study is to estimate as precisely and objectively as possible the frequency of different types of prehistoric sites and activities in various parts of the study area. The potential problems for probability sampling of site rarity and spatial clustering (Schiffer et al. 1978:2) are avoided by careful, staged use of stratification of the study area. The unit of analysis for this study is the quadrat sample unit described below. This is not, however, another example of "non-site" archaeology (Thomas 1975; Nance 1980). Sites, as defined below, are identified and their frequency within a unit of analysis is regarded as a variable of the unit. Summary statistics (e.g. the sample mean and its standard error) can then be used to describe the relative frequency of occurrence per sample unit of sites, or sites with different characteristics. These in turn are used for making inferences about prehistoric activities and their general spatial distribution in the study area. The data presented and analyzed below were collected during the 1979 field season of the Cape Cod National Seashore Archeological Survey. Modifications to this data set are expected as analysis and data collection for the survey continue. Therefore, the summary statistics and inferences presented here can be expected to change, one hopes for the better, in future analyses.

THE CAPE COD NATIONAL SEASHORE ARCHEOLOGICAL SURVEY

The Cape Cod National Seashore (CACO), containing roughly half the land of outer Cape Cod from Eastham north to Provincetown (Figure 6.1), was authorized by Public Law 82-126 in 1961. The purpose of the Seashore is to provide current and future Americans " . . . the opportunity to enjoy outstanding scenic, scientific, historical, and recreational resources . . . and to gain a greater appreciation of this environment and man's relationship to it [National Park Service 1970]." Archaeological sites are among the outstanding scientific and historical resources of the Seashore. They have a unique ability to inform us about human population's relationships to the natural and social environment over long periods of time and about aspects of historic period social conventions and behavior that are often overlooked or distorted in written records.

Two challenges are presented by the Seashore's archaeological resources: effective management and accurate interpretation. In order to manage any resource it is necessary to know with reasonable accuracy the locations, frequency, and characteristics of the

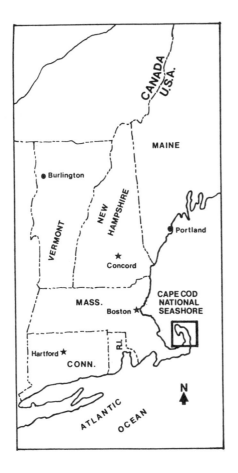

Figure 6.1. Location of Cape Cod National Seashore.

resource. At Cape Cod most archaeological resources are buried by sand or humus, and hidden by dense vegetation. A compilation of archaeological sites that had been discovered in plowed fields and eroded surfaces was made when the National Seashore was created (Moffett 1962). This sample of the archaeological record was drawn from a substantial personal knowledge of collections and eroding sites. Unfortunately, it is haphazard and insufficient as a data base to allow us to estimate with reasonable accuracy the locations, frequency, and characteristics of the archaeological resources within the Seashore.

Accurate interpretation of the archaeological resources also requires data about their locations, frequency, and characteristics. Inferences about the activities carried out at sites must be derived by studying the contents and structure of individual sites and comparing the characteristics of different sites and their chronological and environmental contexts. Accurate understanding of why the activities reconstructed through this analysis occurred is essential for informative interpretation. Data about site contents and structure in the 1962 archaeological report are insufficient for detailed reconstruction and explanation of past human activities within the Seashore.

GOALS AND FIELD STRATEGY

In order to meet these challenges, the National Park Service began a multi-year, multi-stage archaeological survey of the National Seashore in 1979. About 18,000 hectares (44,600 acres) are encompassed by the boundary of the Seashore. This includes marshes, heaths, cliffs, woodlands, fields, sand dunes, tidal flats, submerged land, ponds and streams. About 6900 hectares (17,000 acres) are beneath Cape Cod Bay or the Atlantic Ocean and could not be included in the survey investigation area. An additional 5300 hectares (13,000 acres) are covered by ponds, wetlands, or thick sand dunes. These areas could not be tested adequately by survey techniques and were also excluded from the investigation area. This left approximately 5900 hectares (14,500 acres) constituting the investigation area (Figure 6.2) and serving as the potential population for the survey sampling design. The area is densely vegetated. A substantial percentage of the area is owned privately in small acreage units. In other words, the area presents challenges similar to those surrounding site discovery, field orientation, and accessibility throughout much of the Northeast.

From the initial planning for the survey, it was clear that intensive field investigation of the entire project area was not feasible. It was impossible to investigate even half or a third of the area in enough detail to locate, examine, and interpret all of the archaeological resources. Soil and vegetation covering the resources require the expenditure of a large amount of labor for site discovery, examination, and data collection. Available funds were sufficient for intensive field work in a small fraction of the entire area only. Therefore, it was clear from the beginning that interpretation would have to rely upon a sample of the population of archaeological resources within the study area. This is a common situation in archaeological investigations and not a completely negative one. Being forced to study samples of the archaeological record can push archaeologists to squeeze as much inference as is legitimately possible out of the smallest amount of data. This is not always so, but it can have two

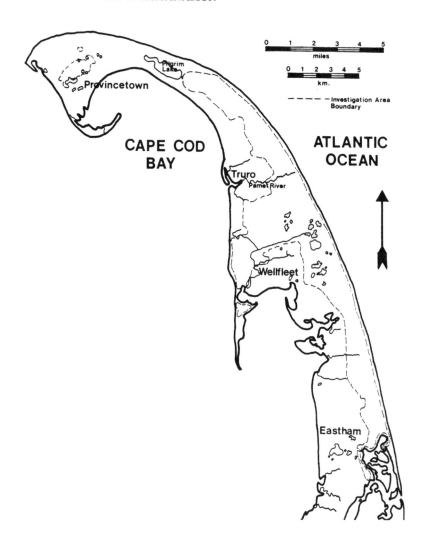

Figure 6.2. CACO archaeological survey investigation area.

positive effects: (1) more archaeological data are preserved *in situ*, and (2) funds expended on data collection are reduced, leaving more for analysis and interpretation or other projects. This happy circumstance results in more of the archaeological record being left for the improved research designs of posterity and a greater spread of scarce funds for appropriate research.

Selection of the part of the project area to be intensively investigated—the sample—could have been done in a variety of ways (e.g. Redman 1974; Plog et al. 1978). Strategies involving probability based selection and several means of judgmental selection were considered. As mentioned above, the value of probability sampling lies in the objectivity it allows in deriving estimates and judging their reliability. For resource management and a large number of research questions such estimates, if obtainable, would be invaluable.

Because both goals of the survey require accurate estimates of the frequency and locations of sites, a sampling design that would allow estimates the precision of which could be judged quantitatively was desirable. This required a design in which selection of the sample units involved a measure of probability. Since some information about the locations of archaeological sites in the investigation area was available, a stratified random design was chosen. Stratification was based upon the known record and environmental variables as recommended by Judge et al. (1975:121-122). Properly stratified samples yield more precise estimates than unstratified samples and often are preferred when possible (Cochran 1977: chap. 5; Redman 1974; Read 1975:58). In addition, archaeological resources in the study area were not expected to be abundant and evenly distributed, the conditions usually required for simple random sampling to be effective (Schiffer et al. 1978).

Locations of archaeological resources from the Seashore area reported in the Massachusetts Historical Commission Archaeological Inventory, the most comprehensive existing list of known sites in the state, were investigated to determine how the stratification should be arranged for effective sampling. The record indicated that over 80% of the reported prehistoric sites were located within 200 m of a fresh water source or a tidal marsh. Casjens (1979) identified a similar correlation for inventoried prehistoric sites in the Concord River valley. Areas with these characteristics were lumped together as Stratum I; areas more than 200 m from present or past sources of fresh water or tidal marshes were designated as Stratum II. Water sources and marshes were identified using 1:24,000 U.S.G.S. topographic maps and a 1962 vegetation map of the Seashore at the same scale.

Sample units were 100 m x 200 m (2 hectares or 4.9 acres)

quadrats. This size was selected for two reasons. First, the initial stratification of the study area differentiated between areas within and areas beyond 200 m of a past or present fresh water source or tidal flat. It was essential that the sample units could cover Stratum I evenly: therefore at least one dimension had to be 200 m. Within Stratum I, sample units were oriented with the 100 m edge along the boundary of the past or present water source or tidal area and the 200 m edge perpendicular to it, running the width of the stratum in order to cover all of the area designated Stratum I. The location of each unit was chosen using points numbered along a line that followed the edge of each water source. Numbers were selected randomly to determine at which point a sample unit would be placed. In Stratum II a grid of points was used to select randomly the location of each sample unit. These were oriented north-south along their long axes.

The second reason for the unit size was that it could be tested by a single crew in a relatively short time. Ordinarily, several units were completed by one crew in a day. Crews usually finished the same day all units they had begun, thus reducing the transportation time devoted to returning for short periods to finish partially completed units. Logistical considerations like this one are part of the practical side to any sampling design (Redman 1974:19-20; Plog 1978; Plog et al. 1978). Square quadrats 200 m on a side were not used because the smaller units allowed more sample units to be done.

A great deal of advance planning was necessary to make this strategy operational. The sample units were selected and mapped on U.S.G.S. 7.5 minute topographic maps. Next they were mapped on paper copies of aerial photo mosaics (scale 1:2400) the Seashore staff uses for recording property lines and land ownership. The air photo mosaics were used for field orientation. Whenever private property was included within a sample unit, the owner's permission to test on or cross over his land had to be obtained. These logistical chores occupied 50-75% of one field supervisor's time during the 1979 season.

SITE DISCOVERY AND EXAMINATION

Almost all of the investigation area for the survey has dense ground cover. Soil and vegetation make sites invisible without subsurface testing. Therefore, it is necessary to test intensively using a subsurface technique. Each sample unit was tested by thirty-two shovel test pits arranged systematically at a 25 m interval (Figure 6.3).

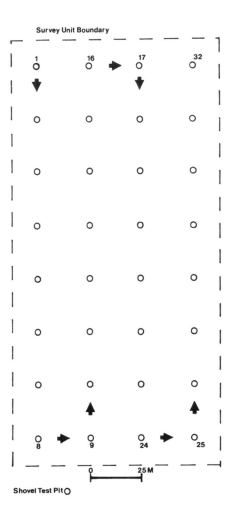

Figure 6.3. Standard sample unit showing the pattern of thirty-two shovel test pits.

The shovel test pits were approximately 40 cm in diameter and dug to culturally sterile glacial sand. Pit contents were screened through .6 cm (¼ inch) mesh hardware cloth.

As already mentioned, unless one discovers all the sites of interest within a sample unit, one is subsampling, not directly sampling (Nance 1979). This has a significant effect on the estimates that can be derived from the sample data. To address the potential subsampling problem in this analysis, two points must be made. First, because of the initial interval between the systematic shovel test pits, it is expected that sites with areas of less than 625 m^2 (25 x 25 m) are underrepresented in the sample. Sites of this magnitude might fall between shovel test pits easily, although some would have been discovered by the shovel tests. Therefore, the estimates of site occurrence based on the sample underestimate the frequency of small area sites. The estimates made in the last two sections of this chapter do not include any sites with areas below 625 m^2.

The second point is that the test technique, in this case shovel test pits with their contents screened, must discover sites effectively when they are excavated within a site area. The effectiveness of shovel test pits was tested during the 1979 field season. Within the site areas tested, 78% of the shovel test pits discovered artifacts. For sites with relatively high average artifact per test values, 100% of the test pits discovered artifacts. Alternative discovery techniques, soil augers (diameter 15 cm) and soil cores (diameter 3 cm), were compared with the shovel test pits for effectiveness (Table 6.1). This check of the techniques indicates that shovel test pits are much more effective than two alternative techniques and that direct

Table 6.1. Evaluation of discovery techniques.

Site Number	Shovel Test Pits		Auger		Core	
19BN300	2/4[a]	50%[b]	3/13[a]	23%[b]	0/9[a]	0%[b]
19BN301 (1st transect)	5/7	71%	11/18	61%	0/14	0%
19BN301 (2nd transect)	4/4	100%	5/11	46%	0/12	0%
19BN305 (1st transect)	4/4	100%	0/9	0%	0/9	0%
19BN305 (2nd transect)	3/5	60%	4/14	29%	0/14	0%
19BN291	2/2	100%	3/3	100%	0/3	0%
19BN169	5/5	100%	8/9	88%	0/9	0%
19BN284	2/2	100%	1/2	50%	0/3	0%
19BN282	4/4	100%	7/13	54%	0/8	0%
19BN292	9/14	64%	12/27	44%	1/19	5%
TOTAL	40/51	78%	54/119	45%	1/100	1%

[a] number of test units with cultural material recovered/number of test units dug.

[b] percentage of test units within site area in which artifacts were discovered.

sampling rather than subsampling of site occurrences (site size > 625 m^2) within each sample unit was accomplished. The test of different discovery techniques confirms the need for the inspection of relatively large volume tests in order to discover most prehistoric sites (Nance 1979; McManamon 1980).

Sites discovered within sample units were tested using additional shovel test pits. When a test pit discovered artifacts, four additional test pits were dug halfway between it and the next ones in the original thirty-two unit grid of shovel test pits. If no cultural material occurred in one of these pits, another was dug between it and the original test pit. This method allowed the consistent and systematic collection of a sample of artifacts from each site area and data to make rough estimates of site size. In the field, site boundaries were usually established when two consecutive shovel tests did not contain artifacts. The operational definition of "artifact" in the field and for this analysis is not limited to bifacial or retouched lithics and pottery. Also included are various kinds of flakes and lithic manufacture or maintenance debris.

TESTING THE STRATIFICATION

As already mentioned, stratification of a study area often improves the precision of estimates made from samples of the area. Stratification, however, poses a danger when it is based on fragmentary information. It is important, therefore, that execution of the sampling strategy be staged, and the appropriateness of the strata reviewed throughout the investigation. As Judge et al. (1975:89) have pointed out, " . . . stratification is an assumption, and must be tested for validity as must any link in the scientific process."

To test the reliability of the survey stratification, the sampling was arranged in stages. A 1% random sample of each stratum was drawn so that estimates could be derived to test the stratification. During the course of drawing the 1% sample, differences in the frequency of archaeological resources in sample units associated with different types of water sources in Stratum I were noticed. Care was then taken to insure that at least 1% random samples were drawn from each of the various subarea types noticed in Stratum I.

For the analysis in this section and analyses of site frequencies presented later, the unit of analysis is not the site but the sample unit. The frequency of prehistoric sites within each sample unit is regarded as a variable. The frequency distribution of values among sample units for this variable can be described by the summary statistics available for any frequency distribution. Here, and elsewhere in this chapter, the sample mean ($\bar{x}$), sample standard deviation (s), and standard error of the sample mean ($s_{\bar{x}}$), are used. Because the sample units are the units of analysis, estimates of site frequencies can be derived using formulas for simple random sampling as long as estimates are for individual stratum, as all are for this chapter. This method avoids the greater constraints imposed on estimation by cluster sampling, which would be the type of sampling in effect if sites, rather than sample units, were the units of analysis.

It is recognized that if these mean frequencies were used to estimate the number of sites within any given stratum the estimate would be artificially high. This is because most sites lie only partially within any single sample unit. It is a common problem facing archaeologists attempting to use probability samples for estimating site frequencies (Plog et al. 1978:395-400; Nance 1980). For this analysis the relative frequencies of different types of sites per sample unit are used for comparisons among different parts of the study area, avoiding the bias that would be injected if absolute numbers of sites were estimated.

Estimates of the mean frequency of prehistoric sites per sample unit for different parts of Stratum I indicate differences among them (Table 6.2). The differences in estimated mean frequency among the subareas are not clear cut because of the relatively large standard errors of the mean. It was possible, however, to use additional information from the 1% sample to distinguish among the Stratum I subareas according to the characteristics of the prehistoric sites found in them. The sites in the Herring and Pamet river areas

Table 6.2. Estimates of prehistoric site frequency for Stratum I subareas from the initial 1% sample.

Area	Number sample units	% of area sampled	Mean frequency of prehistoric sites per sample unit (68% confidence limits)	Revised stratum
Nauset Bay	5	5.8	.80 ± .58	IA
Herring River	3	4.0 (approx)	.67 ± .66	IB
Pamet River	2	4.6	.50 ± .50	IB
Ponds	5	1.4	.40 ± .25	IB
Streams	4	6.4	none discovered	IB
Hollows	2	1.0	none discovered	IC
Interior Wetlands	2	1.3	none discovered	IC

and around the ponds all had very small artifact assemblages (n > 8) and often were within site areas with larger historic period artifact assemblages. The Nauset area, on the other hand, contained a few of this type of prehistoric resource, but for the most part contained sites with larger prehistoric artifact assemblages independent of or with only small amounts of historic period material. The areas along streams and hollows and around interior fresh-water wetlands were different than both the former and latter areas in that they seem to contain less densely distributed prehistoric sites. None were discovered in these areas during the 1% sample.

The differences in mean frequencies of prehistoric sites per sample unit for the different areas, plus the differences among the areas in the kinds or inferred density of prehistoric resources provided both criteria and a justification for refining the stratification. The last column of Table 6.2 shows how the areas were grouped, Table 6.3 shows the recalculated mean frequencies for the new strata, and Figure 6.4 shows the locations of the strata. Logistical concerns and common environmental characteristics suggested that it was better to combine the stream areas with the rivers and ponds, rather than with the hollows and interior fresh-water wetlands. In the revision, Stratum IA includes a small area in the northern part of the study area just south of Pilgrim Lake. Only one sample unit was placed there during the 1% test sampling; however, that unit contained two prehistoric sites. The high site density suggested for this area by this sample unit indicated that the area should be considered together with the Nauset area as Stratum IA.

The mean frequency estimates for the revised strata suggest substantial spatial variation in the density of prehistoric sites. However, the standard errors of the estimated means are still quite high

Table 6.3. Estimates of prehistoric site frequency for the revised strata from the initial 1% sample.

Stratum	Number of sample units	% of stratum sampled	Mean frequency of prehistoric sites per sample unit (68% confidence limits)	$s_{\bar{x}}/\bar{x}$
IA	6	4.8	1.30 ± .74	.57
IB	19	3.4	.32 ± .12	.37
IC	4	1.1	rare	—
II	23	1.1	.04 ± .04	1.00

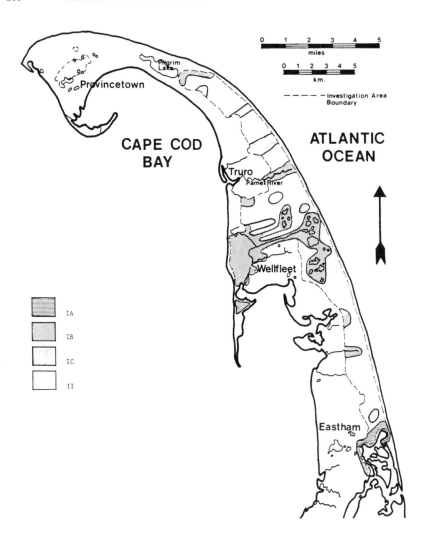

Figure 6.4. CACO archaeological survey investigation area schematic map of sampling strata (areas not to scale).

and the confidence limits relatively low. Following the 1% sample and analysis, a decision was necessary regarding the continuation of a stratified random sampling procedure. The question was whether enough additional sample units could be tested to reduce the standard error substantially and increase the confidence limits to a more reassuring value.

SAMPLE SIZE

Along with the choice of sampling procedure and sample unit size and shape, the choice of an appropriate sample size is necessary for the design of an archaeological sampling strategy. Early attempts to use probability sampling in archaeology involved the choice of a sample fraction based on feasibility or commonly used percentages rather than on the sample size necessary to provide estimates of a given precision. Better informed discussions of archaeological sampling and sample size (e.g. Redman 1974:19-23; Asch 1975; Cowgill 1975:263, 272-273) point out that the sample fraction is relatively unimportant. It is the abundance and variation of the characteristic being studied and number of sample units that determine the precision of estimates based on the sample. As mentioned above, archaeologists also have recognized that reasonably precise estimates of the frequency of rare items, such as sites in some kinds of environments, are likely to require sample sizes well beyond the capacity of most archaeological investigations. The problem of sampling for rare items is not unique to archaeology (Cochran 1977:76-77).

The 1% sample statistics used to test and refine the stratification also were used to calculate sample sizes necessary for reasonably precise estimates of site and site characteristic frequencies in the different strata. The last column of Table 6.3 shows the precision of the 1% sample estimates of the mean. The estimates are not very precise; in all cases the standard error is greater than a third of the sample mean. This means that the sample estimate of the population mean in most cases might not be an accurate estimate of the population mean frequency of sites because a wide range of values have an equally high probability of being the actual population mean. It was desirable to reduce the size of the standard error, increasing the precision of the estimate. This presented a dilemma. Additional sample units had to be investigated to increase the precision, and presumably the accuracy, of the estimates. Random selection of sample units within each stratum was again required. It seemed prudent to determine whether the number of additional sampling units needed to reduce the error to a reasonable level could be investigated given the amount of time remaining in the 1979 field season. Initially, a standard error of ±10% of the sample mean was chosen as a reasonably precise estimate and 80% as a reasonably high confidence limit for the estimate. Cochran (1977:77-78) discusses a method of calculating the necessary sample size for this situation. The following formula can be used:

$$n_o = \frac{t^2 \, s^2}{r^2 \, \bar{x}^2}$$

where

n_o = the estimated necessary sample size,

t = the z score corresponding to the desired confidence limits (for 80% = 1.28),

s = the standard deviation of the 1% sample (here used as an estimate of the population standard deviation),

r = the relative error desired (here 10%), and

$\bar{x}$ = the 1% sample mean (used here as an estimate of the population mean).

For sample size estimates in which n_o/N is appreciable the sample size can be reduced further using the formula

$$n = \frac{n_o}{1 + (n_o/N)}$$

Here N = the number of sample units in each stratum. Using the 1% sample estimates from Table 6.3, the sample sizes necessary to increase the precision and significance level of the estimates as described are listed in Table 6.4. The estimated necessary sample sizes for Strata IA and IB were small enough to be tested during the

Table 6.4. Sample sizes necessary for estimates of mean frequencies of prehistoric sites per sample unit with a ±10% standard error and 80% confidence limits.

Stratum	Estimated sample size
IA	38
IB	22
IC	unable to estimate
II	151

remainder of the 1979 season. The survey effort was concentrated in these strata. In all, thirty-eight sample units were completed in Stratum IA and forty-six in IB. The number done in IB was greater than the estimated necessary sample size shown in Table 6.3 because that estimate is based upon the size needed for the prehistoric site estimate. Greater variation among historic period site frequencies, which are reported elsewhere (Childs 1981; McManamon 1981b), required the larger sample size that was collected.

ANALYSIS OF THE SAMPLE DATA: OVERALL SITE FRE-QUENCIES

Sites were defined originally as areas that contained artifacts. Preliminary analysis allowed additional distinctions among the prehistoric sites. Twenty-six out of the total sixty-five prehistoric sites each contained seven or fewer artifacts, usually in one to three shovel test pits. Often these were within sites that contained historic artifacts. Due to the small sample from these sites, they were not included in the analyses described from this point onward.

Artifact density contour maps were drawn for each site with fifteen or more artifacts (no prehistoric sites contained between eight and fourteen artifacts) using the shovel test pit data. In several cases, clear spatial clustering within site areas was apparent. Boundaries between such clusters were drawn at the three artifact/test pit contour line. The contents and area of each spatial cluster are considered separately in this analysis. Several density contour maps indicated that some sites ought not to have been separated. Their assemblages and areas were combined for the analysis.

The concept of "site" is, as pointed out by Dincauze (1980: 40) relative, and critical to any analysis, such as this one, that aims to describe the general spatial distribution and frequency of activities. This analysis focuses on prehistoric behavior; therefore, the units of analysis should relate to episodes of behavior. The operationally defined sites discovered and examined during the field work do not necessarily do so. In some cases the density contour maps showed two or more spatial clusters of artifacts within a site area; in others, site boundaries cut through such clusters. The spatial clusters are much more congruent with the spaces within which activities, at least those that left a residue of artifacts, occurred. The assemblage of artifacts in each spatial cluster reflects to some extent the type, intensity, diversity, and duration of the activities.

The definition of behaviorally meaningful analytical units within or among archaeological "sites" as identified by field discovery and examination is an essential analytical step. Increasingly, archaeologists in the Northeast must deal with it as the data are investigated to derive descriptions and, ultimately, explanations of behavior (Knoerl 1978; Newell and Dekin 1978; Versaggi 1981). For this analysis each site included in the analysis is a spatial concentration of artifacts defined by the density contour maps, not by the field work alone. Each of these is counted as an occurrence for the frequency estimates.

The frequencies for each sample unit of sites, sites with shell midden (used here to denote a layer of densely packed shell), and sites with prehistoric ceramics, were used to estimate the mean frequency and its standard error per sample unit for each stratum (Table 6.5). The occurrences of these different site types were regarded as variables of the sample units. By using the sample units as the units of analysis, cluster sampling is avoided again. Because simple random sampling was used to select the sample units within each stratum, the statistical calculations of the sample mean and standard error of the mean are simple. Similar estimation procedures have been suggested or used in a variety of archaeological investigations (e.g. Thomas 1975; Rogge and Fuller 1977; Plog 1978; Redman and Anzalone 1980).

The differences among strata are striking. Stratum IA has by far the most dense overall concentration of sites. In addition, sites with shell midden or prehistoric ceramics are very rare in the other strata. These patterns suggest several inferences about the distribution and frequency of prehistoric settlements and activities in the study

Table 6.5. Mean frequency ± s $_{\overline{x}}$ of prehistoric assemblages per sample unit.

| | Stratum | | | |
	IA	IB	IC[b]	II
Assemblages with 15 or more artifacts [a]	1.13 ± .25	.02 ± .02	.05 ± .05	.10 ± .10
Assemblages with shell midden	.29 ± .10	rare	rare	rare
Assemblages with prehistoric ceramics	.25 ± .05	rare	rare	rare

[a] Estimates differ from those used to calculate necessary sample size (Tables 2 and 3) because Table 4 estimates do not include all kinds of prehistoric sites, only relatively large ones (number of artifacts ≥ 15).

[b] Includes data from 1980 field season.

Table 6.6. Sample percentage and acreage in investigation area.

Stratum	Number of sample units		% sample	Acreage in stratum	
	Samples	Available			
IA	38	125	30.4	614	4.2%
IB	46	678	6.6	3322	22.8%
IC [a]	34	295	11.5	1444	9.9%
II	23	1868	1.2	9152	62.9%
				14532	99.8%

[a] Includes data from 1980 field season.

area. The area of Stratum IA, only about 4% of the study area (Table 6.6), was by far the most densely and/or recurrently occupied portion of the study area. It was also the only area in which prehistoric ceramics and shell midden were discovered. Activities associated with ceramics, perhaps certain kinds of food preparation and storage, appear to have been relatively rare in sites outside of the IA area.

The preparation of shellfish meat for storage or consumption seems to have been rare outside of sites in IA. This is expected, because in most of the area outside IA, shellfish processing would not have been feasible due to the distance from shellfish beds. It is more interesting that even within IA, less than 50% of the assemblage areas contain shell midden. Within those assemblages with shell midden, the midden area is a small fraction of the total area. These figures might help place shellfish exploitation as an activity, and its importance to prehistoric groups, in a more balanced perspective. Although more diversified views exist (Salwen 1965; Braun 1974; Dincauze 1974; Luedtke 1980; Snow 1980:178-180), a reading of publications about coastal archaeological resources in the Northeast gives the very distinct impression that shell middens comprise all, or almost all, of the record (e.g. Ritchie 1969; Brennan 1974). The Seashore survey data indicate strongly that midden deposits are relatively rare even in the area where they are most common.

ANALYSIS OF THE SAMPLE DATA: PREHISTORIC LAND USE

The initial estimates of site frequencies thus suggested interesting variation among the strata, especially between Stratum IA and the others. Additional analysis of the contents and structure of the sites was performed to explore further the variation and to see whether it continued to correlate with the strata boundaries. The analysis, which is described fully elsewhere (McManamon, in press), involved two steps. First, the relative frequencies of lithic technology types such as bifaces, flakes, and decortification flakes, were used to form a matrix of Euclidian distances between each pair of sites. A cluster analysis using a furthest neighbor linking method was used to group together sites with similar contents. Following comparisons of lithic assemblage differences among them, these groups were interpreted to represent different kinds of activities, different lengths of occupation, or both.

The second step was an independent analysis of the structural characteristics of each site, for example, mean frequency of chipped lithics/shovel test pit (STP), shell/STP, and fire-cracked rock/STP. Expectations were formulated about the association between high or low scores for the structural variables and the groups of sites interpreted from the lithic assemblage analysis to represent a wide range of activities and lengthy occupation or relatively few activities and short occupation. The hypothesized associations of high structural scores with sites interpreted to represent long-term or recurrent occupations, and low scores with sites interpreted to represent short-term occupations were confirmed. A preliminary classification of site types was developed from this analysis. The types are neither immutable nor comprehensive. Future work is expected to expand and refine the present interpretation; however, it is used here to illuminate prehistoric land use on outer Cape Cod and to provide an example of further use of the estimation approach's usefulness for archaeological interpretation.

A discussion of land use ought to consider at least three characteristics of the use: (1) the kinds of use, (2) the frequency of different kinds of it, and (3) the spatial distribution of use in the investigation area. By kinds of use I mean types and variety of activities. The lithic assemblage contents and assemblage area structural variables suggest a wide range of activities are represented by the entire sample of sites, including lithic tool manufacturing and rejuvenation, food procurement and preparation, and nonlithic equipment manufacturing and maintenance. This range, plus the apparent occurrence of many of the activities at individual sites, suggests that human groups were not exploiting the area seasonally for one or a few abundant resources. The area seems to have been occupied year round. The almost exclusive use of lithic raw materials available in the local glacial outwash soil support this interpretation.

Additional analysis and more precise site examination is

needed to specify the kinds and range of activities represented by the assemblages as well as the seasonal and long-term variation in activities and their distribution. At this time, however, a number of hypotheses can be suggested about the general nature of activities. Five clusters (A, B, C, D, and E) formed by the cluster analysis suggest three patterns of activities. Assemblages in Clusters A and B indicate a wide variety of activities probably involving cutting, scraping, sawing, manufacturing, and maintenance. The wide range is inferred from the large percentage of flakes, which are often good multipurpose tools. The large relative sizes of these assemblages suggests long-term or recurrent activities indicating year-round or regular seasonal occupation. The high percentage of very small debitage in Cluster C assemblages and the overall small sizes of most of these assemblages suggest relatively limited activity areas with a concentration on late-stage lithic manufacturing or lithic tool rejuvenation. Cluster D and E assemblages indicate varied activities though probably not as wide ranging as represented by A and B assemblages, inferred from the moderate percentage of flakes and very small debitage. The small average number of artifacts from E assemblages suggests relatively short activities or occupation.

High scores for structural variables also can be used to infer the general characteristics of human activities at the assemblage areas. High scores for lithics suggest a variety of activities carried out over a relatively long single period or recurrently. For hard-shell clam, high scores indicate centralized, substantial preparation of shellfish for immediate consumption or storage. High fire-cracked rock scores suggest cold weather settlement or an emphasis on food preparation or manufacturing requiring fire.

Combinations of assemblages from particular clusters and high structural scores more definitely suggest particular activities or patterns. High structural scores indicate dense remains and suggest substantial activity. Their association with assemblages in Clusters A or B supports the contention that these are long-term or recurrent occupations. High hard-shell clam scores indicate relatively intense exploitation of this shellfish as part of the settlement's activities. A high score for fire-cracked rock with an A or B assemblage might indicate cold weather occupation in the site.

Cluster C assemblages, if they are short-term activity areas with an emphasis on lithic manufacturing, should be associated with high lithic scores, if any at all. Two out of three high structural scores linked with C assemblages are for high lithic scores, one high hard-shell clam score is the third. The high shell score results from a small midden area that might not be contemporaneous with the remainder of the assemblage area. The high lithic scores indicate areas at which activities common to C assemblages occurred more intensively or in a more confined area.

Cluster D assemblages with high scores suggest activities and occupations similar to those described for A and B assemblages except that the activities probably were less varied. High structural scores are not expected with Cluster E assemblages. Their negative correlation is supported by the results of the observed versus expected comparison. E assemblages seem to reflect short duration, limited activities.

Estimates can be made of the frequency of the activities or patterns of activity using the method discussed in the first section of the analysis (Table 6.7). The relative frequency per unit of area can be used to compare the patterns of activities in different parts of the investigation area. As a whole, Stratum IA has most of the prehistoric assemblages discovered during the 1979 field season. A comparison of the assemblages from the two parts of IA, however, indicates they contain different kinds of assemblages.

The site types represented at Nauset indicate a wide range of activities and settlement types occurred there. Some activities, such as hard-shell clam exploitation, might not have occurred elsewhere in the study area. There is no preponderant activity or type of settlement, although long-term or recurrent occupations tend to occur in the southernmost section and around Salt Pond Bay, with moderate-length occupations more evenly distributed (Figures 6.5 and 6.6). The concentration of settlements in the Nauset area suggests permanent, year-round occupation of this area at least for a part of prehistory. Permanent settlement, if it occurred throughout prehistory, would be contrary to the common interpretation that most human groups in southern New England moved seasonally to exploit various resources (see Chapter 3). The nature of prehistoric settlement in the study area, and Nauset particularly, must be investigated further. The outer Cape's natural environment, however, might have contained a variety of subsistence resources closely spaced, allowing human groups to exploit them from single settlements. Short-term activities or camps away from the base would have been likely, though such foraging, if it occurred, left few remains in Strata IB and IC.

The rarity of moderate-length occupations and especially short-term activities in IB and IC is surprising. Many of the assemblages too small for this analysis (less than fifteen artifacts) are from sample units in IB and IC. They also might represent short-term activities. Including them in the estimation formulas would increase substantially the expected number and density of short-term occupations in IB and IC. Further analysis of the small assemblages as well

Table 6.7. Estimated frequency of settlements and activities (80% confidence limits).

Area	Type of settlement or activity per sample unit					
	Long term or recurrent [1]	Long term or recurrent, possible cold weather [2]	Intensive hard-shell clam exploitation [3]	Moderate length occupation [4]	Short term [5]	Short term, emphasis on late-stage lithic manufacturing [6]
Stratum IA, Nauset (31)	.05 - .34	.05 - .29	.15 - .54	.29 - .69	.15 - .39	.10 - .34
Stratum IA, Pilgrim Spring (7)	rare	rare	rare	.03 - .34	.02 - .34	rare
Stratum IB (46)	rare	rare	rare	rare	.001 - .05	rare
Stratum IC (34)	.003 - .15	rare	rare	rare	.003 - .15	rare
Stratum II (23)	.001 - .20	.001 - .20	rare	rare	rare	rare

( ) = number of sample units in area
[1] Cluster A or B assemblages with high scores for structural variables
[2] Cluster A or B assemblages with high score for fire-cracked rock
[3] Assemblages with high scores for hard-shell clam
[4] Cluster D assemblages
[5] Cluster E assemblages
[6] Cluster C assemblages

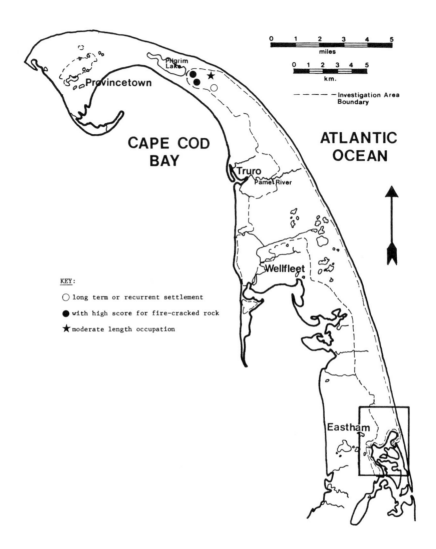

Figure 6.5a. Long term or recurrent settlements and moderate length occupations.

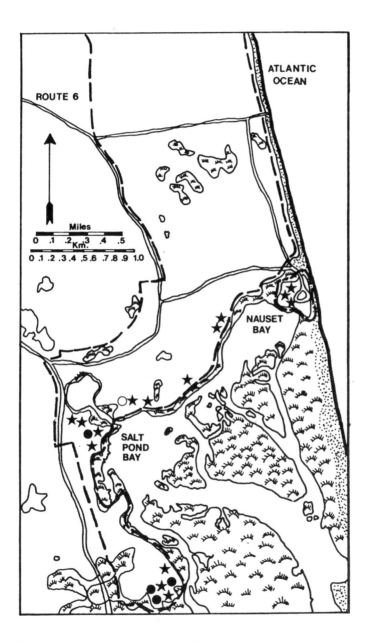

Figure 6.5b. Long term or recurrent settlements and moderate length occupations in the Nauset area (see Figure 6.5a for location and key).

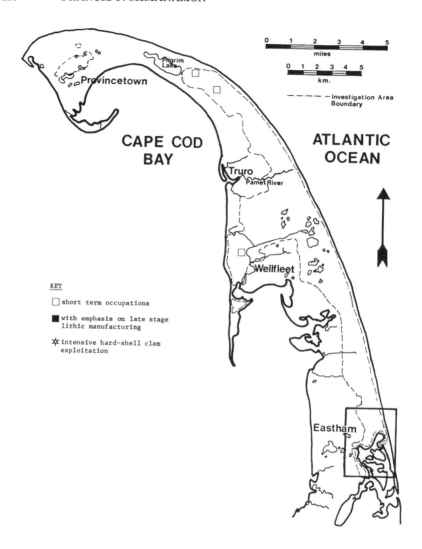

Figure 6.6a. Short term occupations and intensive exploitation of hard-shell clam.

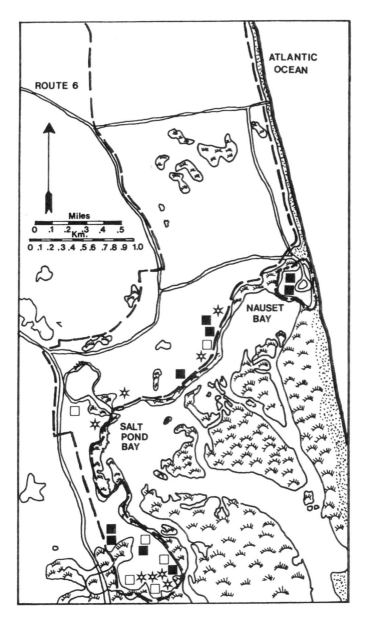

Figure 6.6b. Short term occupations and intensive exploitation of hard-shell clam in the Nauset area (see Figure 6.6a for location and key).

as additional sampling of IB, IC, and II is needed to improve the interpretation of activities and precision of the estimates for these parts of the investigation area.

The high estimates of the frequency of long-term or recurrent settlements for Stratum II are also surprising. The original model for prehistoric settlement implicit in the sample stratification predicted few, if any, large occupations in Stratum II. The estimates, however, suggest that Stratum II, since it contains many more acres than other strata, might contain by far the most recurrent or long-term settlements. Part of this is a function of the poor precision of the estimates for Stratum II due to the relatively small number of sample units from it.

More important, however, are the strata boundaries in the High Head/Pilgrim Spring area at the northern end of the study area. The somewhat arbitrary decision to end Stratum IA 200 m from a current or past water source or tidal flat might be inappropriate in this area. It also is possible that water sources available prehistorically in the Stratum II section of the High Head area have been covered by aeolian sand deposits that cover both prehistoric assemblage areas there. The two prehistoric assemblages discovered in Stratum II are in a sample unit only 300 m from the Stratum IA boundary. A large area of surface-collected material recorded by Moffett (1962) includes these two assemblages and extends into Stratum IA. For these reasons, plus the dissimilarity between the Nauset and Pilgrim Spring portions of IA apparent in Table 6.7, a new stratum might be defined in the High Head/Pilgrim Spring area. If the two sites on High Head were deleted from Stratum II, the estimated frequency and density of all kinds of prehistoric occupations or activities in it would be very low.

The results of the current investigation permit projections of site frequency and density and concomitant interpretations far beyond those possible with the earlier inventory data. It should be obvious, however, that much remains to be explored and refined. The interpretations made above might change completely. Certainly their clarity should be improved with additional data collection and analysis. Even at this stage, however, a relatively detailed empirical behavioral reconstruction can be hypothesized for prehistoric land use. This will serve to generate test implications for additional testing and refinement. It is important to note that much of the reconstruction would be impossible without the rigorous probability sampling strategy, intensive site discovery method, and detailed quantitative assemblage analysis. These are relatively new methods and techniques for archaeological research in the Northeast and other similar parts of the world.

It is the point of this chapter to stress the usefulness of probability sampling and an estimation approach for archaeological survey in the Northeast. To date, archaeological survey in this region has been almost exclusively discovery oriented. That is, the main goal has been to find sites so that one or two could be excavated, or because they were threatened by modern development. As already mentioned, probability sampling is not usually effective or efficient as a method for site discovery. Northeastern archaeologists should realize, however, that site discovery might often be an inappropriate goal. It has led archaeologists to concentrate upon the study of single sites or small groups of sites. Much has been learned about the characteristics of individual sites and some of the behavior that occurred at them. To understand subsistence, social and political systems that involved regular, in some cases seasonal, movement among a number of sites, however, the view from one or a few sites is likely to be insufficient. The extent to which interpretations of settlement and subsistence patterns in all parts of the Northeast ultimately harken to ethnohistorical data or remain uninformatively vague is proof enough of the failure of single site data on this score (see Chapters 1 and 3).

Estimation, because it can determine and quantify the frequency of a range of site types in a study area, has a great potential for describing and helping to explain cultural phenomena such as settlement, subsistence, and political systems. Estimates of the frequency of archaeological assemblages or site variables indicate how frequently certain kinds of activities or behavior occurred. Shifts in the frequency of occurrence over space or time and their correlation with other shifts ultimately can help explain the factors that influence human behavior.

Probability sampling and estimation are particularly important in the Northeast because archaeologists cannot expect to sample completely even relatively small areas of several hundred hectares. In order to learn the frequency and distribution of resources in areas of any significant size, estimation is the only approach. The preliminary results from the Cape Cod National Seashore Archeological Survey illustrate the potential and appropriateness of the approach. It requires careful planning and rigorous, dedicated execution, but the ability to learn with quantified precision the nature of the archaeological record in an area of interest is worth the effort.

ACKNOWLEDGEMENTS

The research reported here has been funded by the National Park Service through its Cultural Resources Preservation Program. This research is part of the Service's continuing effort to inventory, assess, and understand the archaeological remains under its jurisdiction. Special thanks for their support of this project are due to Ross Holland, Doug Scovill, Charlie Clapper, and Herb Olsen, Superintendent of the National Seashore. All of the individuals who have worked on the CACO Archeological Survey deserve thanks for their efforts. Of particular importance for the data and analysis presented here has been the diligence of Chris Borstel, Jim Bradley, Terry Childs, and Elena Filios who have served as supervisors for the project at one time or another. George Cowgill, Al Dekin, Bob Paynter, Dean Snow, and Chuck Redman generously provided advice and comments on earlier versions of this article or the Survey planning. I hope they agree with my use of their suggestions. Irene Duff has skillfully and patiently typed numerous drafts of this and other papers and deserves great credit. Carol A. Pierce and recently Adalie Mae Pierce-McManamon have tolerated my late hours and forgotten chores because of the Survey. My thanks to all of them and the unnamed others for their help.

REFERENCES

Asch, D.L.
1975   On sample size problems and the uses of nonprobabilistic sampling. In *Sampling in archaeology*, edited by J.W. Mueller, pp. 170-191. University of Arizona Press, Tucson.
Braun, D.P.
1974   Explanatory models for the evolution of coastal adaptation in prehistoric eastern New England. *American Antiquity* 39(4):582-596.
Brennan, L.A.
1974   The lower Hudson: A decade of shell middens. *Archaeology of Eastern North America* 2(1):81-93.
Casjens, L.
1979   *Archaeological site catchments and settlement patterns in the Concord River watershed, northeastern Massachusetts.* Report to the Massachusetts Historical Commission, Boston.
Casjens, L., R. Barber, G. Bawden, M. Roberts, and F. Turchon.
1980   Approaches to site discovery in New England forests. In Discovering and examining archaeological sites: Strategies for areas with dense ground cover, compiled by F.P. McManamon and D.J. Ives. *American Archaeological Reports No. 14.* University of Missouri, Columbia.
Childs, S.T.
1981   *Historic period land use and settlement on outer Cape Cod: An exploratory analysis from the 1979 survey of Cape Cod National Seashore.* Unpublished manuscript on file, Division of Cultural Resources, North Atlantic Regional Office, National Park Service, Boston.

Cochran, W.G.
   1977   *Sampling techniques* (3rd ed.). Wiley, New York.
Cowgill, G.L.
   1975   A selection of samplers: Comments on archaeo-statistics. In *Sampling in archaeology*, edited by J.W. Mueller, pp. 258-274. University of Arizona Press, Tucson.
Dincauze, D.F.
   1974   An introduction to archaeology in the greater Boston area. *Archaeology of Eastern North America* 2:39-66.
   1980   Research priorities in northeastern archaeology. In Proceedings of the conference on northeastern archaeology, edited by James A. Moore. *Research Reports* 19:29-48. Department of Anthropology, University of Massachusetts, Amherst.
Hole, B.L.
   1980   Sampling in archaeology: A critique. *Annual Review of Anthropology* 9:217-234.
Judge, W.J., J.J. Ebert, and R.K. Hitchcock
   1975   Sampling in regional archaeological survey. In *Sampling in archaeology*, edited by J.W. Mueller, pp. 82-123. University of Arizona Press, Tucson.
Knoerl, J.J.
   1980   Site resolution and intra-site variability. In Discovering and examining archaeological sites: Strategies for areas with dense ground cover, compiled by F.P. McManamon and D.J. Ives. *American Archaeological Reports No. 14.* University of Missouri, Columbia.
Lovis, W.A.
   1976   Quartersections and forests: An example of probability sampling in the northeastern woodlands. *American Antiquity* 41(3):364-372.
Luedtke, B.
   1980   The Calf Island site and the Late Prehistoric period in Boston Harbor. *Man in the Northeast* 20:25-76.
McManamon, F.P.
   1978   Site identification in the Northeast. In Conservation archaeology in the Northeast: Toward a research orientation, edited by A.E. Spiess, pp. 79-86. *Peabody Museum Bulletin* 3.
   1980   Site discovery: Past and future directions. In Discovering and examining archaeological sites: Strategies for areas with dense ground cover, compiled by F.P. McManamon and D.J. Ives. *American Archaeological Reports No. 14.* University of Missouri, Columbia.
   1981a Parameter estimation and site discovery in the Northeast. *Contract Abstracts and CRM Archeology* 1(3):43-48.
   1981b The Cape Cod National Seashore archeological survey. *Man in the Northeast* 22: (in press).
   n.d.   Prehistoric land use on outer Cape Cod. *Journal of Field Archaeology* 9(1): (in press).

Moffett, R.
1962   *Notes on the archeological survey of the Cape Cod National Seashore.*
        Unpublished manuscript on file, Division of Cultural Resources, North
        Atlantic Regional Office, National Park Service, Boston.
Mueller, J.W.
1978   Pioneering practitioners of contemporary sampling: Comments on the
        state of the art in New England cultural resource management. In
        Conservation archaeology in the Northeast: Toward a research orienta-
        tion, edited by A.E. Spiess, pp. 107-112. *Peabody Museum Bulletin*
        3.
Nance, J.D.
1979   Regional subsampling and statistical inference in forested habitats.
        American Antiquity 44:172-176.
1980   Non-site sampling in the lower Cumberland River valley, Kentucky.
        Mid-Continental Journal of Archaeology 5(2):169-191.
National Park Service
1970   *Cape Cod National Seashore master plan.* Unpublished manuscript on
        file, Division of Cultural Resources, North Atlantic Regional Office,
        National Park Service, Boston.
Newell, R.R., and A.A. Dekin, Jr.
1978   An integrative strategy for the definition of behaviorally meaningful
        archaeological units. *Palaeohistoria* 20:7-38.
Plog, S.
1978   Sampling in archaeological surveys: A critique. *American Antiquity*
        43:280-285.
Plog, S., F. Plog, and W. Wait
1978   Decision making in modern surveys. In *Advances in archaeological
        method and theory* 1:384-421, edited by M.B. Schiffer. Academic
        Press, New York.
Read, D.W.
1975   Regional sampling. In *Sampling in Archaeology*, edited by J.W.
        Mueller, pp. 45-60. University of Arizona Press, Tucson.
Redman, C.L.
1974   Archeological sampling strategies. *Addison-Wesley Modular Publica-
        tion in Anthropology No. 55.*
Redman, C.L., and R.D. Anzalone
1980   Discovering architectural patterning at a complex site. *American
        Antiquity* 45(2):284-290.
Ritchie, W.A.
1969   *The archaeology of Martha's Vineyard.* Natural History Press, Garden
        City, New York.
Rogge, A.E., and S.L. Fuller
1977   Probabilistic survey sampling: Making parameter estimates. In *Conser-
        vation archaeology*, edited by M.B. Schiffer and G.J. Gummerman,
        pp. 227-238. Academic Press, New York.

Salwen, B.
  1965   *Sea levels and the Archaic archaeology of the northeast coast of the United States.* Ph.D. dissertation, Department of Anthropology, Columbia University. University Microfilms No. 65-13,990, Ann Arbor.
Schiffer, M.B., A. Sullivan, and T. Klinger
  1978   The design of archaeological surveys. *World Archaeology* 10(1):2-28.
Snow, D.R.
  1980   *The archaeology of New England.* Academic Press, New York.
Thomas, D.H.
  1975   Nonsite sampling in archaeology: Up the creek without a site. In *Sampling in archaeology*, edited by J.W. Mueller, pp. 61-81. University of Arizona, Tucson.
Thorbahn, P.
  1980   Site survey in New England: A field experiment in sampling theory and research design. In Discovering and examining archaeological sites: Strategies for areas with dense ground cover, compiled by F.P. McManamon and D.J. Ives. *American Archaeological Reports No. 14.* University of Missouri, Columbia.
Versaggi, N.M.
  1980   The analysis of intra-site variability. *Contract Abstracts and CRM Archeology* 1(3):31-39.

7

BIOCULTURAL ADAPTATION: NEW DIRECTIONS IN NORTHEASTERN ANTHROPOLOGY

D.L. SCHINDLER, G.J. ARMELAGOS, and M.P. BUMSTED
*University of Massachusetts
at Amherst*

Human skeletal remains have been underutilized in reconstructing the adaptations of prehistoric populations. Traditionally, skeletal material has been used to assess the racial affinities of prehistoric groups without considering other dimensions such as their adaptations. Often, physical anthropologists have not extended their analysis beyond morphological considerations. This limited use of skeletal material has been characteristic of American archaeology in general and Northeastern archaeology in particular. We will attempt to (1) examine the historical factors that influenced the typological racial approach in analyzing skeletal material, (2) suggest an alternative methodology for analysis of material that focuses on biocultural adaptation, (3) illustrate the importance of integrating archaeology and biological anthropology in the biocultural perspective, and (4) examine the potential of a biocultural perspective for research in the Northeast.

TYPOLOGICAL ANALYSIS OF SKELETAL POPULATION

One of the essential questions of early archaeological analyses centered around the intersite relationships of excavated materials. The standard method of analysis entailed typological reconstruction of diagnostic artifacts after which temporal and chronological comparisons were made with other collections of artifacts. When artifacts or groups of artifacts were determined to be similar, the assumption was made that this similarity reflected a general relationship between the artifacts and between the people making them. Unfortunately, many sites lacked diagnostic artifacts and archaeologists were therefore unable to determine the relationships between sites. However, skeletal material was recovered in many of these sites. Physical anthropologists, eager to accumulate collections of skeletal material, offered to undertake a racial analysis that could be used to establish relationships between populations. Typological similarities were used to establish affinities between populations, and these biological affinities were then used to reconstruct the culture history for the area.

The cranial index was, and remains, the most frequently used skeletal measure of biological affinity. The continued use of the cranial index is surprising, because as early as 1911, Franz Boas demonstrated the instability of the cephalic index and its inappropriate use in racial analysis. Specifically, he showed that the cephalic indices of immigrant family members born and raised in the New World were significantly different from those of siblings born and raised in Europe.

From 1925 until the late 1940s, E. A. Hooton developed a method of typological analysis that greatly influenced the study of skeletal biology. Hooton believed that an individual could be typed with respect to racial morphology, and that this information would reveal the biological history of the population. Hooton's (1930) *The Indians of Pecos Pueblo*, a study in which he examined the racial history of an archaeological population, was an influential classic of the period. As an example of the extent to which the racial-typological approach could be stretched, Hooton defined a "pseudo-negroid" type within the Pecos Pueblo population. He was cautious in stating that an "undiluted Negro type" would obviously be different from the "full African Negro type" and that there need not be a biological link between these types. However, according to Hooton these similarities existed and demanded explanation. Hooton succumbed to the obvious interpretation by stating that the presence of "pseudo-negroids" could be explained as a result of "earlier invaders who worked their way up Northeast Asia across the Bering Straits down the New World, and carried with them some minor infusion of Negroid blood which had trickled in from the tropical parts of the Old World [Hooton 1930:356]." Many more recent investigators have also, unfortunately, fallen prey to similarly "obvious" interpretations.

During the early 1950s there were significant changes in the race concept as physical anthropologists incorporated the concept of population into their methodological framework. One might have expected significant shifts in methodology in which populations and mechanisms for altering their structure (natural selection, mutation, gene flow, and drift) would gradually become the focus of physical anthropological studies. However, just as human biologists maintained their traditional focus on taxonomy following the Darwinian revolution, the development of population biology did not drastically alter the approach of the physical anthropologist.

The racial history of Amerindian populations, beginning with George Neumann (1952) and through the reanalysis by Bass (1964) and Long (1966), continued to be a major focus of study. In an attempt to explain the peopling of the New World, Neumann developed a model containing essentially three levels. At a broad continental level, Neumann placed all Amerindian populations within what has been traditionally referred to as the Mongoloid subspecies of *Homo sapiens*. Neumann suggested that there were several waves of immigration into the New World. As each new wave entered, two situations were possible. As a new group moved into the center, or core area (of more dense habitation), it would perhaps mix with previous inhabitants. In general however, the older groups (inhabitants) would move out into marginal or peripheral areas before such contacts developed. Thus, all groups remained relatively distinctive, or morphologically "pure." Within a temporal framework, he proposed that all Amerindian populations could be dealt with in terms of (1) an earlier phylogenetically more primitive Paleoamerind, (2) a more recent derived or modified Mesoamerind, and (3) a most recent immigrant Cenoamerind series (Neumann 1959:66).

In addition to this temporal arrangement, Neumann categorized the Amerindian populations into a series of eight races, according to their geographic locations, cultural associations, and morphological similarities. Groups of skeletons from relatively isolated cultural contexts formed the basis of the eight varieties. Mixtures were attributed to population movements of the eight main varieties into areas already inhabited, creating mixtures, but with the main types remaining essentially "pure." By applying both racial and temporal classifications simultaneously, Neumann was able to generate a descriptive typology of interpopulational variation.

Each of Neumann's varietal series of races was defined by a series of quantitative and metric cranial features which would, ideally, separate each race from every other. To illustrate Neumann's classification, it is useful to consider one of his types that is relevant to Northeastern archaeology. The Lenapid variety was a relatively late arrival in the northeastern woodland area, and was supposedly preceded by the Otamid population in the northern Plains, Minnesota, central Illinois, the Ohio Valley, New York State, and in New

England. The Lenapid people, according to Neumann, can be described as having relatively large skulls with a cranial index of 75.39. The cranial proportions are at the lower border of mesocrania and high in relation to cranial length. Viewed from above, the vault is ovoid to ellipsoid in form but never as full as the European cranium in the temporal region. They are above the medium level in muscularity, brow ridges, slope of the frontal bone, and position of the occiput.

The Lenapid face is moderately rugged and is considered moderate in size when compared to the brain case. Prognathism is submedium to medium and the mandibles tend to be moderate to large, having a bilateral chin with only a small degree of gonial eversion. The subjective nature (e.g. "submedium to medium" prognathism) of such descriptions is obvious and lacks any interpretive value. The inadequacies of such analytical procedures are discussed more fully below.

While no attempts were made to determine the relationships of such features to one another, or the nature of their intrapopulational variation, such anatomical features were defined as racial because they appeared to distinguish populations. Such definitions provide no explanations of the traits themselves. Once a morphological feature becomes defined as representing a specific racial type, the only possible explanation of its occurrence in other populations is racial admixture as a result of migration. This view incorrectly portrays human populations as internally static units, changing only as a function of gene flow.

In 1959, Edward Hunt, a student of Hooton, presented an extremely critical evaluation of Hooton's typological analysis, which had a significant impact on the use of typology. Hunt could find no genetic reason "why putatively 'ancestral' morphological types should persist in a hybrid population more often than one might expect by chance [Hunt 1959:81]." Hunt was especially critical of the use of morphological types from geographically distant populations in establishing cultural history. On the other hand, Hunt stated that "where chronology and cultural affiliation are well known, it is still possible to justify the limited use of regional physical types for historical purposes [Hunt 1959:74]." Specifically, Hunt was impressed with Neumann's classification of North American cranial material which, he noted, was based on Neumann's personal study of 10,000 skulls. Since Neumann's study was based on samples with an archaeological context, rather than the individual crania, Hunt (1959:74) found his analysis "provisionally convincing." It should be noted, however, that Neumann's actual analysis utilized only a small number of the total 10,000 crania in the formulation of his classification. For example, his Otamid variety was based on measurements from eighteen crania, while another variety was based on fifteen specimens.

A number of researchers have attempted to extend the Neumann classification through the use of more sophisticated statistical analyses (Aikens 1967; Bass 1964; Long 1966; Wilkinson 1971; Robbins and Neumann 1972). William Bass's (1964) analysis of the relationship between the Plains populations originally described by Neumann, for example, is the first of a series of reanalyses of Neumann's original classification. Although Bass criticized Neumann for serious inadequacies in his sample size and sampling technique, in addition to the overall limitations of his racial categories, Bass brought no new theoretical insights to the problems.

Long (1966) utilized Neumann's typological approach in an attempt to understand cranial changes in Amerindian populations within a microevolutionary context. Long undertook a series of discriminant function analyses and rejected much of Neumann's earlier typology, while at the same time introducing a new Iroquoian type. As an alternative hypothesis to Neumann's migration theory, Long proposed that "All relations discovered in this study can be explained by microevolution, occasionally involving genetic drift but more frequently involving the mixing of groups . . . [Long 1966: 462]." Long proposed further that "Multiple discriminant analysis can probably best be used to define major groups based on the degree of 'fit' of individuals from closely related cultures. Such groups would be homogeneous for 1) a limited geographic area, 2) a limited time period, and/or 3) a limited cultural or linguistic affiliation . . . [Long 1966:462]."

Propositions and definitions such as these, by rationalizing a continued focus on interpopulational variation, bring us no closer to an understanding of the nature of human variation than Neumann's original classification. There is no discussion of the features incorporated as variables into the analysis that would provide any means of understanding their relationships to one another. Such understanding is a necessary prerequisite to any consideration of their microevolutionary change. While Long pointed out that certain variables were given more weight than others on the basis of their interpopulational variation, no systematic attempt was made to determine the source or nature of the observed variation.

Other criticisms have been even more devastating. For example Hardy and Van Gerven (1976) demonstrated that Neumann's (1952) description of an Indian Knoll variety as Iswanid and the Fort Ancient Muskogid (Robbins and Neumann 1972) failed to consider the relationship of size factors in their racial assessments. Neumann and coworkers believed that these two groups were different because

sixteen of nineteen t-tests for differences in measurements were significant at the .05 level. Hardy and Van Gerven, using principal-
components analysis and analysis of covariation, were able to show
that by holding size factors constant, only four of the variables were
significantly different. Thus, two groups originally thought to be
unrelated were found to be more closely related after size factors
had been held constant.

With the increasing availability of high-speed computers a
whole series of multivariate statistical techniques has become available to most physical anthropologists. It remains clear, however, that
a theoretical and methodological orientation toward the analysis of
interpopulational variation has continued. As a consequence, old
measurements and taxonomies continue to be reanalyzed with little
new insight gained into the nature of human variation (e.g. Birkby
1966; Crichton 1966; Rightmire 1970a, 1970b).

Even when multivariate techniques are used, elements of the
typological approach remain. Interpretations of skeletal remains
that use racial categories, even in the context of multivariate methodology, often resort to typological analysis. For example, it should be
pointed out that when we discuss the origins of "the Negro" or the
"Asian component" of the American Indian, we are especially prone
to slip into typological thinking. Just as much of racial analysis of
contemporary populations can be typological when using genetic
traits, skeletal biologists can be typologists even when they speak of
the variation that exists within a skeletal series.

Finally, there has been an increase in the use of discrete traits
for analyzing population relationships. Skeletal biologists have utilized noncontinuous variants of the teeth and bony skeleton to
establish biological distances between populations (Armelagos 1974:
i-ii; Berry and Berry, 1967, 1972a, 1972b; Finnegan and Faust 1974).
However, there are serious problems in defining even the most common discrete traits that may be intimately related to nongenetically
determined (canalized) development (Howe and Parsons 1967).
Thus, the appearance of discrete skeletal traits may be as much a
function of nongenetic factors as genetic factors. For this reason, the
use of discrete traits to obtain genetic differences or similarities may
not be as useful as many researchers believe.

The use of discrete traits reflects the notion that the determination of racial affinity can best be undertaken with features that
are under strong genetic control. In this way, the relationship between groups could be measured in more precise genetic units. It is
not likely that we will be able to find skeletal traits which reflect
genetic makeup of the population. Indeed, even if we are able to
discover traits which reflect the genetic background, we may not be

able to assess racial history.

The validity of the genetic approach to the analysis of human racial history has been discussed in more detail by geneticists Weiss and Maruyama (1976). They assess the major views concerning the analysis of racial history and the methods used for such analysis, including the traditional approach (which used anthropometrics) and the population genetics approach. According to them, the genetic approach to reconstructing racial history is certainly no less ambiguous and problematic than anthropometry. They state, more specifically that " . . . not only is the classification into major races a tenuous pursuit, but . . . there really may have been no effective separation between the populations taken to represent the major races. What then is the meaning of genetic separation times? They really are nothing other than simple transformations of genetic distance, and add no definitive empirical support to any position regarding human evolutiòn [Weiss and Maruyama 1976:47]."

There can be little doubt that human osteology has been and continues to be dominated by an overriding concern for the description of biological differences between populations, the result of which has been an ever-growing number of taxonomic definitions. However, because little attempt has been made to systematically analyze the nature of skeletal variation within human populations, such definitions have served only to generate a series of broad typological categories in the absence of any understanding of the lower order processes such categories assume.

BIOCULTURAL ADAPTATION

The limitations of the racial model can be demonstrated in the interpretation of archaeological populations from a number of geographic regions. For example, in the Nile Valley racial typologies based on skeletal remains have played an integral role in reconstructing the history of the region. This approach, which has been used since the middle of the last century (Morton 1844), emphasized the cyclical resurgence of caucasoid and negroid racial groups to explain the cultural changes in the Nile Valley. Various researchers (Batrawi 1935, 1945, 1946; Elliot-Smith and Jones 1910; Morant 1925) have viewed two racial types as indigenous to the valley. In their reconstructions, they saw a lower Egyptian or caucasoid type and an upper Egyptian or negroid type as playing a crucial role in the history of the region. From their perspective, periods of cultural growth and decline were assumed to correspond to periods of greater and lesser caucasoid influence (MacGaffey 1966). The goal of research became the search for "negroid" elements during the various cultural periods (Van Gerven et al. 1973).

Recent studies cast doubt on our ability to invoke the waxing and waning of caucasoid and negroid genes as an explanation of the biological transformation of Nubian populations. Greene (1966), using sixteen discrete traits under strong genetic control, was not able to demonstrate any significant shifting in the frequency of those traits that would suggest major changes in gene flow. Analysis of discrete cranial traits (Berry et al. 1967; Berry and Berry 1973) reported similar findings. Furthermore, cranio-facial changes which have occurred during the last 12,000 years may be related to changes in subsistence. A decrease in robusticity of the entire cranio-facial complex, the movement of the face to a position more inferior and posterior, an increase in cranial height, and a decrease in cranial length all have been associated with changes in subsistence (Carlson et al. 1974; Carlson 1976a, 1976b; Carlson and Van Gerven 1977; Van Gerven et al. 1977).

A model has been proposed to explain these morphological changes. Carlson (1976a, 1976b) and Carlson and Van Gerven (1977) have suggested that changes in masticatory (chewing) function would reduce the muscular stress on jaws and teeth. The reduced neuro-muscular activity would reduce mechanical stimulation of periosteal membranes resulting in a decrease in robusticity.

While the analysis of subsistence change and its impact on morphology represents an important perspective in understanding biocultural adaptation, it would be difficult to apply these methods to the small samples in the Northeast. However, the analysis of materials from Sudanese Nubia and elsewhere demonstrate problems inherent in racial typology and suggest alternative methods which may provide a more fruitful approach to the material.

There have been numerous studies that use skeletal features to measure the biological adaptation of the group. In a model proposed by Goodman (Huss-Ashmore et al. 1982) skeletal indicators can be used to measure stressors that result in physiological disruption. In the Goodman model (Figure 7.1), the environment is the source of constraints (i.e. agents that can disrupt physiological stability), which affect the ability of the organism to adjust to its environment. The culture (as seen in technology, social organization, and ideology) provides a buffer from the environmental constraints. While the culture is often successful in buffering the individual or population from the stressors in the environment, it can also fail to inhibit the stressors and there are often instances where the cultural system itself is the producer of stressors.

The impact of potential stressors on an individual population

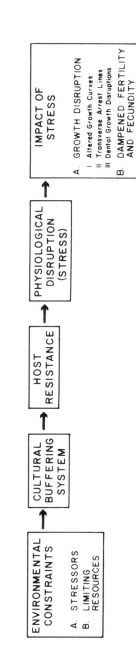

Figure 7.7. Model of biocultural adaptation (after Goodman 1980).

is mediated by a variety of host resistance factors. The general health of the individual and characteristics of the target organ can influence the magnitude of physiological disruption (stress). When the cultural system fails to protect the individuals, and their resistance is inadequate to meet the challenge of the stressors, then there is likely to be physiological disruption. The magnitude of the disruption will be determined by the magnitude of the stressor, the success of the culture as a buffer, and the ability of the individual to resist the stressor.

The analysis of physiological disruptions can be measured on a number of levels. For example, altered patterns of growth, shifts in fertility and fecundity, patterns of disease, and patterns of mortality have been successfully applied in interpretations of prehistoric biocultural adaptation. The intensity and thoroughness of analysis depends on the objectives of the researcher. In some instances, the analysis of a single pathological condition may deserve intensive investigation. The discovery of a single individual with hydrocephaly who lives to reach his or her teenage years reveals much about the culture. A hydrocephalic individual requires significant care to survive and the fact that the individual survived provides information about the society's ability to maintain individuals who are seriously debilitated.

While a single pathological condition can provide insights into a society's ability to care for the ill, the interpretation of biocultural adaptation usually requires a more intensive population analysis. A thorough analysis of a single pathological condition can provide insights into a group's adaptation. A number of researchers (Hengen 1971; El-Najjar et al. 1976; Carlson et al. 1974) have discussed the occurrence and distribution of porotic hyperostosis (a skeletal lesion) in attempting to interpret the existence of iron deficiency anemia in prehistoric populations from Europe, the American Southwest, and North Africa.

A more comprehensive understanding of biocultural adaptation requires the consideration of a number of pathological conditions. For example, the occurrence of artificial interference (e.g. cranial deformation), congenital defects, trauma, infectious disease, and nutritional defects can provide a more complete interpretation of biocultural adaptation.

EXAMPLES FROM OUTSIDE THE NORTHEAST

We will use two case studies of paleopathology as analytical tools. The first example centers on a prehistoric population from Sudanese Nubia; the second deals with the Dickson Mounds population from the Illinois River Valley. The Nubian populations span three periods totaling 1950 years: Meroitic (350 B.C. - A.D. 350), X-Group (A.D. 350-550), and Christian (A.D. 550-1400). We will use two examples from the analysis of Nubian paleopathology, traumatic lesions, and nutritional deficiencies to illustrate biocultural adaptation in these groups.

THE NUBIAN CASE

The incidence of traumatic lesions provides an index of the cause of injury or stress in a culture. The location of traumatic fractures can be an indicator of accidental and/or purposeful aggressive action. Fractures near the wrist of the radius or ulna (bones of the forearm) result from falls when the arm is extended to break the fall. Fractures of both bones of the forearm at midshaft are most likely to occur when an individual raises their arm to protect his face from a blow. This "parry fracture" may be used as an index of strife in a society, while the frequency of fractures near the wrist can be an index of clumsiness. A pattern of multiple injuries and the distribution of injuries in males and females can further aid in interpreting whether the injuries were accidental or inflicted. In the Nubian series there was a doubling of postcranial traumatic lesions during the Christian Period. The increase was primarily among females. The finding of two women with severe multiple injuries, likely to have been the results of beatings, may indicate a change in status. While the sample is too small to make a general statement, it does suggest that the status of women was declining.

The determination of nutritional deficiencies in prehistoric populations is extremely difficult. Attempts have been made to describe specific nutritional deficiencies such as scurvy (Vitamin C deficiency) or rickets (Vitamin D deficiency) with little success. However, as Steinbock (1976:322) notes, malnutrition rarely selects for only one vital component and we are more likely to find multiple deficiencies of several nutrients than individual or single nutrient deficiencies.

There is excellent evidence to suggest that the prehistoric Nubians were suffering from iron deficiency anemia (Carlson et al. 1974). Porotic hyperostosis, a condition in which there is a thickening of normally thin bones such as the skullcap, ribs, and sternum, is due to an anemia. The thin bones of the skeleton are a major source of red blood cell production, and there is an increase in red blood cell production in response to anemia. While porotic hyperostosis may result from any anemia, the lesions in the Nubian populations

were restricted to the superior border of the orbits, which is characteristic of relatively mild anemias caused by nutritional deficiencies
(Hengen 1971). The pattern of involvement also supports this interpretation. The high frequencies in the younger age groups (2-6 years)
and among young adult females suggest that individuals being breast
fed were especially susceptible to the condition after weaning. A
reconstruction of Nubian diet indicates that their reliance on millet
and sorghum, cereal grains that are poor sources of iron, contributed
to the anemia.

While the discovery of porotic hyperostosis suggests that
nutritional deficiencies existed in Nubian populations, other stress
indicators should confirm the existence of nutritional stress. Huss-
Ashmore (1978) and Martin and Armelagos (1979) were able to
show that altered patterns of growth and development in children,
severe juvenile osteoporosis in children, and premature osteoporosis
in young adult females, were related to nutrition.

Osteoporosis is a bone pathology that is characterized by a
decrease in bone mass. While osteoporosis has been thought to be
related to the aging process, there is abundant evidence to show that
it can occur in juveniles (Garn 1970) and young adult females (Martin
and Armelagos 1979). The occurrence of osteoporosis in the younger
age segments of the population suggests a response to nutritional
stress. In the Nubian juveniles, the actual pattern of long bone
growth or the relative percent growth did not give indisputable evidence of growth retardation. A comparison of the thickness of the
cortex of the bone when compared to the length or diameter of bone
suggested serious nutritional problems. While the lengths and the
diameters of the long bones were being maintained, the bones were
becoming very thin. In a sense, the lengths and diameters were being
maintained at the expense of the thickness. Minerals were being
diverted from the walls of long bones for this maintenance. Microscopic analysis of the juveniles experiencing osteoporosis revealed
that bone was being resorbed at a greater rate than expected.

Similar evidence of premature osteoporosis was found in
young adult females. They displayed a significant amount of long
bone loss in the 20-29 year age period. Microscopic analysis revealed
that these females had cortical bone that was very porous and that
the bone present was not well mineralized.

The occurrence of premature osteoporosis in young females
is most likely to be the result of nutritional stress during lactation.
While bone is often deposited during pregnancy (the fetus uses little
calcium) it is resorbed during prolonged lactation, and females can be
deprived of 300 mg of calcium and 500 calories daily. Multiparous
females are expecially at risk since their reserves of nutrients are

likely to become depleted, resulting in poor bone maintenance and blood loss.

THE DICKSON MOUNDS CASE

Biocultural analysis has also been successfully applied to the analysis of prehistoric adaptation in the New World. During the course of a 400 year period, populations at the Dickson Mounds underwent a rapid change in subsistence. The archaeological record demonstrates a change from the Late Woodland through a transition period (Mississippian Acculturated Late Woodland) to the Middle Mississippian period. During this time, there was a shift to intensive agriculture (Lallo 1973).

This shift in adaptation could be expected to result in dramatic changes in ecological relationships, such as increased reliance on agricultural products, increase in population size and density, and an increase in trade. These changes in cultural and social adaptations would increase the potential for nutritional deficiencies, infectious disease, and mortality. The increase in nutritional disease is significant. The frequency of iron deficiency anemia (as measured by porotic hyperostosis) quadrupled from 13.6% in the Late Woodland to 51.5% in the Middle Mississippian period (Lallo et al. 1977). The pattern of involvement, age 1-3 and young adult females, reflects a pattern similar to that found in the Nubian populations.

The infectious lesions, as measured by changes resulting from inflammation of the outer periosteum, increased from 27% in the Late Woodland to 81% in the Middle Mississippian period. Among the adults, the infectious lesions begin earlier in the Middle Mississippian period and are much more severe. Among the children, there is a synergistic relationship between nutritional deficiencies and infectious lesions. There is an increase in individuals with both lesions, and these individuals show more severe manifestations of each condition.

There are other more subtle changes that can be used to measure the impact of subsistence changes. Defects in dental enamel (enamel hypoplasia) increase as agriculture intensifies (Goodman et al. 1980). Similarly, evidence of growth disruptions in long bones (Harris line) increase under the same conditions of intensification. The shift to intensive agriculture is likely to have been a major contributing factor to the increase of nutritional and infectious lesions. Maize is very low in lysine, an essential amino acid.

It is also possible to use enamel hypoplasia to retrospectively analyze childhood stress in adults who have survived these stresses.

Enamel hypoplasia provides a record of earlier metabolic events. By measuring the location of the enamel hypoplasia from the cemento-enamel junction and using information on the rate of tooth growth, it is possible to determine the age at which the stresses occurred. Goodman et al. (1980) have demonstrated that adults experienced considerable stress during their childhoods (between ages 2 and 4.5).

The individuals who have survived childhood stress experience a reduction in longevity. Individuals who have one hypoplastic line show a nearly five year decrease in longevity (Goodman and Armelagos, n.d.). There is an overall increase in mortality with the shift in subsistence. Use of life table analysis shows that age-specific mortality increases at every age period.

The Nubian and Dickson Mounds studies illustrate the richness of skeletal studies in understanding adaptability. Buikstra (1977) has used similar methods for a regional approach to analyzing prehistoric adaptation in the lower Illinois River valley.

CHEMICAL ANALYSIS

The types of analyses just described are based on the macroscopic and microscopic studies of bone. Complementary analyses that show promise are chemical studies of bone. Elemental and isotopic composition (major, minor, and trace elements; stable isotopes of carbon, nitrogen, and oxygen) will all have some value in the determination of major components of an individual's diet. Some elements or isotopes have a greater association with a specific group of foods than with other food groups. The use of these new techniques for determining only the presence or absence of a food, such as maize or shellfish, is limited. The strength of chemical studies lies in the association of elemental or isotopic groups with the disease patterns, metabolic disturbances, and causal links between the host and environment.

Collagen is a structurally stable protein. Because collagen is synthesized in stages, its composition reflects diet during the various phases of individual development. Chemical degrading of the molecule in the laboratory can reveal defects in the molecular make-up due to dietary deficiencies. Recovery of the collagen formed during various stages of development can provide information for assessing dietary composition over the lifespan of the individual.

ELEMENTAL ANALYSIS

Chemical analysis of major, minor, and trace elements is an important technique for assessing paleonutrition (see Huss-Ashmore et al. 1982). Such analysis has attempted to determine the impact of toxic levels, deficiency states, or dietary composition. Gilbert (1975) and Wing and Brown (1979) provide general discussions of the potential of trace mineral analysis for paleonutrition. The incorporation of trace minerals into bones and teeth has been examined in a number of prehistoric populations (Boaz and Hampel 1978; Brown 1973, 1974; Gilbert 1975; Schoeninger 1979a, 1979b; Stedt 1979; Szpunar et al. 1978).

Although there have been a large number of elements tested, most studies have focused on variation in zinc, copper, manganese, magnesium, and strontium. These studies suggest that zinc and copper would increase in populations with a high dietary meat intake, while manganese, magnesium, and strontium would be higher in populations in which plant foods comprise a greater proportion of the diet.

Gilbert (1975) analyzed five trace minerals (Zn, Cu, Sr, Mn, and Mg) in seventy-five individuals from the Dickson Mound population in Illinois. Zinc concentrations did discriminate between the populations in the predicted fashion. Since zinc is related to protein consumption, decrease in zinc levels would be expected in the maize-reliant Middle Mississippian population. Gilbert also found that zinc levels were related to the occurrence of pathology in some of the groups. For example, among the Late Woodland populations there was a negative correlation between zinc concentration and the occurrence of pathology. Bahou (1975) expanded on this aspect of the study and found a relationship between trace elements and other pathologies.

The analysis of strontium has also been used to discriminate between meat and plant eaters. While strontium and calcium react chemically in a similar fashion, most animals actively discriminate against strontium through renal excretion. Plants, however, accumulate strontium in their leaves and stems. Toots and Voorhies (1965) have applied strontium analysis to discriminate between herbivores and carnivores in paleontological samples.

Brown (1973, 1974) has pioneered the use of strontium-calcium analysis as a dietary indicator. In addition, she was able to assess differential access to meat by subgroups within the culture. In prehistoric populations from Chalcatzingo, Mexico, Schoeninger found that individuals with the highest status had the lowest mean bone strontium levels (indicating more meat in diet) while burials without grave goods had the highest mean bone strontium levels (Schoeninger 1979a, 1979b). Thus, status differences as reflected by differential access to meat can be determined.

Stedt (1979) measured thirteen elements (Na, K, Li, P, Ca, Mg, Ba, Al, Fe, Mn, Cu, Zn, and Pb) but found no conclusive evidence of trace element differences that could be related to diet, or individual age, or sex. Stedt believes that factors affecting her results include the variability of trace elements in separate bones of the body (Gilbert 1975), variation in trace elements in different fractions of the same bone (Kuhn 1979), physiological state prior to death, and the diagenetic effects of soil and fossilization processes (Stedt 1979: 89). In addition, the use of samples from a large number of sites may have increased the variability found.

Other factors complicating elemental analysis include the *in vivo* interactions between elements that may affect their distribution in bones. In addition, bone mineral usually shows differences resulting from organic and inorganic exchanges which occur between the soil and bones after death. The University of Arizona Geoscience Laboratory is developing techniques to extract cytianeous carbonates from the original bone mineral. Bone collagen, unlike bone mineral is more stable in the post-mortem environment. Collagen assessment may thus give a more reliable indication of dietary composition. Collagen and mineral formation are different processes, but they should be generally comparable. The molecular structure of collagen may degrade over time with an eventual loss of total collagen (Hon 1965, 1967; Wyckoff 1972).

An additional examination of collagen for individual dietary assessment is available through stable isotope analysis. Although the stable isotopes of nitrogen, oxygen, and carbon are apt to be of greatest anthropological interest, the existing knowledge of the natural biogeochemical variation in stable carbon isotopes (^{12}C and ^{13}C) make these isotopes of immediate interest.

The ratio of ^{13}C to ^{12}C in plant or animal tissues reflects the environment (the carbon source) of the organism. The source of carbon is either atmospheric or aquatic in plants, and dietary in animals.

Nearly 99% of the earth's carbon is composed of the stable isotope ^{12}C while a little over 1% is composed of ^{13}C. The C13 value is the ratio of ^{13}C to ^{12}C compared to a standard, usually negative and expressed in thousandths, for example -38%0. (Bumsted 1980a; Lerman 1975). Carbon in plants is metabolized through three major pathways: C_3 (Calvin), C_4 (Hatch-Slack), and CAM (Crassulacean acid metabolism). During photosynthesis, plants will preferentially take up ^{12}C over ^{13}C. While C13 values for plants may range from 0 to -38%0, naturally occurring ratios are highly predictable with a bimodal distribution reflecting the metabolic pathway of the plant. C_4 (Hatch-Slack) plants take up more ^{13}C than do C_3 plants and will therefore have a higher (less negative) $^{13}C/^{12}C$ ratio. The modal value for C_4 plants is -12%0 while for C_3 plants the mode is -28%0. CAM plants, with the ability to use both C_3 and C_4 pathways, are intermediate in value. Specific values depend on growth conditions.

The application of stable carbon isotope analysis to paleonutrition is based on controlled animal studies. This research has demonstrated that as carbon is passed along the food chain, the isotopic composition of animals continues to reflect the relative isotopic composition of their diet (DeNiro 1977; DeNiro and Epstein 1978a, 1978b; Bender et al. 1981).

The plants that comprise the diet of animals will have distinct C13 values. Maize, a tropical New World cultigen, is a C_4 plant. On the other hand, the native flora of North American temperate environments is comprised of primarily C_3 varieties. Therefore, a shift from indigenous gathered plants (C_3) to cultivated plants such as maize (C_4) will result in a shift in dietary isotopic values. Because many marine food sources are enriched in ^{13}C (Have C_4-like isotopic values), one may be able to distinguish a marine resource strategy from an inland foraging strategy in an area such as New England. Unlike radioactive ^{14}C, $^{13}C/^{12}C$ ratios do not change after the death of an organism. Archaeological remains, food refuse, soil humus, or skeletal remains can be used for dietary reconstruction.

Interest in carbon isotopes to date has focused on their use in correcting ^{14}C dates and in environmental reconstruction. Bender (1968) and Stuiver (1978) have used C13 analysis to correct radiocarbon dates. There have also been a number of attempts to apply stable isotope analysis to environmental reconstruction (Teeri and Stowe 1976; Lerman and Troughton 1975; DeNiro and Epstein 1978a; Mazany 1978; Tieszen et al. 1979).

There have been only a few published stable carbon isotope studies that are explicitly anthropological (Craig and Craig 1972; Herz and Wenner 1978; Brothwell and Burleigh 1977; Vogel and Van der Merwe 1977; Burleigh and Brothwell 1978; DeNiro and Epstein 1978a; MacNeish 1978; Van der Merwe and Vogel 1978; Bender et al. 1981). Of these studies, the last six consider the problem of dietary reconstruction. These six studies have focused on the interpretation of a maize (horticultural) component. Other workers are examining marine components in Costa Rican (Norr, pers. comm.) and South African prehistoric diets (Van de Merwe, pers. comm.).

These studies indicate that stable isotope analysis can be of use in reconstructing the diets of prehistoric populations. However, the actual determination of proportion of maize in diets is still controversial, and methods for this should be tested further. Reliable assessment of marine diets or of marine/maize diets is further away from routine.

While previous studies have dealt with the question of the importance of maize in the diet, there is a potential for using stable carbon isotopes to determine nutritional deficiencies in archaeological groups. For example, we may now be able to test the relationship of the intensity of maize use to the increase in nutritional and infectious lesions in a skeletal population.

The effective use of stable carbon isotopes in paleonutritional research requires information on variation of ^{13}C values within a population and the impact of variation on the health of individuals in the group. Preliminary studies by Vogel, Van de Merwe, and colleagues indicate that there are sex differences with respect to the use of maize. The effects of these dietary differences remain to be studied. The simultaneous analysis of isotopes, elements, and specific nutritional diseases should clarify many questions about the effects of increased reliance on maize and other cereal grains on nutritional health.

Neither isotopic nor elemental analysis can provide an instant answer to perplexing archaeological questions related to subsistence. The technology involved can determine the quantity of the element or isotope of interest but can neither assess the relevance of such a measure, nor assign any biocultural meaning to the value. As with more traditional soil and palaeobotanical studies, chemical analysis relies on situations of contrast—natural versus cultural, C_4 versus C_3, meat versus vegetable protein, and so on. Samples of on-site and off-site soil and archaeological organic remains (postulated dietary components) properly collected and stored are required.

A BIOCULTURAL PERSPECTIVE FOR THE NORTHEAST

While biological anthropology can obviously make a valuable contribution to archaeological studies of cultural adaptation, the question of its applicability in the Northeast remains. The biocultural perspective has seen little use, especially in the Northeast, although it is proposed here as an appropriate direction for this region. Two primary factors support this perspective: (1) availability and suitability of biological materials in the Northeast, and (2) regional analyses. Before discussing these however, it is instructive to briefly examine the historical background of archaeological research involving analysis of human skeletal materials in the Northeast.

Much of the skeletal material collected in the nineteenth and twentieth centuries seems to have come from accidental discoveries made in farming activities and urbanization. Interest in human skeletons, like that in artifacts, previously focused on determining the origins and identities of the indigenous American peoples. Explanations ranged from New World origins to Egypt and the Mediterranean, and identified the people as anyone from the Lost Tribes of Israel to the survivors of Atlantis. Although this focus on determining the geographic origins of New World peoples has disappeared from American archaeology, the notion of using skeletal remains to identify biological (and hence cultural) populations continues to dominate archaeological use of these materials.

Northeastern archaeology is guilty of almost totally neglecting human skeletal remains as important and integral parts of both living and archaeological systems. The primary role of skeletal material in the Northeast, thus far, has been in the reconstruction of culture history. Site-oriented archaeology has used biological analyses of morphological traits to establish or support intersite relationships based primarily on nonbiological criteria, specifically lithic tool technology. The assumption seems to be that if a biological relationship between human skeletons can be established, then the relationship between associated artifact types can also be viewed as biological. Such biological analyses (Schindler n.d.; Oschinsky 1960, 1964; Szathmary and Ossenberg 1978; Laughlin 1966) played an important role in separating and defining prehistoric Eskimo and Indian sites in the Northeastern Arctic and sub-Arctic regions. Ritchie (1969), in interpreting the prehistory of New York State used skeletal materials to reconstruct physical appearance. From this base, biological populations were constructed, providing support for materially defined cultural units. This misapplication of biological analysis is most visible in his characterization of the Lamoka Lake and Brewerton cultures as representing biologically distinct populations. A "typical Lamoka adult male" was said to be "of medium height (about five feet five or six inches), slender and gracile build; with a long, narrow, oval, and high-vaulted head; a high and narrow face, with little malar (cheekbone) or alveolar (lower face) projection; a well-formed palate with a regular arrangement of teeth; a relatively narrow nose, and eyes in medium-high sockets, under weak to moderately developed brow ridges [Ritchie 1969:46]." The Brewerton people were said to be in sharp contrast physically to the Lamoka Lake people. His examination of dental wear and pathologies was somewhat more enlightened, and consideration was given to possible dietary causes of pathology.

The early literature of Northeastern archaeology reflects this site-orientation and the narrow consideration given to human skeletal remains. Unfortunately, the focus of more recent archaeological research has not been much broader. By and large, the site is still the unit of analysis.

Interest in Northeastern skeletal materials has not been intense, but a few early descriptive studies were made by Wilson (1862) and Carr (1880). More extensive and influential has been the work of Hrdlicka (1927) and Knight (1915), however these works are also primarily craniometric descriptions. In an attempt to synthesize the data on Northeastern skeletal materials, Howells (1946) used the cranial index as his primary indicator of biological affinity. As discussed earlier, this measure has been recognized as ineffective for such studies.

Lane and Sublett (1972) used nonmetric traits to genetically distinguish social units or kin groups of historic period Seneca Indians from the Allegheny Reservation. They used their analysis to test for residential patterns as determined archaeologically. Ethnohistorical data supported the conclusions of the biological analysis.

In an earlier work, Sublett (1966) used demographic, dental, craniometric, morphological, and genetic variation attributes to reconstruct a generalized physical type (with a calculated range of variability) for the Seneca. This type was then compared to data from the Iroquoian groups in an effort to determine biological relationships between the member groups of the League of the Iroquois. The analytical perspective of this study was primarily geographical, and the direct historical approach was extremely important. The skeletal material, more than 500 individuals, spans approximately 800 years from prehistoric times up to A.D. 1800. Ethnohistorical sources were used to document trends in discrete traits indicating regional microevolutionary processes. A more recent application of biological analysis by Bellantoni and Harris (1980) attempts to use craniometric data to support established population boundaries as defined by material culture. The results of the craniometric analysis, using the Penrose (1954) statistic to assess intergroup relationships (Constandse-Westermann 1972), support the material culture distinctions between the Ontario Iroquois and the populations occupying the New England, New York, and Middle Atlantic areas. The inappropriateness of craniometric analysis for establishing the cultural affiliations of skeletal remains has already been discussed. The important contribution of Harris and Bellantoni's work is not in the analyses which they performed, but in their use of a regional approach to the research.

The call has already been made to move away from the

particularism of the culture-historical approach and to begin addressing larger anthropological questions. A regional approach in the Northeast that makes full use of the material and biological components of the archaeological record, as well as developments in the application of models from other fields, is the only means by which anthropological archaeology can fruitfully proceed. It is, however, premature to urge Northeastern archaeologists to adopt regional strategies if, for the most part, they have no research orientation other than that of the culture-historian (see Chapter 2).

A number of problems confront the anthropologist in trying to apply a regional, biocultural approach in the Northeast. Availability of biological materials, legal restriction, and the changing nature of the data base are all issues that must be confronted and dealt with. Each of these concerns will be addressed below in light of the Northeast's potential to significantly contribute to answering the "big questions" in anthropology.

In January 1980, a questionnaire survey of twelve museums and sixteen university departments (50% response) indicated that there is a considerable amount of human skeletal material from New England sites available for analysis. As a result of the archaeological neglect of skeletal materials in the Northeast, many of the early individual finds or collections are poorly documented, incomplete, or lost. Some relatively large samples, systematically excavated and well documented as a result of modern archaeological interest, exist at larger institutions. However, the majority of materials, even those of recent excavation, are poorly curated and undocumented. All await study by physical anthropologists working on Northeastern problems. Many museums and institutions in the Northeast also indicated that they were understaffed, and few had curators trained in osteological identification and analysis. A more detailed regional survey of skeletal resources needs to be conducted, in many cases by personal visit. Regional archaeological surveys of professional, amateur, and private individuals should include questions concerning skeletal materials.

In many respects, the archaeological literature and the survey paint a dismal picture of the Northeast's potential for biocultural studies (Bumsted 1980b). The data base is composed primarily of isolated finds, many of which lack contextual information and the skeletal remains have not been properly curated. Biocultural inference from isolated finds is more limited than that from large populations, but with proper temporal and spatial controls, populations can be assembled from such individuals. Methods of statistical, archaeological, and biological data manipulation are being developed to strengthen these inferences. Our skeletal survey ran across one such assembled population—82 individuals could be identified from one geographic area. The individuals were recovered over the past 120 years as isolated finds. Unfortunately, all but about 47 individuals were lost over these same 120 years.

In addition to synthesizing currently available data, provision must be made for skeletal materials that have yet to be excavated. In the field, archaeologists have generally regarded the discovery of human burials as exciting in the first moment, but the excitement rapidly fades. Human skeletal material is cumbersome to handle, and slows down the work pace considerably if it is to be removed from the ground properly. Mapping, recording, and handling procedures for skeletal material are difficult, time-consuming, and generally unfamiliar to most archaeologists. As a result, the potential information available from skeletal materials, in situ, is not always collected. Inadequate curation of the material in the field also adds to the loss of potential information.

Archaeologists have become accustomed to calling on the services of specialists in other fields. In fact introductory textbooks stress the importance of this multidisciplinary aspect of archaeology in dealing with problems and questions that the archaeologist is not fully capable of handling. The field human osteologist, a person trained in human skeletal analysis and also a competent field archaeologist, is also a specialist whose services should be called upon when human burials are encountered in the field. This is especially important in an area like the Northeast where undisturbed sites are few and preservation of bone is usually poor. The services provided by a human osteologist are most certainly as important as are those of the geologist, botanist, or zoologist.

Archaeologists and biological anthropologists are confronted today by a host of legal and ethical problems. The excavation and study of human remains has become a sensitive issue and rightly so. As anthropologists, we have a self-imposed charge to protect and preserve the Native American way of life. We have also charged to ourselves the task of learning as much as possible about the lifestyles of these peoples, both for the benefit of Native American cultures, and in an effort to answer the larger, pancultural questions of anthropological research. The goals of anthropologists and the Native American community do not have to conflict, but at this point in our history, we find that they are diametrically opposed. A full discussion of these complicated ethical issues cannot be undertaken here. It is important however, that as anthropologists, we be as sensitive to these issues as possible.

The Heritage Conservation and Recreation Service of the U.S. Department of the Interior has set up a general policy for the disposition of human remains. Iowa, Maine, and other states have also adopted specific policies on this matter. Massachusetts General Laws (Chapter 9, Section 27C) also provide for the recovery, study, and subsequent disposal of ancient (150+ years old) human remains found on public lands. Such individual policies and the lack of specific federal policies provide for neither the protection of Native American Indian rights nor for the proper removal and study of human remains by qualified anthropologists. Regulation on the federal level is needed to standardize the treatment of human remains when found on both public and private lands.

The participation of Native American representatives in forming and implementing policies is essential and cooperation of Native Americans and anthropologists is needed for future work. Where aboriginal sites are to be destroyed by construction on public or private lands, or where human remains are found accidentally in the course of such work, it should be recognized that qualified archaeologists and biological anthropologists, working with Native American representatives, are the most appropriate people to recover and handle such materials.

CONCLUSION

We have (1) examined the historical factors that influenced the typological approach in analyzing human skeletal remains, (2) discussed the problems in using this particularistic approach and suggested an alternative methodology for analysis of materials which focuses on biocultural adaptation, (3) illustrated the importance of the biocultural perspective in integrating archaeology and biological anthropology, and (4) examined the potential of a biocultural perspective for research in the Northeast.

The value of a culture-historical approach is not being denied; it is the inappropriateness of skeletal analyses in this context that is seriously questioned. The application of skeletal analyses to the development of racial typologies was an attempt to identify "races" of Native Americans, and thereby to delineate "cultural units" or spheres of both cultural and biological interaction. The application of these cultural units to reconstructions of culture history is equally problematic.

The use of skeletal indicators in identifying stresses related to biological and associated cultural factors has been demonstrated as a more effective means of addressing questions of biocultural adaptation. Analyses of altered patterns of growth and development, shifts in fertility and fecundity, patterns of disease and patterns of mortality can be successfully applied to interpretations of prehistoric adaptation.

The application of such a framework involves a much closer working relationship between biological anthropologists and archaeologists than is generally found to exist today. The changing nature of our resource base demands a more unified approach to anthropology in the Northeast. A shift in research directions away from culture historical approaches on the part of both biological anthropologists and archaeologists must accompany this integration. The nature of the biological remains will necessitate a regional approach in applying a biocultural perspective to the area. The systematic analysis of biological remains has the potential for understanding the foundations of adaptation of groups in the Northeast and to contribute significantly to the theoretical concerns of anthropological archaeology.

REFERENCES

Aikens, C.M.
    1967   Plains relationships of the Fremont culture: A hypothesis. *American Antiquity* 32(2):198-209.
Armelagos, G.J.
    1974   Forward. In Bibliography of human and nonhuman non-metric variation, compiled by Michael Finnegan and M.A. Faust. *Research Reports* 14:i-ii. Department of Anthropology, University of Massachusetts, Amherst.
Bahou, W.F.
    1975   *The relationships of particular trace elements to various bone pathologies in the Dickson Mounds skeletal population.* Senior Honors Thesis. University of Massachusetts, Amherst.
Bass, W.M.
    1964   The variation in physical types of the prehistoric Plains Indians. *Plains Anthropologist* (Memoir 1) 9(24).
Batrawi, A.M.
    1935   *Report on the human remains, Mission Archaeologique de Nubie 1929-1934.* Government Press, Cairo.
    1945   The racial history of Egypt and Nubia, Part I. *Journal of the Royal Anthropological Institute* 75:81-102.
    1946   The racial history of Egypt and Nubia, Part II. *Journal of the Royal Anthropological Institute* 76:132-156.
Bellantoni, N.F., and E.F. Harris
    1980   *Anthropological relationships among prehistoric northeastern Amerindians.* Paper presented to the Northeast Anthropological Association, Amherst, Massachusetts.

Bender, M.M.
1968 Mass spectrometric studies of carbon 13 variations in corn and other grasses. *Radiocarbon* 10:468-472.
Bender, M.M., D.A. Baerreis, and R.L. Steventon
1981 Further light on carbon isotopes and Hopewell agriculture. *American Antiquity* 46(2):346-353.
Berry, A.C., and R.J. Berry
1967 Epigenetic variation in the human cranium. *Journal of Anatomy* 101: 361-379.
1972a Epigenetic polymorphism in the Primate skeleton. In *Comparative genetics in Monkeys, Apes, and Man,* edited by A.B. Chiarelli. Academic Press, New York.
1972b Origins and relationships of the ancient Egyptians based on a study of non-metrical variations in the skull. *Journal of Human Evolution* 1(2): 199-208.
1973 "Origins and relations of the ancient Egyptians." In *Population Biology of Ancient Egyptians,* edited by D.R. Brothwell and B.A. Chiarelli, pp. 200-208. Academic Press, New York.
Berry, A.C., R.J. Berry, and P.J. Ucko
1967 Genetical change in ancient Egypt. *Man* 2:551-568.
Birkby, W.H.
1966 An evaluation of race and sex from cranial measurements. *American Journal of Physical Anthropology* 24:21-28.
Boaz, N.T., and J. Hampel
1978 Strontium content of fossil tooth enamel and diet in early hominids. *Journal of Paleontology* 52:928-933.
Brothwell, D., and R. Burleigh
1977 On sinking Otavalo man. *Journal of Archaeological Science* 4:291-294.
Brown, A.B.
1973 *Bone strontium as a dietary indicator in human skeletal populations.* Ph.D. dissertation, University of Michigan, Ann Arbor.
1974 Bone strontium as a dietary indicator in human skeletal populations. *Contributions to Geology* 13:85-87.
Buikstra, J.E.
1977 Biocultural dimensions of archaeological study: A regional perspective. In *Biocultural adaptation in Prehistoric America,* edited by R.L. Blakely, pp. 67-84. University of Georgia Press, Athens, Georgia.
Bumsted, M.P.
1980a The potential of stable carbon isotopes in bioarchaeological anthropology. In Biocultural adaptation: Comprehensive approaches to skeletal analyses, edited by Debra L. Martin and M. Pamela Bumsted. *Research Reports* (in press), Department of Anthropology, University of Massachusetts, Amherst.
1980b CRM and the physical anthropologist. *American Society for Conservation Archaeology Newsletter* 7(2):2-9.

Burleigh, R., and D. Brothwell
    1978   Studies on Amerindian dogs, 1: Carbon isotopes in relation to maize in the diet of domestic dogs from early Peru and Ecuador. *Journal of Archaeological Science* 5:355-362.
Carlson, D.S.
    1976a Temporal variation in prehistoric Nubian crania. *American Journal of Physical Anthropology* 45:467-484.
    1976b Patterns of morphological variation in the human midface and upper face. In *Factors affecting the growth of the midface*, edited by J.A. McNamara, Jr., pp. 277-299. Center for Human Growth and Development Craniofacial Growth Series, Monograph No. 6, Ann Arbor, Michigan.
Carlson, D.S., G.J. Armelagos, and D.P. Van Gerven
    1974   Factors influencing the etiology of cribra orbitalia in prehistoric Nubia. *Journal of Human Evolution* 3:405-410.
Carlson, D.S., and D.P. Van Gerven
    1977   Masticatory function and post-Pleistocene evolution in Nubia. *American Journal of Physical Anthropology* 46:495-506.
Carr, L.
    1880   Notes on the crania of New England Indians. *Anniversary Memoirs of the Boston Society of Natural History*, Boston.
Constandse-Westermann, T.S.
    1972   *Coefficients of biological distance.* Anthropological Publications, Oosterhout, The Netherlands.
Craig, H., and V. Craig
    1972   Greek marbles: Determination of provenance by isotopic analysis. *Science* 176:401-403.
Crichton, J.M.
    1966   A multiple discriminant analysis of Egyptian and African Negro crania. *Papers of the Peabody Museum of Archaeology and Ethnology* 57:43-67.
DeNiro, M.J.
    1977   *I. Carbon isotope distribution in food chains, II. Mechanism of carbon isotope fractionation associated with lipid synthesis.* Ph.D. dissertation, California Institute of Technology.
DeNiro, M.J., and S. Epstein
    1978a Dietary analysis from $^{13}C/^{12}C$ ratios of carbonate and collagen fractions of bone. *U.S. Geological Survey Open File Report* 78-701:90-91.
    1978b Influence of diet on the distribution of carbon isotopes in animals. *Geochimica et Cosmochimica Acta* 42:495-506.
Dincauze, D.F.
    1980   Research priorities in northeastern archaeology. In Proceedings of the conference on northeastern archaeology, edited by James A. Moore. *Research Reports* 19:29-48. Department of Anthropology, University of Massachusetts, Amherst.

Elliot-Smith, G., and J.F. Jones
  1910   Reports on the human remains. In *Archaeological survey of Nubia report for 1907-1908*. Government Press, Cairo.
El-Najjar, M.Y., D.J. Ryan, C.G. Turner, III, and B. Lozoff
  1976   The etiology of porotic hyperostosis among the prehistoric Anasazi Indians of southwestern United States. *American Journal of Physical Anthropology* 44:477-488.
Finnegan, M., and M.A. Faust (compilers)
  1974   Bibliography of human and nonhuman nonmetric variation. *Research Reports* 14. Department of Anthropology, University of Massachusetts, Amherst.
Garn, S.M.
  1970   *The earlier gain and later loss of cortical bone in nutritional perspective*. C.C. Thomas, Springfield, Illinois.
Gilbert, R.
  1975   *Trace element analyses of three skeletal Amerindian populations at Dickson Mounds*. Ph.D. dissertation, University of Massachusetts, Amherst.
Goodman, A., and G.J. Armelagos
  n.d.   *Childhood stress indicators and decreased adult longevity in a prehistoric population*. Manuscript on file, University of Massachusetts, Amherst.
Goodman, A., G.J. Armelagos, and J. Rose
  1980   Enamel hypoplasias as indicators of stress in three prehistoric populations from Illinois. *Human Biology* 52(3):515-528.
Greene, D.L.
  1966   Dentition and the biological relationships of some Meroitic, X-Group and Christian populations from Wadi Halfa, Sudan *Kush* 14:285-288.
Hardy, V., and D.P. Van Gerven
  1976   The effect of size variation on univariate assessments of morphological difference in human crania. *American Journal of Physical Anthropology* 44(1):79-82.
Hengen, O.P.
  1971   Cribra orbitalia pathogenesis and probable etiology. *Homo* 22(2): 57-76.
Herz, N., and D.B. Wenner
  1978   Assembly of Greek marble inscriptions by isotopic methods. *Science* 199:1070-1072.
Ho, T.
  1965   The amino acid composition of bone and tooth proteins in Late Pleistocene mammals. *Proceedings of the National Academy of Sciences* 54:26-31.
  1967   The amino acids of bone and dentine collagens in Pleistocene mammals. *Biochimica et Biophysica Acta* 133:568-573.
Hooton, E.A.
  1930   The Indians of Pecos Pueblo: A study of their skeletal remains. *Papers of the Southwestern Expedition* 4. Yale University Press, New Haven.

Howe, W.L., and Parsons, P.A.
   1967   Genotype and environment in the determination of minor skeletal variants and body weight in mice. *Journal of Embryology and Experimental Morphology* 17(2):283-292.
Howells, W.W.
   1946   Physical types of the Northeast. In Man in northeastern North America, edited by Frederick Johnson. *Papers of the Robert S. Peabody Foundation for Archaeology* 3:168-178.
Hrdlicka, A.
   1927   Catalogue of human crania in the United States National Museum collections. *Proceedings of the United States National Museum* 69:1-127.
Hunt, E.E.
   1959   Anthropometry, genetics and racial history. *American Anthropologist* 61:64-87.
Huss-Ashmore, R.
   1978   Nutritional determination in a Nubian skeletal population. *American Journal of Physical Anthropology* 48:407.
Huss-Ashmore, R., A.H. Goodman, and G.J. Armelagos
   1982   Nutritional inference from paleopathology. *Advances in archaeological method and theory*, edited by M.B. Schiffer, in press. Academic Press, New York.
Knight, M.
   1915   The craniometry of southern New England Indians. *Memoirs of the Connecticut Academy of Arts and Sciences*, Vol. 4.
Kuhn, J.K.
   1979   *Trace and minor elemental analyses of Sicilian skeletons by x-ray fluorescence.* Paper presented to the American Association of Physical Anthropologists, San Francisco.
Lallo, J.W.
   1973   *The skeletal biology of three prehistoric American Indian populations from Dickson Mound.* Ph.D. dissertation, University of Massachusetts, Amherst.
Lallo, J.W., G.J. Armelagos, and R.P. Mensforth
   1977   The role of diet, disease, and physiology in the origin of porotic hyperostosis. *Human Biology* 49:471-483.
Lane, R.A., and A.J. Sublett
   1972   Osteology of social organization residence pattern. *American Antiquity* 37(2):186-201.
Laughlin, W.S.
   1966   Genetic and anthropological characteristics of Arctic populations. In *The biology of human adaptability*, edited by P.T. Baker and J.S. Weiner. Oxford University Press, London.
Lerman, J.C.
   1975   How to interpret variations in the carbon isotope ratio of plants: Biologic and environmental effects. In *Environmental and biological control of photosynthesis*, edited by R. Marcelle, pp. 323-335. W. Junk, The Hague.

Lerman, J.C., and J.H. Troughton
  1975 Carbon isotope discrimination by photosynthesis: Implications for the bio- and geosciences. In *Proceedings of the Second International Conference on Stable Isotopes,* edited by E.R. Klein and P.D. Klein, pp. 630-644. USERDA, Argonne.
Long, J.K.
  1966 A test of multiple discriminant analysis as a means of determining evolutionary changes and intergroup relationships in physical anthropology. *American Anthropologist* 68(2):444-464.
MacGaffey, W.
  1966 Concepts of race in the histiography of northeast Africa. *Journal of African History* 7(1):1-17.
MacNeish, R.
  1978 Energy and culture in ancient Tehuacan. Unpublished manuscript in the author's possession.
Martin, D.L., and G.J. Armelagos
  1979 Morphometrics of compact bone: An example from Sudanese Nubia. *American Journal of Physical Anthropology* 51:571-578.
Mazany, T.
  1978 *Isotope dendroclimatology: Natural stable carbon isotope analysis of tree rings from an archaeological site.* Paper presented to the 4th International Conference on Geochronology, Cosmochronology, and Isotope Geology, Snowmass-at-Aspen, Colorado.
Morant, G.M.
  1925 A study of Egyptian craniology from prehistoric to Roman times. *Biometrica* 17:1-52.
Morton, S.G.
  1844 Crania aegyptica. *Transactions of the American Philosophical Society* 9.
Neumann, G.K.
  1952 Archeology and race in the American Indian. In *Archeology of eastern United States,* edited by James B. Griffin, pp. 13-34. University of Chicago Press, Chicago.
  1959 Origin of the Indians of the middle Mississippi area. *Proceedings of the Indiana Academy of Sciences* 69:66-68.
Oschinsky, L.
  1960 Two recently discovered human mandibles from Cape Dorset sites on Sugluk and Mansel Islands. *Anthropologia* 2.
  1964 *The most ancient Eskimos.* Canadian Research Centre for Anthropology, Ottawa.
Penrose, L.S.
  1954 Distance, size, and shape. *Annals of Eugenics* 18:337-343.
Rightmire, G.P.
  1970a Iron Age skulls from southern Africa reassessed by multiple discriminant analysis. *American Journal of Physical Anthropology* 33:147-168.

1970b Bushman, Hottentot and South African Negro crania studied by distance and discrimination. *American Journal of Physical Anthropology* 33:169-196.

Ritchie, W.A.
1969 *The archaeology of New York State* (2nd ed.). Natural History Press, Garden City, New York.

Robbins, L.M., and G.K. Neumann
1972 The prehistoric people of the Fort Ancient culture of the central Ohio Valley. *University of Michigan Museum of Anthropology Anthropological Papers* 47.

Schindler, D.L.
n.d. *Definitions of culture and cultural boundaries in the northeast.* Unpublished manuscript on file, University of Massachusetts, Amherst.

Schoeninger, M.J.
1979a Dietary reconstruction at Chalcatzingo, a Formative period site in Morelos, Mexico. *University of Michigan Museum of Anthropology Technical Reports* 9.
1979b Diet and statue at Chalcatzingo: Some empirical and technical aspects of strontium analysis. *American Journal of Physical Anthropology* 51:295-310.

Stedt, P.G.
1979 *Trace element analysis of two prehistoric populations: The Fremont and the Anasazi.* M.A. thesis, San Diego State University.

Steinbock, R.T.
1976 *Paleopathological diagnosis and interpretation. Bone diseases in ancient human populations.* Charles C. Thomas, Springfield.

Stuiver, M.
1978 Carbon-14 dating: A comparison of beta and ion counting. *Science* 202:881-883.

Sublett, A.J.
1966 *Seneca physical type and changes through time.* Ph.D. dissertation, State University of New York, Buffalo.

Szathmary, E.J.E., and N.S. Ossenberg
1978 Are the biological differences between North American Indians and Eskimos truly profound? *Current Anthropology* 19(4).

Szpunar, C., J.B. Lambert, and J.E. Buikstra
1978 Analysis of excavated bone by atomic absorption. *American Journal of Physical Anthropology* 48:199-202.

Teeri, J.A., and L.G. Stowe
1976 Climatic patterns and the distribution of C_4 grasses in North America. *Oecologia* 23:1-12.

Tieszen, L., D. Hein, S. Qvortrup, J. Troughton, and S. Imbamba
1979 Use of ^{13}C values to determine vegetation selectivity in East African herbivores. *Oecologia* 37:351-359.

Toots, H., and M.R. Voorhies
1965 Strontium in fossil bones and the reconstruction of food chains. *Science* 149:854-855.

Van der Merwe, N., and J.C. Vogel
    1978 ^{13}C content of human collagen as a measure of prehistoric diet in Woodland North America. *Nature* 276:815-816.
Van Gerven, D.P., G.J. Armelagos, and A. Rohr
    1977   Continuity and change in cranial morphology of three Nubian archaeological populations. *Man* 12:270-277.
Van Gerven, D.P., D.S. Carlson, and G.J. Armelagos
    1973   Racial history and bio-cultural adaptation of Nubian archaeological populations. *Journal of African History* 14:555-564.
Vogel, J.C., and N.J. Van der Merwe
    1977   Isotopic evidence for early maize cultivation in New York State. *American Antiquity* 42(2):238-242.
Weiss, K.M., and T. Maruyama
    1976   Archeology, population genetics and studies of human racial ancestry. *American Journal of Physical Anthropology* 44(1):31-49.
Wilkinson, R.G.
    1971   Prehistoric biological relationships in the Great Lakes region. *University of Michigan Museum of Anthropology Anthropological Papers* 43.
Wilson, D.
    1862   *Prehistoric man.* Macmillan, London.
Wing, E.S., and A.B. Brown
    1979   *Paleonutrition: Method and theory in prehistoric foodways.* Academic Press, New York.
Wyckoff, R.W.G.
    1972   *The biochemistry of animal fossils.* Scientechnica, Bristol.

The original excavations and analysis of Nubian materials were supported by National Science Foundation Grants GS7, GS286, and GS557. Subsequent analysis of the Nubian skeletal series was supported by National Institute of Health grant NIH-1-RO1-02771-01. Stable isotope research was supported by a University of Massachusetts biomedical research support grant and National Science Foundation Doctoral Dissertation Improvement Grant BNS80-16652.

INDEX

Thomas F. King, Patricia Parker Hickman, and Gary Berg. **Anthropology in Historic Preservation: Caring for Culture's Clutter**

Richard E. Blanton. **Monte Albán: Settlement Patterns at the Ancient Zapotec Capital**

R. E. Taylor and Clement W. Meighan. **Chronologies in New World Archaeology**

Bruce D. Smith. **Prehistoric Patterns of Human Behavior: A Case Study in the Mississippi Valley**

Barbara L. Stark and Barbara Voorhies (Eds.). **Prehistoric Coastal Adaptations: The Economy and Ecology of Maritime Middle America**

Charles L. Redman, Mary Jane Berman, Edward V. Curtin, William T. Langhorne, Nina M. Versaggi, and Jeffery C. Wanser (Eds.). **Social Archeology: Beyond Subsistence and Dating**

Bruce D. Smith (Ed.). **Mississippian Settlement Patterns**

Lewis R. Binford. **Nunamiut Ethnoarchaeology**

J. Barto Arnold III and Robert Weddle. **The Nautical Archeology of Padre Island: The Spanish Shipwrecks of 1554**

Sarunas Milisauskas. **European Prehistory**

Brian Hayden (Ed.). **Lithic Use-Wear Analysis**

William T. Sanders, Jeffrey R. Parsons, and Robert S. Santley. **The Basin of Mexico: Ecological Processes in the Evolution of a Civilization**

David L. Clarke. **Analytical Archaeologist: Collected Papers of David L. Clarke. Edited and Introduced by His Colleagues**

Arthur E. Spiess. **Reindeer and Caribou Hunters: An Archaeological Study**

Elizabeth S. Wing and Antoinette B. Brown. **Paleonutrition: Method and Theory in Prehistoric Foodways.**

John W. Rick. **Prehistoric Hunters of the High Andes**

Timothy K. Earle and Andrew L. Christenson (Eds.). **Modeling Change in Prehistoric Economics**

Thomas F. Lynch (Ed.). **Guitarrero Cave: Early Man in the Andes**

Fred Wendorf and Romuald Schild. **Prehistory of the Eastern Sahara**

Henri Laville, Jean-Philippe Rigaud, and James Sackett. **Rock Shelters of the Perigord: Stratigraphy and Archaeological Succession**

Duane C. Anderson and Holmes A. Semken, Jr. (Eds.). **The Cherokee Excavations: Holocene Ecology and Human Adaptations in Northwestern Iowa**

Anna Curtenius Roosevelt. **Parmana: Prehistoric Maize and Manioc Subsistence along the Amazon and Orinoco**

Fekri A. Hassan. **Demographic Archaeology**

G. Barker. **Landscape and Society: Prehistoric Central Italy**

Lewis R. Binford. **Bones: Ancient Men and Modern Myths**

Richard A. Gould and Michael B. Schiffer (Eds.). **Modern Material Culture: The Archaeology of Us**

Muriel Porter Weaver. **The Aztecs, Maya, and Their Predecessors: Archaeology of Mesoamerica, 2nd edition**

Arthur S. Keene. Prehistoric Foraging in a Temperate Forest: A Linear Programming Model

Ross H. Cordy. **A Study of Prehistoric Social Change: The Development of Complex Societies in the Hawaiian Islands**

C. Melvin Aikens and Takayasu Higuchi. Prehistory of Japan

Kent V. Flannery (Ed.). Maya Subsistence: Studies in Memory of Dennis E. Puleston

Dean R. Snow (Ed.). **Foundations of Northeast Archaeology**

in preparation

Charles S. Spencer. **The Cuicatlán Cañada and the Rise of Monte Albán**

Steadman Upham. **Polities and Power: An Economic and Political History of the Western Pueblo**

Vincas P. Steponaitis. **Ceramics, Chronology, and Community Patterns: An Archaeological Study at Moundville**

Michael J. O'Brien, Robert E. Warren, & Dennis E. Lewarch (Eds.). **The Cannon Reservoir Human Ecology Project: An Archaeological Study of Cultural Adaptations in the Southern Prairie Peninsula**